CONVERSATIONS ON LOVE

Natasha Lunn

VIKING

an imprint of

PENGUIN BOOKS

VIKING

UK | USA | Canada | Ireland | Australia
India | New Zealand | South Africa

Viking is part of the Penguin Random House group of companies
whose addresses can be found at global.penguinrandomhouse.com.

Penguin
Random House
UK

First published 2021

001

Copyright © Natasha Lunn, 2021

The moral right of the author has been asserted

Certain names and identifying characteristics of some people described
in this book have been changed to protect their privacy.

The author and publisher are grateful to the following for their kind permission to reproduce
copyright material: Jeanette Winterson and Jonathan Cape, for the lines on p. vii from
The PowerBook by Jeanette Winterson, published by Jonathan Cape, 2000, and reproduced by
permission of the Random House Group Ltd ©; Dalkey Press/Deep Vellum Publishing, for
the line on p. 3 from *Eros the Bittersweet* by Anne Carson; Penguin Books Ltd, for the line on
p. 45 from *Olive, Again* by Elizabeth Strout, published by Penguin Books 2019, 2020, Viking
2019; Lou Barlow, for the line on p. 45 from 'Brand New Love'; Cheryl Strayed and Atlantic
Books, for the lines on p. 93 from *Tiny Beautiful Things*; Dani Shapiro and Knopf Publishing
Group, for the line on p. 95 from *Hourglass: Time, Memory, Marriage*; Faber and Faber Ltd, for
the line on p. 153 from *High Tide in Tucson: Essays from Now or Never* by Barbara Kingsolver;
Hilary Mantel and HarperCollins, for the line on p. 201 from *Giving Up the Ghost* by Hilary
Mantel; Penguin Classics, for the line on p. 275 from the translation of *Letters to a Young Poet*
by Rainer Maria Rilke (Penguin Classics) reproduced with kind permission from Charlie
Louth; Kobalt Music Group Ltd, for the lines on p. 281 from 'For You' by Laura Marling.

Every effort has been made to trace copyright holders of material reproduced in this book.
We would be pleased to rectify any omissions in subsequent reprints or editions should they
be drawn to our attention.

Set in 12.6/15.4pt Fournier MT Pro
Typeset by Jouve (UK), Milton Keynes
Printed and bound in Great Britain by Clays Ltd, Elcograf S.p.A.

The authorized representative in the EEA is Penguin Random House Ireland,
Morrison Chambers, 32 Nassau Street, Dublin D02 YH68

A CIP catalogue record for this book is available from the British Library

ISBN: 978-0-241-44873-1

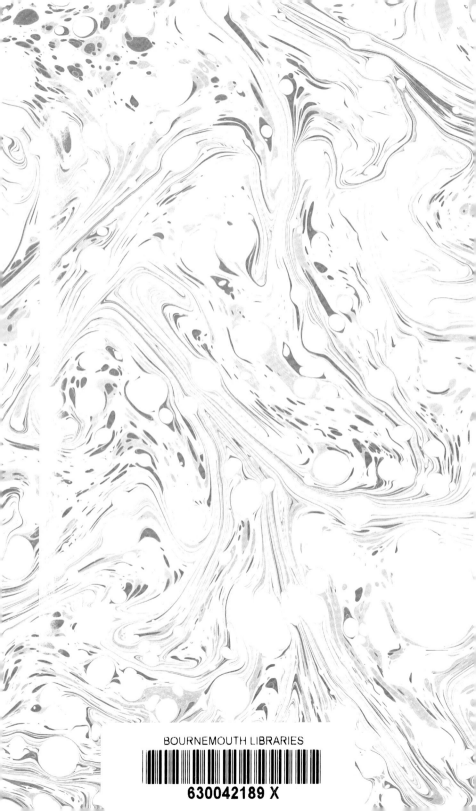

CONVERSATIONS ON LOVE

For anyone who feels lost in longing

'The stories we sit up late to hear are love stories. It seems that we cannot know enough about this riddle of our lives. We go back and back to the same scenes, the same words, trying to scrape out the meaning. Nothing could be more familiar than love. Nothing else eludes us so completely.'

(Jeanette Winterson, The PowerBook)

Contents

Introduction

For years, I was committed to longing. Longing for a reply to a text message, for an 'I love you', or for a man to look at me a certain way. If I was in a relationship, I longed for it to last, and if I wasn't, I longed to find one. My longing was a restlessness that spread out into my life like a mist. I could not see anything clearly with it there.

I used to think it was love that I was longing for, but I was wrong. I was obsessed with the idea of love, not the truth of it. All those years and nights I spent asking, 'When will I find love?' I never paused to think about what precisely it was. Do many of us? We don't learn about love at school, we don't research it, or take a test in it, or review it once a year. We're encouraged to learn about economics and grammar and geography, but not to know about love. It seems strange to me, how we expect so much from love, and yet devote so little time to understanding it. Like wanting to dive into the sea but having no interest in learning how to swim.

And yet, whether we think about it or not, love leaks in and out of all of our lives, every day, freely, cruelly and beautifully. I watch a video of my friend's six-week-old baby wriggling in the bath one hour before reading a quiet email from a woman whose third round of IVF has just failed. I think about two new engagements, another that was called off, another that never happened. I listen to the friend trying to build a new life after an unexpected divorce, the friend who is grieving a parent, the giggly optimism of another friend tentatively unwrapping a brand-new love. On and on it wilts and blooms, the love in all of our lives. Unknowable and undefinable. Or so I thought.

For a long time, I assumed love was the source of my unhappiness. I wanted to understand why it felt beyond my capabilities. Why could I walk away from a job I was unhappy with, but not from a bad relationship? Why did I have agency in every other aspect of my life, and not in love? Why did I assume marriage would be the end of something, and not the beginning? My suspicion that I had misunderstood love completely was what Elizabeth Gilbert once described as a 'breadcrumb of curiosity', a clue that I needed to pick up and follow.

That's why, for the last four years, I've asked writers and therapists and experts about their experiences of love in an email newsletter called *Conversations on Love*. I've listened to people talk about their love for a person, for a city, for a poem, for a tree. I've listened to a man say he wished he'd slept with more people and a woman say that sex is the dream life of a marriage. I've listened to people share stories about sustaining a 26-year-long friendship across different countries, about falling in love while losing a child or grieving a sibling, about seeing babies born in war zones and about learning to find romance in solitude. Each one was a reminder that love was possible, and that my understanding of it had been limited.

While I was having these conversations, love was leaking in and out of my life too. The interviews expanded my idea of what love could be, and what it could look like, but it wasn't until I started trying to conceive after a miscarriage that I began to see how much more I had to learn. Because although I thought I'd outgrown my propensity towards longing, there were many similarities between my longing for a baby in my thirties and my longing for a boyfriend the decade before. Both made me more focused on the love I didn't have rather than the love I did. Both sometimes tipped me towards self-pity. Both made me compare myself to others and feel like there was an area of happiness in life I was excluded from. I used to look longingly at couples holding hands on Sundays, but now I fixated on women pushing buggies round the local park. The thing I was longing for had changed, but the restless, searching feelings were the same. I understood then there would always be something to long for in love if I continued to see it in this narrow way – a boyfriend, a marriage, a baby, a second baby, a grandchild, another decade on this Earth with my mother, father or husband. So I began to ask more questions. I began to write this book.

Every day, you will be asking your own questions about love too. Maybe you are looking for a relationship or, in a secret place in your heart, asking whether you should leave one. Maybe you are in a long-term partnership, wondering how to sustain love through life's many storms. Maybe you are a parent and you want to be a better one; or you've lost a parent, and that loss suddenly seems to dwarf everything else. On the surface what we want and need from love are different. But I have found that our individual questions are often rooted in three bigger ones: How do we find love? How do we sustain it? And how do we survive when we lose it? These are the questions I want to explore in the pages ahead.

It's no exaggeration to say the conversations about love

I've had have changed my life. They helped me to see through the mist of longing, to see the love that was already in my life, all along. They've also convinced me that, although love *is* in many ways unknowable, it is useful for us to try to define it. As bell hooks wrote in *All About Love*, 'Learning faulty definitions of love when we are quite young makes it difficult to be loving as we grow older' and 'a good definition marks our starting point and lets us know where we want to end up'.

And we do need to start learning more about love, I think, just as we would any other skill, because it can determine the course of a life. As Dr Julianne Holt-Lunstad found in her study on the link between social connection and lifespan, people with strong social relationships are 50 per cent less likely to die prematurely than people with weak social relationships.* Despite the lack of attention it gets – contrast the number of pages a newspaper devotes to politics or finance or travel compared to relationships – there are few things more serious, more important than love. A lack of it can cause so much damage. A wealth of it can heal us.

Although the conversations in this book are stories about love, they are also about the way humans are drawn together and disappointed by each other, how they hurt and mend, how they keep moving forward, even when they think they can't, trying to grasp some meaning from what life takes away from them. My hope is that they can be for you what they have been for me: a reminder to not let the people you love slip into the background; an invitation to take love more seriously; and an

* Quoted in Vivek H. Murthy, *Together: Loneliness, Health and What Happens When We Find Connection*, Profile Books, 2020, page 13.

encouragement to make something meaningful out of the life you have been given. One of the characters in Hilary Mantel's novel *A Place of Greater Safety* said (in real life), 'Love is stronger, more lasting than fear.' And when I interviewed Hilary she told me that 'one reason to write is to try to find out if that is so'. This is what I am trying to find out too. Is love stronger than the fear of uncertainty? Than the fear of change? Than the fear of death? Answering these questions is a never-ending task, and this is one of the greatest lessons I have learnt: love is a lifelong project, a story that we can't skip to the end of. How lucky are we, to know we will never finish it? Because there is never a final page, only a series of beginnings. This is one of them.

How do we find love?

'Life is not a problem to be solved,
but a mystery to be lived.'

(M. Scott Peck)

Romantic Fantasy vs Reality

'When I desire you a part of me is gone . . .'
(Anne Carson, Eros the Bittersweet*)*

The first time I kissed Ben was the first time I kissed anyone. I was fourteen and uncertain of everything: what music I liked, what brand of school shoes to wear, what sort of person I wanted to be. The only thing I was certain of was wanting him. At a time when all the choices in the world were stretched out in front of me, and I could easily make the wrong ones, it was a relief to have so little control over something. It was as if the feeling chose me.

I met him a year before our first kiss in the ABC cinema. I was thirteen and he was twelve, six months younger than me. He came over to my house to hang out with my younger brother because they went to the same school. When I saw him, he was spinning a lemon-yellow yo-yo at the top of the stairs outside my bedroom. 'Hi,' he said. 'Hello,' I said. And that was it; two words were enough to set a fifteen-year-long crush in motion. Going forward, I collected details of his existence like forensic evidence: the exact position of a freckle on his arm, the way he spread butter on toast, how he squinted when he smiled, whenever he smiled. It was in longing for him to notice me that I learnt love was something that either happened to you or didn't. A gift that was either bestowed or held back.

Our flings over the years were brief and inconsistent: he cheated on me when we were fourteen, we were drawn back together at sixteen – the only time we ever nervously said 'I love you' – and again at eighteen. These were not periods in which we ever spent significant amounts of time together, only a collection of days and nights on which we kissed, watched old *Star Wars* VHS tapes and sometimes drove around empty country lanes at night. The fact that we never had a real relationship was of little importance. Our story existed in ambiguity, and in all the things we would never say.

The longer, more thrilling chapters were written in my mind, not in reality. My imaginary narrative formed a nostalgic will-they-won't-they romance – modelled on Dawson and Joey's – that was constantly on the precipice of happening and yet never quite seemed to. There was always a mutual misunderstanding (a text message misinterpreted) or an act of fate (my parents' disapproval; another girl) that thwarted our latest reconciliation. Why did I keep trying to make it work? When he kissed another girl at school it was my first experience of rejection, which dented my self-worth at a formative age. From then on his affection felt like a prize I could win back, one that might mean I was lovable. A part of me that longed to recreate my parents' relationship kept Ben in my orbit too. They met at school when they were fifteen, and their model of love, more romantic than any novel on my bookshelf, was the earliest one I had. If I put Ben on a pedestal, I put the idea of an everlasting teenage love on a higher one.

How many of us have these stories of adolescent infatuation, in which longing is more important than knowing, and fantasy trumps reality? This kind of young love is often constructed with beautiful intensity, which is understandable in your teenage years, when you are rich in time and ruled by hormones. Maybe such fixation is even a form of creativity – how a youthful imagination can take the scant details of an ordinary connection and build another world inside it. So I don't regret my first romantic fantasy. But I do regret the template for love that I drew from it, and all the subsequent years I spent trying to mould myself to fit it.

Throughout our university years, Ben and I continued to pass inconsistent affection back and forth. He posted me home-made CDs and cryptic notes I stored in shoeboxes beneath my bed. He sent nostalgic emails which my boyfriend at the time discovered and got angry about. In my memory this was the first time he wanted me more than I wanted him, but he may have a different story. (There are always two.) Still, when I was homesick I slept in his faded black H&M T-shirt, because he had become a memory of home, a tie to a past version of myself that was reassuring to flick back to whenever I felt confused in the present.

The irony is, I was confused because I had carried over the unhelpful lessons from this teenage infatuation into other relationships in my twenties. My pattern was often the same: I'd date someone new, idealize them, keep parts of myself hidden, and perform the role of a woman more palatable than I believed myself to be. This woman never asked for anything. Often I dated someone for months – sometimes over a year – without ever becoming 'boyfriend' and 'girlfriend', or progressing into real intimacy. And like Ben, even when these men hinted at their feelings for me, they never quite named them. As Marianne says when Eleanor asks if Willoughby ever said 'I love you' in *Sense and Sensibility*: 'It was every day implied, but never professedly declared. Sometimes I thought it had been – but it never was.'

When you are not being honest in a relationship – to another person or to yourself – it is a little like screwing on the top of a jam jar when the ridges are out of line. An onlooker might think you are screwing it on just fine, but you can feel a stiffness developing that warns you it's not on properly, and you know then that, however hard you try to keep turning it, the lid will never tightly seal. In this way I could always feel something in these relationships was out of sync from the beginning. Moving through the motions of intimacy with this dread pulling at the back of my mind was an anxious state to exist in, always suspecting that a person did not want to be with me but being too afraid to ask. It meant I got so good at pretending I didn't need anything that I forgot how to be myself. It also meant I mistook instability for attraction, because the scraps of affection men tossed me were more thrilling for their inconsistency: the surprise of a text message at 1.30 a.m. that said, 'Are you out?x', or the promise of a drunken 'I love you' never mentioned again when sober. The men I dated never called the relationships off, but never fully committed to them either. They always had one foot in and one foot out, like my friend's boyfriend who moved into her flat but still kept most of his belongings at his family's home.

More consistent than any affection was a careless – perhaps unintentional – cruelty that I silently accepted and used as further proof that I was unlovable. Like the time a man told me my lips were always dry while kissing me in bed, or when another said I wore too much make-up, or when yet another said, 'Insecurity is the most unattractive quality in a woman,' after I'd summoned up the courage to ask why he took so long to reply to my messages. I learnt that the loneliest place of all is lying in bed at night next to someone who makes you feel small, with your back to theirs, still hoping they will turn over and put their arms around you.

At the time, I recognized this suppressing of the self as a private, graceless shame; only now do I understand it to be an unoriginal problem. I've spoken to countless people who – despite feeling confident at work, with family, with friends – have lost themselves in relationships. Have squashed their personalities into a different shape and forgotten their own needs and desires in an attempt to second-guess a partner's. This shrinking of the self starts in small ways: pretending you want to see a horror film at the cinema; making Spotify playlists of songs that might impress them instead of the ones you really want to listen to; buying a dress you can't afford just because you think they'll like it. But soon, you're saying no to plans with friends just to keep an evening free on the off-chance they might ask to see you at the last minute. You're acting like it's not a big deal that they didn't show up at your birthday until 11 p.m. You're pretending you don't need relationship labels or consistent communication or the small acts of kindness that make you feel loved. You're pretending you don't need anything at all.

When I asked psychiatrist Dr Megan Poe why people lose their sense of self in relationships, she said it's sometimes because they're trying to 'echo-locate the other and not reveal the self' and merge with them. According to Dr Poe, who used to teach a course on love at New York University, 'People think, if I'm matching the other person then we're a match, but that makes them more insecure because they're not being themselves.' This behaviour also means the other person gets confused, because they don't recognize who you've become. 'When a lot of false selves emerge it can get really foggy,' Dr Poe said, 'and inevitably the other person thinks, where are they? I can't find the person I originally fell for.'

In a commencement speech at Douglass College in 1977, Adrienne Rich said that responsibility to yourself 'means insisting that those to whom you give your friendship and love are able to respect your mind. It means being able to say, with Charlotte Brontë's Jane Eyre: "I have an inward treasure born with me, which can keep me alive if all the extraneous delights should be withheld or offered only at a price I cannot afford to give."' When I looked up the original Jane Eyre line I found the one that precedes Rich's quote: 'I can live alone, if self-respect, and circumstances require me to do so.' Reading both lines together, I realized I'd done the opposite to Jane. I'd lost sight of my inward treasure (and therefore my ability to walk away) and, as a result, had traded in my self-respect. And for what? Not for love, but for a gut feeling that told me the men I dated were extraordinary humans, always cleverer and more interesting than I was. (It was no coincidence that I often dated journalists, advertising creatives and writers – all careers I wanted but had not at that point been brave enough to pursue.) It wasn't until I interviewed clinical psychologist Dr Frank Tallis years later that I understood how misleading that gut feeling could be. Because, as Tallis told me, we often 'aggrandize our own confusion or lack of insight' when we have no evidence of real intimacy. We reach for words like 'chemistry' or 'gut feeling' because we have nothing tangible to base a feeling on – no examples of kindness or care or connection, just a magnetic draw. Tallis said this lack of evidence 'becomes fuel for romantic mysticism. You think, I can't explain it, so therefore it must be fate, it must be profound. But that's just one false inference feeding another, and each inference takes you further away from reality.' As I listened to his explanation I winced with recognition, remembering all the times I felt mystically drawn to someone without any real knowledge of who they were. But I did not understand this at the time, and so I continued to erase pieces of myself to sustain relationships that had no roots in the real world.

Even during those years, as we fell in and out of relationships with other people, Ben and I kept in touch. Our parents were – and still are – very close, so we'd grown up going on family holidays together and still returned home to villages five minutes apart. Occasionally we flirted or kissed or talked for hours on the phone at night. Sometimes I called him because I was lonely. Sometimes I think he called me because he was lost. Mostly we were friends who used each other for attention, but once in our late twenties we reunited for a brief romance, which only lasted a month or two. It felt like we were grown-ups pretending to be thirteen again in a way that made me sad. And as I traced the differences between our adult and teenage bodies in bed – his softer, fuller stomach; my larger, dimpled thighs – I couldn't tell if I was trying to find a person I once knew, or one I had never really known at all. Both of us, I think, were looking for answers to the problems of adulthood and intimacy in each other; a place where we would never find them.

A year later we went for the drink which would be our last alone. On the pavement outside a Soho bar afterwards, I saw that somewhere in the night air between us was a decision that wasn't really about the person standing in front of me at all. It was between immaturity and growing up, between fantasy and reality. Did I want to keep avoiding intimacy and lean back into the safety of a nostalgic crush that didn't require me to do anything differently? No. I wanted to form *real* relationships that existed in the real world. To do so would require courage and self-understanding, maybe a little lone-liness, and a lot of responsibility. Part of that responsibility meant not calling Ben for attention whenever I felt alone. It meant understanding the role I was playing in idealizing men instead of really seeing them, and finding the inward treasure I had lost in the process. It meant, as bell hooks wrote in *All About Love*, wanting to know 'the meaning of love beyond the realm of fantasy – beyond what we imagine can happen'. I still believed the act of showing yourself fully to a new person was a risk, but somewhere inside me a fresh knowledge was unfolding: that the risk of not doing so – of never being seen, of never expressing needs, of never giving and accepting real love – was far greater. After years of feeling passive in love, I understood then that we do have a choice, even if it's difficult to see. Mine was this: to stay in the fantasies inside my head, or to climb out and live.

*

It's a strange feeling, thinking about who you were in past relationships: a mix of sadness and humour, of mortification and frustration. But as well as learning to laugh with friends at some of the more embarrassing stories – one of the few upsides to errors in dating – the shame I once felt has been replaced with compassion for the younger version of myself who so desperately wanted to find love, and was looking for it in all the wrong places.

Part of me still regrets how many years I squandered worrying that I had 'failed' at love or that I would never find it. Another part is terrified by the fact that I was so infatuated with a fantasy that when the opportunity for real love was right in front of me – when I met the man who I would one day choose to marry – I very nearly missed him. But I also know these earlier 'failings' are what led me here. As Hilary Mantel told me when I interviewed her, 'Some mistakes have to be made, they are creative errors.' And she was right; it was in all those clumsy mistakes and years of longing that I found the root of the first question in this book: how do we find love?

I think before we try to answer that question, it's useful to look more closely at it. Because how can we work out how to find love without asking what that word really means? That's what I will explore in the conversations ahead: how might our definition of love impact how and where and if we find it? Which clichés can help us, and which should we ditch? And are we more or less in control of finding love than we think? The answers won't include a dating-app strategy or a percentage-based study of where you're most likely to meet a partner. But I hope they will be an invitation to see love in a more expansive way, and to find examples of it we might be overlooking.

*

When I was searching for love in my twenties, there seemed to be two types of people who were looking for romantic relationships: those who easily fell into them and were content in the spaces between when they were – albeit briefly – single.

And those who found falling in love an impossible task, who couldn't seem to find happiness on their own, but couldn't get past the starting-block stage of a relationship either. I had always been in the latter camp. So when an unhelpful colleague said, 'When someone is single for a long period of time and they don't want to be, there's usually a reason,' I held on to her words as evidence there must be a reason I was single too. Was I too needy? Too intense? I didn't suspect part of the problem might be not who I was, but the context within which I viewed the search for love.

When I began interviewing people about relationships, I realized how many others fell into the trap of putting too much focus on romantic love. Lots blamed their obsession with romance on the old fairy-tale narratives in popular culture. Undoubtedly, these stories played a part for me. But there was also an unhealthy story about solitude that had somewhere seeped into my view of love. Why did I once believe that being alone was a tragedy? And what effect did that fear have on my search for love? I hoped the philosopher and the School of Life founder Alain de Botton would have the answers.

Alain was one of the first people I interviewed about love, because he was one of the first people to encourage me to see its complexity. From his novel *Essays in Love*, I learnt about infatuation: the fantasies and false starts, the obsessions and stories we project on to each other. And later from his book *The Course of Love*, I learnt about the challenges of intimacy long after the initial sheen of desire has worn off. Few people chronicle love with as much meticulous rigour and pragmatism as Alain. So I was not surprised to find that he cut to the heart of why – for some of us – the search for love is such a vulnerable experience.

The psychology of being alone, with Alain de Botton

NL: People fall into the trap of seeing romantic love as the answer to their problems. How does that misunderstanding make the search for a relationship more difficult?

AdB: It suggests that if the search for a partner didn't work out then it would be a tragedy, that your life would essentially have been wasted. That sets up a frantic, unhelpful backdrop to the search for love. The best frame of mind to be in – for anything you want – is an ability to walk away from it, were it not to come right. Otherwise you put yourself at the mercy of chance and people abusing your desperation. So the capacity to say, 'I could be alone,' is strangely one of the most important guarantees of one day being with somebody else in a happy way.

The psychology of being alone is interesting, because it can be experienced as more or less humiliating, depending on the story we tell ourselves. If you're alone on a Monday night, for example, you don't feel particularly bad about it. You think, I've had a hard day at work, there's a long week ahead, I'll spend time on my own. Whereas if you're alone on a Saturday night, you can think, what's wrong with me? Everybody else is out having a lovely life with other people.

Often we have crude models of the lives of others, which aggravate our despair of being on our own. We tend to imagine, when we're alone, that everybody is in a happy relationship other than us. It's easy to think, I'm the only vaguely decent person to whom this has happened. And that's not true; lots of dignified and capable people have, for one reason or another, found themselves on their own. It doesn't have to be a tragedy.

But it can feel lonely when your coupled friends disappear on a weekend in a way they don't during the week. How do you think we can change the way we see those weekends?

First of all, it's about pinpointing where the problem lies. The problem is not being alone. It's being alone when you have a story in your head about human beings, and the proper place of companionship within our story. Instead of going out to learn dancing simply to avoid Saturday-night agony, you could change the story in your head about what being alone means. Because if being in your own company is fine on a Monday and a tragedy on a Saturday, the problem is not the objective fact of being alone, it's the story you're telling yourself.

You once told me when we use the word 'love', what we're really talking about is connection. That made me think of times I felt I didn't have love in my life, when actually I did. Is it helpful to re-evaluate what the word 'love' means?

Yes, or what it is we're really seeking within love. Someone might feel their life is incomplete without a relationship. But if you ask, 'What is it about your relationship-less state that is so desperate?' often you find smaller areas of discomfort that can be addressed in other ways. Someone might say they want love, and then when they're forced to think about why, it's because they want connection. Is that dependent on having a relationship? Not necessarily, because you can have connection outside a relationship. Then another person might say, 'I want intellectual stimulation.' Well, does that depend on a relationship? Again, not necessarily. A lot of things we reserve for relationships are available elsewhere. For example, there's a tragic misalignment of the hierarchy of friendships and relationships. It's odd how we've relegated friendship so far down the line. It hasn't always been this way: in early-nineteenth-century Germany having a good friend was seen as more important than having a lover, and much closer to the roots of happiness.

A topic I'm getting different points of view on is the cliché that you have to love yourself before you can love someone else. I'm wondering if, rather than self-love, perhaps self-understanding is a more useful goal. Where do you stand on this?

I'd place the emphasis on self-understanding too, and the capacity to communicate it. If somebody said, 'I don't adore myself, but I'm interested in myself and I can communicate the truth about myself to other people,' that would be more reassuring than somebody who said, 'I'm perfect.' Acknowledging your brokenness, pain and insufficiency is a rather romantic thing to do. Actually, an overemphatic self-admiration cuts you off from other people, whereas an engagement with your own vulnerability is key to building a bond. When it comes to self-love it's not so much about loving yourself, but accepting that all human beings have their less impressive sides, and so your less impressive sides don't cut you off from the possibility of having a good relationship. They don't mean that you're a terrible person who doesn't deserve love. They just mean you are part of the human family.

If you don't value or understand yourself, is there more risk you could lose yourself in a relationship?

It sounds odd that you could lose touch with your own self. How could that be possible? You are you; how could you become less you by being in contact with somebody else? But we receive data from our senses and emotional selves, which can be overruled by data we get from other people. A classic example is if you say, 'I'm a bit sad,' and another person goes, 'No, you're not, you're fine. You're doing so well.' You might then think, my point of view is not legitimate. They are right, I'm fine. When actually, it might be important for you to step back and acknowledge that things *are* difficult.

One way of looking at the risk of losing yourself is through the prism of self-love or self-hatred, but another is asking, how much fidelity are you going to bring to being certain of your own feelings? And how many of your feelings are going to be overruled by stories that come in from the outside? Because, frequently, anyone you're in a relationship with has a view on what's right for you, or what's right or wrong in the world. And the capacity to say, 'That's interesting, but I've got my own reality, and I'm not sure that fits in,' depends on whether that's a muscle that's been exercised in childhood. Often it hasn't been, because many aspects of a child's reality are overruled by parents. A child might say, 'I want to kill Granny. She's so stupid.' And the parent might say, 'No you don't, you love her.' Actually, a wiser parent would say, 'I suppose we do all sometimes get a bit angry with others, maybe she disappointed you in some way. What way might that be?' Then the child might get in touch with their feelings to understand why, and they can talk about it. But people run away from more disturbing feelings in their children and encourage them to cut themselves off from them. Then, as an adult, they might not feel their feelings are legitimate.

In my early twenties, what got me into trouble in relationships was following a mysterious gut feeling. Why do you think that leads to unhelpful situations in love?

Our emotions are not entirely reliable: they tend to overshoot or undershoot the target. Think, for example, of fear. We tend to be afraid of the wrong things and overlook the real things we should be afraid of. We're afraid of ghosts, but we're not that afraid of how short our lives are, or that we've neglected our true talents. We're not great at knowing what there is to fear, nor are we great at knowing what there is to love (and in what quantities). If a rather charming candidate comes into view, we can slightly lose our faculties. We imagine who they are, how our lives are going to be together for ever, and that they are the fount of total happiness. At times like these, it's useful to recognize that we're in a crush. There should be another side of our mind that is aware this is going on. That side should be sympathetic to the enthusiasm, but still maintain a grip on reality, so that you're still aware that the other person is a stranger. That one good evening or one good weekend is not everything. That these feelings are not entirely reliable predictors of the future. I think those two sides are compatible: one can enjoy the crush just as one can go to a horror film, when one side of your mind is terrified (because you're thinking, oh my God, the monster is going to beat us) but the other side is going, *no, it's a film, it's not real.* We can play a similar sort of observer and feeler division in the early stages of love.

When you are in the middle of an intense crush, though, it can be difficult to know that it is a fantasy. What are the signs of that?

It's the scale of the idealization. If you've forgotten you've just met another human being, not a divine creature, then ultimately that person's going to be very frustrating when you realize they are just another flawed person. So having a certain pessimism about what people are like is useful. But I think that's compatible with kindness and enthusiasm. One of the best models of love is how parents love their children. Parents *really* love their children. At the same time, sometimes they don't like them – they get bored of them, they think they're awful, they want a break from them. And all those things go on in the love that an adult might have for another, too: sometimes we're fed up and aware of somebody's glaring faults, but still very much on their side. They annoy us and we still love them.

That makes me think idealizing someone is the opposite of love, because it means refusing to see the whole of them?

Yes, you're not witnessing them properly. No one really wants to be idealized – we want to be seen and accepted and forgiven, and to know that we can be ourselves in our less edifying moments. So to be on the receiving end of somebody's idealizing feelings is alienating. It looks like we're being seen and admired like never before, but actually, many important parts of us are being forgotten.

A big question in love I'm wrestling with is control. Because in some ways I think we are more in control in love than we have been led to believe, and it's important to know that our role isn't passive. On the other hand, I wonder if we also need to bring the idea of luck back into love, because you can be open and self-aware and want to meet someone, and it still might not happen when you hoped it would.

You don't have to be religious to believe that chance has a huge role to play and that, really, another person's life is a great mystery. There's only so much you can do to influence them. You can think that by saying the right things, or by reading every book on the subject matter, you will somehow reduce your chances of failure and increase your control. But that's only partially true. You can't tell where somebody else is in their life. They might just not fancy you, which is deeply unfortunate, but something to be accepted, not fought over, like bad weather. We don't control the weather, nor do we control other people's capacity to find us attractive. So yes, what's helpful is a certain reserve in us all to accept that, even if we were to be alone, it would be OK. To get there, we need to talk to more people: people who've divorced and would probably tell you never to get into a long-term relationship; older people who've spent a lifetime alone and content; priests and nuns and monks. We need to stop tying ourselves so narrowly to this punitive vision that we've got to date in our twenties, find the ideal partner by twenty-eight, and have our first child at thirty-one, otherwise our life will be miserable. If that sort of narrative happens, it'll be great in some ways and it'll be awful in others. We need to show more imagination about what a good life might look like.

What do you wish you'd known about finding love?

To be calmer about the whole process. And that things would work out or they wouldn't, and even then, that would be fine too. This black and white model of 'it's got to be like this and then it will be perfect' just doesn't work. It doesn't matter who you meet or when you meet them; there's pain and joy on each side of the ledger. So don't stick rigidly to one story about what your life means, because it's likely to be wrong. In fact, there are many ways of living this life.

*

If I'd had this conversation ten years earlier, it would have softened the edges of my loneliness. Alain made me see the situation of being alone not as an unflattering reflection of my 'less impressive sides', but as an unimaginative story I was telling about connection.

All the times I had been casually rejected, I realize now, were either future blessings or facts to be accepted, rather than resisted. I had wasted energy trying to keep these relationships afloat; there was no need to waste more asking why someone didn't love me, or what I could have done differently to change the outcome. The only outcome was the one that happened. And as Alain pointed out, 'There's pain and joy on each side of the ledger.' If I'd stayed with someone I'd met in my early twenties, moved to the seaside, got a dog and had a baby at thirty, there would have been wonderful and mundane chapters to that story, just as there were wonderful and mundane chapters to the life I lived during those years instead. For every depressing date, there was a precious friendship formed. For every lonely Sunday, a new ambition discovered.

In my earliest efforts at love, imagination was a thief that stole truth and perspective and time. It was a distraction from reality, which made me see love where there wasn't any. But Alain made me wonder if there was a way to use imagination to expand our idea of love, rather than to obscure it. Could we imagine the many different ways there are to live a life? Could we imagine all the potential sorrows and joys in all those different stories? Perhaps, if we could, we would see that there are no 'right' or 'wrong' stories after all – just the lives in front of us, full of possibilities.

*

Alain convinced me that searching for love from a place of fear was not a good beginning to any love story. It meant motivations were often selfish – to avoid loneliness; to outsource happiness – and would lead in the wrong direction. As the psychiatrist M. Scott Peck wrote, 'If being loved is your goal, you will fail to achieve it.' It was this line that encouraged me to speak to somebody who had managed to create a meaningful life outside of a romantic relationship, who had pulled back from a singular desire to be loved and accessed all the different forms of connection available to them. Because it is one thing to know that you need to de-centre the search for romantic love in your life, and another entirely to actually do it. I think the author Ayisha Malik is someone who has.

In Ayisha's debut novel *Sofia Khan is Not Obliged*, and its sequel *The Other Half of Happiness*, she not only explored what it was like to date as a Muslim woman, but captured the humour, heartbreak and necessary self-awareness involved in anyone's search for love. So when we first spoke, I expected our conversation to focus on dating. Instead, I discovered

Ayisha has an expansive view of love. She finds it everywhere: in work, in faith, in family, in friendships and in her continued investment in self-understanding and philosophy. I put to her the question I wish I'd asked myself two decades ago: how did she free herself from the powerful myth of romantic love, and learn to find connection in so many places?

No one person can see the whole of who you are, with Ayisha Malik

NL: What was your view of love when you were younger?

AM: I had a narrow, idealized version of what a love story looked like and it always involved the search for a romantic partner. As I grew older, I learnt that the expectation that someone will save you from who you are, or from what you have or don't have, is a fallacy. Expecting someone to fill in a hole that's within you? That's expecting too much of any one person. That's not your friend's job or your partner's job. That's your job.

Can you pinpoint when your understanding of love expanded?

Part of that lesson was finding a love story with my friends in my twenties, when I realized how profound, heartfelt, generous and consistent those friendships could be. Rain or shine, two o'clock in the morning, whatever we needed, we were there to talk each other through it. Those friends encouraged me to interrogate who I was as a person: what I believed, why I believed it.

The other part was a more gradual understanding that

nothing is consistent, and no one is perfect. Everyone is going to disappoint you, even your parents. Once I accepted that, I stopped expecting I would meet someone who would save me or make my life easier. I am a fairly grounded, well-rounded person; I don't need a hero. If I do meet someone, he will be a normal human being who is trying to figure out his way through the world, who is flawed and who will make mistakes, just as I will.

Was part of that acceptance understanding that there are many ways to love and be loved, outside of a relationship?

Yes, I found love in friendships and in work and in my faith. I said earlier that nothing is consistent, but that's not entirely true. Even through teen angst and my lonely twenties, even when friends or family felt uncertain, God has been solid and consistent in a way that absolutely nothing else in life has. I know it's not a fashionable thing to say. People might ask, 'How can any rational being believe in one God?' It sounds crazy when you talk about an omnipotent being who controls the universe. But for me, faith *is* about love. It's something I can rely on. It's something that gives me a sense of belonging. It's there, whether I feel it or not, even in times of despair. When you feel completely alone and at sea, a short prayer can give you the strength to go somewhere inside yourself to find love.

Have you ever felt distant from your faith?

I did feel removed from it for a while. For a long time my only aim was to be a successful writer. But I noticed that with each success there was a paring back of my spirituality. I remember praying one day, and speaking to God, and saying that if my success was going to come at the price of my spirituality, then I didn't want it. I would rather have peace and self-knowledge than be constantly struggling to succeed within a structure that is set up to keep you wanting more and more. Because we live in a very individualistic society, we focus on what we want and what we deserve, and we can forget the world doesn't owe us anything. There are billions of people on this Earth and, in the grand scheme of things, you are but a tiny part of the whole. My faith is a compass that reminds me of that. It is constantly humbling and helpful.

As well as being a form of love in your life, how has your faith shaped the way you see love more generally?

It has helped me to relinquish control over how my love story or life might pan out. Giving up that control is about having faith that things happened as they're meant to, and if a plan doesn't go accordingly that's because there's something else waiting for you – you just don't know what it is yet. I recently listened to a podcast about Stoicism and I saw the connection to Islam. In both, there's this idea of understanding that all you have control over is how you react to a situation and how you treat others. So faith has shaped the way I see love because it's shifted my focus from myself as an individual to the other people around me. It's shown me that meaning in life comes from the kindness and compassion you show to others, and also from a deep, peaceful acceptance that allows you to look disaster and joy in the eye with the same kind of level-headedness.

I think understanding my lack of control in love is one of the things I've struggled with. Because we often have the illusion of control, and that can be confusing.

Absolutely. We're tricked or fooled into believing we have control. Let's take dating. It's such a fraught process. You're concentrating so hard on finding someone to build this certain life with, and then you meet someone and you're like, oh, they're nice, I like them, they like me. But before you can even reach the next stage you're already thinking about what you'll lose if you lose them – you're losing the idea of the future. You're so focused on that that you can ignore signs that this person might not be right for you. But when you relinquish control over how things happen, it lessens that fear of losing something. Which is important, because that fear of loss can force people to make bad decisions when it comes to love.

You said that, as well as friends and faith, work was a form of love in your life too. How so?

A friend once asked me, 'If you had the choice between marrying the love of your life and writing, what would you choose?' And I said writing. I think maybe it is the love of my life, because what you get from it is an understanding of the human condition. We're all searching for the truth, and I find it in words. As a writer, you're also showing the readers parts of yourself. It's only looking back that I see the purpose I've found in work might have been the love I was seeking. Because everyone wants to belong, and while you can have that anchor in your family, you split time with those people. They're not quite everything to you. I guess that's what people seek in a partner; they need to feel anchored to that person in an inextricable way. But I get that feeling with writing, because whatever peaks and troughs life may bring, I feel bound to it and grounded by it. I'm still open to a romantic relationship, but I want love to be a part of the puzzle that is my life. I don't need it to be the full picture.

That's the point a lot of us want to get to, but other people's expectations can make it difficult. Was there a time when you felt under societal pressure to have a relationship? And if so, how did you free yourself from that?

Even if you're completely fine with being single, the minute someone pities you, you think, am I not living the way I'm meant to? We spend our whole lives trying to meet targets set by someone else. We lose sight of who we are, because we're so busy chasing external things. In love that means people search for what's outside of them (a romantic partner) and lose sight of what's inside them (a potential for self-development and understanding).

There is a rigid framework in which you're supposed to have done certain things by a certain age. That was so deeply enshrined in my subconscious that I didn't question it. I started dating in my early twenties because it was something I thought I *should* be doing, not because I wanted to. I dreamt about wanting it. I watched films about wanting it. But in reality I wasn't ready for a relationship. I also saw the process of my sister being introduced to 'suitors' and I knew I wouldn't go through that, because most of the arranged marriages that I saw were a complete disaster. My father passed away when we were young, so because my mum was raising two daughters on her own there was pressure on her to make sure her eldest daughter married. She just knew I wasn't going to do that. But I still have that pressure. Just the other day my brother-in-law said, 'Ayisha, it's time to get married.' And when I go to weddings or family gatherings people often point out that I'm not. Part of trying to figure out what you really want from life is ensuring you're selective about who you surround yourself with, so now I largely refuse to go to places where I know I'll be interrogated about not being married, because there's no love or concern there. It's just nosiness.

When it comes to dating, I've found a way to do it on my own terms. I've never desperately wanted to have kids. So because I don't have the burden of wanting to be a mother, that allows dating to be about finding a person who I want to actually be with. It frees me up to be more chilled about the process.

What advice would you give someone who is struggling to create meaning in their life outside of a relationship?

Figure out what you're looking for outside of yourself that you've not found within. Are you looking for a relationship because you genuinely want one? Or because you don't love yourself and you think that if you meet someone who loves you it will validate your self-worth? Sometimes people do get into relationships to validate what they think they lack. A lot of it is self-interrogation. On the other hand, being contentedly single is a huge blessing, but you want to be sure that you're not making decisions out of apathy or comfort or fear. We can be so cynical about love that sometimes I wonder whether we end up shooting ourselves in the foot. This idea of – I'm using air quotes – 'I'm a strong independent woman who doesn't need a man' can also be dangerous, because being strong doesn't mean you don't need people. We're not born to be alone. We need community, however we choose to find it: with a partner, with friends, with family. I think there's a danger of pulling away from love in order to own your feminism, when, actually, you learn to understand yourself in relation to people around you. You can find independence through connection too.

What do you wish you'd known about finding love?

I spent a lot of time thinking that love was loading an expectation on to one person to see me for who I am and love me regardless. But actually, that's completely untenable for any one person, whether it's your partner or your sibling or your best friend. You can be seen by various people in different ways, and no one person, not even your parents, can really see the whole of who you are. So it's about finding *all* the different people you can love, and seeing the positivity each of them brings to your life.

*

I have often asked why, for nearly a decade, I clung on to miserable relationships until the other person walked away. Why do we sometimes choose to hurt ourselves more in the future by denying a painful truth in the present? So many of us do. Nearly all my friends have too. One dated a man who committed to events with her family – a wedding, a christening – and then cancelled at the last minute. Another remained in a relationship with a man who forgot every important life milestone – a job interview, a driving test, her mother's heart surgery – even though she had gone to every gig or football match that had been important to him. One friend stayed with someone who gave her thoughtless gifts, like a weird spoon or one maraca, and another dated a man who would ask her out on a specific day, then never arrange a time or place, so she would spend that day anxiously waiting, before being forced to text and ask if it was still on.

When I was having similar experiences in dating, I wish I'd known that there is more to fear inside a relationship that shrinks you than in a life outside of it. And that one approach to fighting that fear is looking for different ways to feel less alone. Speaking to Ayisha made me see that when we stop relying on one person to make us happy, we not only find more confidence to question a relationship that isn't working; we live a more varied and interesting life. As she said, no one person can see the whole of who we are.

I'd learnt, too, that building a strong romantic relationship required self-sufficiency and self-understanding: two things I had lost in earlier relationships. Before I could find them, as Ayisha explained, I had to figure out what I was looking for outside of myself that I had not found within, then understand who I was in the present in relation to my past.

*

After four years of interviewing people about love, I had discovered how many of us share a secret fear of not being good enough. Even so, I was still surprised to discover the psychotherapist Philippa Perry once felt it too. The author of the bestselling *The Book You Wish Your Parents Had Read (and Your Children Will Be Glad That You Did)* is someone I, and thousands of others, turn to to understand how our childhood shapes our adult relationships. So hearing that she too had once believed she was not worthy of love was a reminder that problems like these are not unique reports on our individual failings, just ordinary human experiences we share.

I wanted to find out how we could see through the mess of all these misunderstandings – of ourselves and of others – and begin to build a love that was real, and not a fantasy. I had experienced the tumultuous first months of an unhappy relationship, but what did the beginnings of a good one look like?

Nobody is right for anyone, with Philippa Perry

NL: What are the benefits to falling in love slowly?

PP: What makes a satisfactory coupling is not thinking, he or she is right for me, from the start. Nobody is right for anyone. Actually, what makes somebody right is commitment. Then when you're committed to each other and you have true dialogue, that means you allow the other to impact upon you and they allow you to impact on them. You're not rigid and unchanging; you are moved by each other. It's like two stones rubbing together until suddenly they fit. You have your initial years of sexual attraction and then something deeper can hook in. Rather than having a relationship with your fantasy of that person you begin to have a real relationship with them; you've impacted each other enough to actually *know* each other. And to know someone is to love them. So you make someone the right person and they make you the right person. There isn't someone the right shape out there for every person – that has to happen in relationships. That's why relationships get better, because we allow mutual impact.

Was meeting your husband Grayson an instant attraction or a more gradual one?

We went to the same evening class and I thought, oh, what an uncouth young man. I even went for a drink with a couple of other blokes from that class before I went for a drink with him. There wasn't an initial attraction at all. But over six months, we had a meeting of the minds that turned into love. That seems a more satisfactory way of going about it, really. The only chance of meeting someone for one date and thinking you want to meet up again is if you've got 'chemistry', which is great for a hook-up, but not an indicator of long-term love. Meeting someone often happens in a place where you get used to being around them. You like or love someone when you like or love yourself when you're with them – and that takes a long time to know. You have to let them in.

Why do you think people find the early stage of love so difficult?

Sometimes you want to become the other person's fantasy, so you don't lose them. You can be knocked out of shape a bit, and that's different from mutual impact. That's adaption, which is bad because you're morphing out of shape to please the other. Whereas when you allow mutual impact, you're not putting on an act to please the other – you allow impact because it's the flow of dialogue, and hopefully you're both doing it.

I wanted to talk about mutual erotic transference. Could you explain what it is and how it can affect us when we meet someone?

We tend to connect to what is familiar because what we recognize makes us feel good. Our body has a memory that isn't conscious: maybe the way Nanny's hair fell across her forehead, or what it felt like to be given a piggyback on Dad's back. We haven't got a memory of those feelings because they were never put into words – they are pre-verbal memories. But that doesn't mean they don't resonate with us deeply when we see or feel them again. For example, suppose two young people look at each other and, although he doesn't know it, she reminds him of his mother's ankles. He will have a familiar sensation that feels like coming home. Although these are pre-verbal memories they feel *right*, so someone might think, I knew as soon as I saw him that he was for me. It might be the sound of a laugh, or the way someone punctuates their sentences, that the body hooks on to. It's the ghost of a memory, and when we latch on to ghosts of memories (especially if they have good associations) they make us feel great.

Do you think there's a danger in some relationships of falling into a pattern where one is the responsible parent figure, and the other becomes the child?

Yes, that's not good! In every relationship you have different roles and it's good to share them. The most dominant ones are what I call 'the dreamer' and 'the accountant'. Somebody has all the great dreams (Let's go to Thailand for a year! Let's start a new business! I've got a fantastic idea for making a film!) and the other will do the logistics (sorting out the tax; paying the bills; booking the flights). In my first relationship I was the dreamer and my husband sorted out the tax and paid the bills. In my current relationship, I'm forced continually into the role of accountant while Grayson does the dreaming – and I fight it. Otherwise I would be ripping open envelopes and making lists, with no space for my own creativity. I fight for that space to be the dreamer.

There are tough patches in a relationship and then there are bad relationships. What do you think are the signs that you've fallen into the latter?

When you start to feel lonely. If you're seen more or less how you see yourself – or perhaps expanded by how someone else sees you – then you feel met in a relationship. If you're diminished, then you don't feel met. If you're not seen at all, and someone continues having a relationship with their fantasy of you instead of with you, then that's lonely. And if that's a negative fantasy? It's toxic.

Have you ever been in a relationship in which you didn't feel seen?

When I met my first husband I began to believe I would be nothing without him, because I never felt good enough. He had great cheekbones, but he didn't have much respect for me. None, really. My friends at work said, 'I don't think he's good for you.'

I also thought nobody would want to be friends with me, and they only wanted to be friends with him, because he was so clever. My friends kept saying, 'No! We're *your* friend. We're not friends with you because of him.' But I couldn't hear it.

One weekend when he was away I invited friends over for lunch. I was erecting a collapsible table and trapped a bit of skin on my hand in it. It split open; there was blood everywhere. I rang my friends and said, 'I've got to cancel, I'm afraid; I'm going to the hospital.' And I couldn't believe it: they came to the hospital and were kind to me all day. Then, when my husband came home and saw my bandaged hand, he said, 'Oh Christ, you've always done something, haven't you.' And instead of being sucked into it, I thought, that's very different to the kindness my friends showed me. Hmm, I don't like this. I better get out. It was easy once I'd had that realization. It was like I woke up.

If someone you spend a lot of time with tells you you're not worth much, that begins to dent your confidence. So when friends said to me about my first husband, 'Er, no, it's you I'm friends with,' it was really good for me. That happened in my late twenties, when I was enjoying work with a nice bunch of people. I began to have a different view of myself and I saw that I didn't like who I was with my first husband. Because when you like who you are when you are with another person, you realize how important it is to be around people who make you feel that way. They reflect your goodness back to you, and you know you've got it.

I think one reason people stay in relationships like those is because they feel undeserving of love. Where do you think that comes from?

I think it's because it felt to the child who was forming – whether it was true or not – that love was conditional on them being a certain way. They might think, if you knew the real me, you wouldn't love me, because they felt the real 'me' wasn't loved. If you grew up with parents who were always rushed or harassed, they might only have given praise because you were trying to be a different person in order to get attention. What happens then is you make a shiny shell that appeals to people to make yourself feel great, but that shell is a fabrication, a sort of forced identity, rather than your inner being.

When people first come to therapy they say in many ways the same sentence, which is, 'If you really knew me, you wouldn't like me.' So I say, 'Show me that nasty part.' By encouraging people to say their negative thoughts out loud it reassures them they are not an awful person. Often someone feels those things, not because of something bad they've done, but due to a free-floating shame that exists because they learnt as a child to believe they were bad.

Other than therapy, how can we cultivate kindness for ourselves despite those negative thoughts?

Everybody's got a critical or anxious inner voice. It helps to write it down, to turn all the 'what ifs?' into 'so whats'. A friend or partner can also challenge you when you're being neurotic, because being able to hear other people's ideas of you – if they come from a place of goodwill – is therapeutic.

It's about finding someone you can be 'you' around without performing, without being the party person or the successful I'm-in-control-of-everything person. Someone you can experiment with being vulnerable in front of and accepted by. That can make you feel like a new 'you'. And when you take the risk to be vulnerable with another person, and they accept you as you are, it's amazing.

Why is it difficult for some people to ask for their needs to be met in a relationship?

For the last hundred years or so we've trained children not to ask for anything, because it's a nuisance. Children are told, 'Those that ask don't get.' And then as an adult they think they'd be selfish if they said, 'It makes me feel better when you text before you go to sleep to say goodnight.' It doesn't sound much to ask, does it? But somehow it feels enormous, because of small comments like, 'I've told you twice not to call me after bedtime.' Parents don't do this hatefully. They think they're doing it so you don't become an annoying little asker, but it makes you into one. Because if you don't ask for your needs to be met, they won't be, and that can make you needy.

Is finding love in friendships or community, as well as a relationship, an important part of building self-esteem?

The idea that connection has to come entirely from one other person is bollocks. Obviously I like being married, otherwise I wouldn't have been married to the same bloke for thirty years. He's a constantly curious person, I love him and being with him, but to put couple love above agape [charitable love for strangers or God], philia [a friendship bond] and storge [love between parents and children] is not helpful. We need more than couple love, because it can be too inward-looking without other forms of connection. So it's important to ask, what loving things can you do towards your friend group or community? How can you put down your barriers so you can be welcomed into those relationships?

Maybe, then, it's more about putting our efforts into finding different forms of love rather than thinking, I need to be content on my own.

If you look at hunter-gatherer tribes, people are rarely on their own. We're pack animals and this idea that we have to go on solo holidays all the time and make it alone in a super-human way? It's bollocks. If you don't like being alone, you don't like it, and that's all right. Forcing yourself to do something when every cell in your body is screaming 'no' just leads to panic. It's difficult to know the difference between forcing yourself to do something that's not good for you, and being scared of doing something that is good for you. If the fear is excitement, then feel it and do it anyway. But if it's about the massive amount of willpower that's required to do something out of societal pressure, then that's different.

What do you wish you'd known about love?

That I needn't worry about not being good enough. And that love is about finding a home. Our parents aren't going to live for ever, so I think we need to find a tribe, a family, a community or a group that feels like home. A place where we feel seen, and where we can see.

*

In my twenties, I lost myself in romantic relationships. So, in my thirties, I was determined not to change for anyone. But Philippa showed me that part of falling in love *is* letting another person have an impact on you. You're not rigid and unchanging, she told me, you're altered by each other, 'like two stones rubbing together until suddenly they fit'. The important distinction? When you want to change to keep a partner interested, that's 'adaption', which is bad because you're bending your identity to please another. Whereas when you change alongside another person, that's 'mutual impact', because you're not putting on an act to please anyone. Instead, you're growing, individually and together.

*

Truth, I think, is the core of love. As a woman called Gill Hammond told me, 'When you can get to the truth, even if it doesn't resolve the actual issue, you are connected in some way.' And when we don't tell the truth – when we perform or pretend in love, or try on different versions of ourselves to get someone's approval – we invite loneliness in. Although we are trying to attract love, really we're blocking it. Instead of trying to be known and seen, we are hiding, holding back.

The obvious solution is to not pretend to be someone you're not, while still allowing space for the person you are dating to get to know you (and vice versa). Most of us know this. Some of us still avoid it. Because being yourself in a relationship is a risk. It means showing someone the real bits of who you are – the spots beneath the make-up; the self-doubt beneath the cynicism – and finding the courage to say, 'This is me. Take it or leave it,' and to really mean it.

The author Juno Dawson is someone who took that risk and who was prepared to walk away in order to be fully herself. It was a decision she reached after years of doing the opposite: for the first twenty-nine years of her life Juno presented to the world as a man. It wasn't until she transitioned that she could finally live as herself, as a woman, and stop putting on a performance in her relationships – and in her life. So I wanted to know: how did being her true self change her experiences in dating? And did this honesty make it easier for her to let real love in?

The gap between who we are and who we pretend to be,
with Juno Dawson

NL: Did the feeling of not fully understanding yourself, before you transitioned, make it more difficult to let love into your life?

JD: It was as if there was always something on the tip of my tongue that I didn't understand. Now it's obvious, because if you're being introduced as 'my boyfriend', or being proposed to as someone's future 'husband', those are very gendered roles. I was unable to see myself in them. And I couldn't understand what anyone would see in me, because falling in love with me as a man, when I felt like a woman, was a facade. It's difficult for all of us not to put on a performance on dates, and my act was trying to be somebody that I wasn't: a man. So when I knew I was going to transition, I thought, I might never have another boyfriend again, but at least I will be myself. I might die alone, but I will die as a woman. I knew that even if another man never wanted me, I was doing the right thing. I had my friends, I had my dog, I had a pretty good life. It was more important to be fully myself and be single than it was to pretend. (Perhaps that is a good lesson for all of us.) And so, thankfully, I made that choice, and it turned out there was a world of love waiting for me post-transition.

Do you think that, whoever you met, a relationship would never have worked before that point?

Looking back, love pre-transition was always going to be impossible. It wasn't that I was being too choosy. Or picking the wrong men. I just had more work to do on myself before I could find love. I dated two lovely guys in particular who were everything I was looking for, but there was still something missing. That hole had nothing to do with who I dated; it was about me and how I was hiding from myself.

Even when I decided to stop hiding, transitioning was a slow, hard, frustrating process. There were waiting lists and medical procedures, pills and doctors and eighteen months of therapy. It's a tabloid myth that you go to your GP and go through a tunnel and pop out as a woman. I did a lot of work with my therapist about why I felt a crushing sense of dissatisfaction. It got to the point where I said, 'Look, I've got to try this, we've been talking about it for a year now, I need to start living as Juno to see what happens.' And if that had made me miserable, maybe things would have turned out differently. But I got happier and happier, and I've never looked back.

How did dating feel different after you'd transitioned?

It's like you've finally solved a riddle. I spent the first twenty-nine years of my life wrestling with a huge conundrum. When that was no longer there, I had more headspace for other things, including love. When I started dating in my thirties, it was the first time I could go on a date and not pretend. I sat down and said, 'Hi there, my body is about to go through this enormous transformation and my life is very messy. This is me.' One guy said, 'Cool. That's honest. Let's see what happens.' And off we went. I was shocked, because I didn't think anyone would be interested, especially in somebody who was in such early days of transitioning. He was a lovely guy, but it was too soon, and I needed to prioritize myself. But four years later when I met Max [Juno's fiancé], I'd figured out who I was, and my life was calmer. I was also in my late thirties, so I was done playing games. Perhaps that degree of maturity helped as well.

When you met Max, did it feel different to other relationships?

When we met I was seething from a shitty relationship with an absolute timewaster. He made me into a crazy nightmare person who couldn't sleep, because I didn't know if he was going to reply to my messages for three days. That's an important lesson in love: no one is too busy to reply to a fucking text message!

After that I reinstalled Tinder, and Max had obviously liked me in the interim while I'd not had the app. I agreed to go for a drink, but I was still in a bad mood. At that point, I wished harm to all of mankind and I assumed that when I got back from a work trip it would probably run its course. But then we went out for pizza and had a good date. I saw how clever and kind he was. I thought, this isn't a conversation I could have with just anyone. And a few months later he had a health crisis, which meant he nearly went blind after a detached retina surgery went wrong. It was then I understood how much I cared for him.

What I would say is that this relationship isn't necessarily different – I'm different. There's so much emotional literacy that goes into being with someone: instead of dramas, there are compromises. Instead of tantrums and storming out, you learn how to read signals and when to back off and which hills to die on. These are all things that are difficult to navigate without self-understanding. They are what we should be teaching in schools, I think.

What do you wish you'd known about finding love?

It's like mixing paint: sometimes when you mix two people together they make a horrible colour. Some people do bring out the absolute worst colours in you and, if that's the case, it's the relationship that's flawed, not you. You're not meant to lose sleep or cry over love. You shouldn't have to fight for it. If it feels like a fight, don't waste your time.

*

Juno reminded me that we have to keep trying to understand the truth of how we feel – the real reason why a small criticism upsets us, or why we sulk when we are feeling insecure. There will always be temptations to hide from ourselves. The important thing is to notice them, to resist them, and to keep finding ways to be honest in our relationships. (Oh, and to also remember the lesson that could save many years of unnecessary suffering: that no one is ever too busy to reply to a text message.)

The Unbearable Unknown

*'I think our job – maybe even our "duty"
– is to – To bear the burden of the mystery
with as much grace as we can.'*
(*Elizabeth Strout*, Olive, Again)

One Sunday morning, in a cafe two streets away from where I lived, a man sat down on the table next to mine. I sketched out a vision of who he might be with the few details available: a kind-looking face; a clean, navy wool jumper that it might be tempting to borrow; the book he was reading (*The Runaway Jury*). He seemed the sort of person who would show polite enthusiasm when your parents told the same story for the third time, who would clean the brown juice out of the bottom of the bin rather than ignoring it and putting another black bag over the top. The type of partner who would say 'You can do anything!' when you doubted yourself, and really mean it; who would reply to text messages as soon as he received them. This would probably be how I met someone, I thought. Not on a dating app, but in real life, sitting in a cafe on a Sunday morning, striking up a conversation about a John Grisham plot from a nearby table. I remembered that, as Lou Barlow sang, 'Anyone could be your brand-new love.' Then a woman – his girlfriend – walked in, sat down opposite him and said, 'Sorry I'm late.' I stared straight into my laptop screen and mentally climbed back down from the picture I'd built in my head of this kind-looking man. This was how I spent the twilight of my twenties: always believing I was *just on the edge* of meeting someone, seeing opportunities everywhere, then feeling a little pathetic when they never quite materialized in reality. The searching was a constant distraction, as if talking to a friend at a party and looking over their shoulder at who might be coming through the door next. Except, instead of a conversation, I was missing my life.

Long before I'd heard Alain de Botton question why we should feel more alone on weekends than any other day, Sundays tended to pass more slowly than the rest. To avoid a limp start to the morning, it was important to have a reason to get up early, to shower, to put on some proper clothes and leave the flat, so I often came to this little Mediterranean cafe with my laptop and the Sunday papers. 'Table for one?' the same waiter always asked. 'Yes please,' I'd always say. 'Near a plug!' Even though the other people in the cafe were strangers, it was nice to be in their company. A tender smile or a warm question asked made me feel connected to something, even if I wasn't yet sure exactly what that feeling was.

At this point, all but one of my closest friends were in relationships. Those who were too busy to meet up on Sundays often lamented their lack of time. They longed for more hours in the day. They had toddlers' party bags to fill, in-laws to entertain, Sunday roasts to assemble. They had less time, so they appreciated it more; I had too much of it to fill, so appreciated it less. I knew time was a precious thing to be used more productively: I was alive, I could do anything, write, volunteer, start yoga, go to a gallery, a pottery class, somewhere I might make new friends. I resented time for underlining my loneliness, and I resented myself for wasting it.

The obvious story was that I was unhappy being single. Beneath that, a private fear that I always would be; and worse, an anxiety born from not knowing either way. The simple fact of the unknown was one I could not resist wrestling with. Like hauling a heavy suitcase up the stairs at a station, I imagined it would be easier if there were an end point in sight, because when you can see the top of the station stairs or the finishing line of a run, it's easy to dig deep for an extra bit of strength to get there. What I found tiring about looking for a romantic relationship was that there was no way of knowing for certain if there would ever be an end point. I would tell friends, 'I don't mind if I don't meet anyone for another ten years, I just want to know that it will happen *one* day.'

It's easy to see now how short-sighted my approach to this portion of life was. How focused I was on receiving love, instead of giving it; on waiting for it, instead of building it. Many of the things I was looking for a relationship to provide – physical company; connection; the opportunity to be a mother – were actually available to me without one. And yet, at the time, I could not see the role I played in my own loneliness, and so I lived in the shadow of a relationship I didn't know if I would ever have.

Have you ever felt the unbearable weight of not knowing? Have you ever thought, if only I could get a guarantee that I would one day get what I long for, then I would be able to relax? Or, even if I knew that I would never get it, then at least I could design a different sort of life, instead of wasting energy on waiting for what could be just around the corner: A longed-for relationship? A pregnancy? A job in a certain industry?

Unless you believe in psychics, all of us will face some measure of this uncertainty – it's part and parcel of existence. Maybe there is comfort in knowing that, whatever we have or don't have compared to each other, we share this same vulnerability to randomness. Every day we wake up with no clue of when we might die or what might happen when we do. How easily we forget this big question, woven through everything. How small, by comparison, the other questions are. Not any less important, but perhaps more manageable in the context of it.

On another Sunday around this time, I visited my granny. Hers used to be a chaotic home, always messy, full of people. It became quieter when her children moved out, more so since my grandpa and her dogs died. In her eighties, problems with her legs meant that it was difficult for her to go anywhere and, other than visits from family, she relied on television for company. 'The thing is, Natasha,' she said to me that morning, 'most of my friends have died now. That's the way it happens. That's the way of it.' In that split second, in that still house, I realized that for my granny time really did move slowly. She was in the inevitable stage of ageing when deteriorating health steals experience, and death steals friends, and a once noisy life becomes quiet.

On the drive home I thought about how the unknowns of my life I was thrashing against were possibilities too. I looked back on all I did not know as a toddler, as a child, as a teenager; all the wonderful stretches of life ahead. I wondered if the ugliest shade of unhappiness comes, not directly from what you lack, but from wanting a different life to the one you're living. Perhaps that feeling is not a state of longing after all, but a way of seeing. A choice disguised in a lack of one.

I needed to ask, what would a better way of seeing look

like? And how do you move forward when uncertainty tempts you towards cynicism? The answers, I think, are in something the author Sheila Heti told me in an interview when I asked her about the question of whether or not to have children. The important thing, she explained, was not to make the 'right' or 'best' decision, but 'to closely bind yourself to whatever you're living'. She said, 'You make your life meaningful by applying meaning to it – it's not just inevitably meaningful as a result of the choices you've made.' We were discussing this in the context of choice, but I think it applies to circumstance too. The romantic relationship or family I wanted would not make my life meaningful; only I could.

This meant seeing my genuine loneliness as a sign that I needed to change something (by making new, meaningful connections), but seeing my solitude as a separate opportunity. The difference between the two is something the former Surgeon General under Barack Obama, Vivek H. Murthy, explains in his book *Together*. There are plenty of moments when we are in solitude, connected to nature or purpose or meaning, and we don't feel lonely. There are also plenty when we are with other people and are what Vivek calls 'emotionally alone', as I had felt in former relationships. He writes, 'When we feel lonely, we're unhappy and long to escape this emotional pain. Solitude, by contrast, is a state of peaceful aloneness . . . it is an opportunity for self-reflection and a chance to connect to ourselves without distraction or disturbance.' This distinction made me see that, as well as being a burden, my longing for love made me more alive to small moments of beauty in solitude: the transcendental strings in a happy-sad song; the precise power of a sentence perfectly assembled; the way half a dozen petals fell off a rose with no warning, twirling in the air before settling on the ground. Maybe not having something you want wakes you up to another kind of romance. And when life forces you to live in the intensity of the unknown, between two possible futures, it's also a chance to develop the inner resources and love that will serve you well in the years ahead.

Part of me wants to share this epiphany with my younger self, sitting in that cafe, feeling silly for picturing a meet-cute with another woman's boyfriend. To tell her, too, that one day she will sit at the exact same table, eating pancakes with a primary schoolteacher she's been seeing recently who she will grow to love. And that, even then, even though that will be wonderful, it will only be one of many memorable mornings she will spend in that cafe. There will be the coffee with a new friend who will become a great love; the one time she will come there to grieve; the breakfast she will share with her brother in the sunshine when they first decide to move into a flat together round the corner. And then all the Sunday mornings she will come there on her own, to write this book, to understand – finally – the difference between loneliness and solitude, and the romance of trying to find meaning in the latter. But perhaps I would not tell her, even if I could, because to do so would be to steal the strange, complicated, sometimes tiring gifts of the unknown. The thrill of all the places she has yet to go, all the faces she has yet to know.

Maybe, then, this is how you try to bear the burden of the mystery with grace: by finding humility where you once saw self-pity, and opportunity where you once saw absence. By saying, 'Even if I don't get what I want, I have a good life,' then paying closer attention to the small details that make that life beautiful. And by never forgetting that not knowing what will happen next also means that anything could.

*

As it turned out, I did find a new love in that decade; she just happened to be a friend, not a lover. I met Marisa when I was twenty-seven, when she interviewed me for an internship at a women's magazine. Though she left the company to work at a newspaper soon after I got the job, we continued to find ways to make our lives overlap.

I remember those years as a period of falling in love – laughing over tumblers of lukewarm white wine in Soho pubs, evenings that would end with a bored barman turning on the lights and asking us to leave. There were never enough hours in the night to say everything we wanted to. We'd become the sort of couple I loathed in the pizza restaurant where I waitressed at the time. One night we only took the hint to leave when we smelt the bleach, because they'd already started mopping the floor around us.

Despite its romantic beginning, ours was not a giddy girl crush, but a friendship based on understanding and being understood. If I felt then that the men I dated saw me only as a faint pencil sketch of a person, Marisa, by contrast, didn't just see me clearly but brought out all the colours. When you spend time around a friend who makes you feel this way, you're left with a lingering sense of peace. Their questions nudge you closer to knowing yourself, their love shrinks your insecurities. And so, in the space of loving and feeling loved by Marisa, I learnt to value myself.

Many people I've spoken to have reflected on finding a

similar mooring in friendship. Ayisha Malik credited her friendships in her twenties with expanding her view of love, and Philippa Perry revealed how being truly valued by friends at work gave her the courage to walk away from her first marriage. Our experiences echo something philosopher Simon May discovers about Aristotle's view of friendship-love – known to the Ancient Greeks as philia – in his book *Love: A History*. May finds philia is something that draws you closer to self-knowledge and deepens self-esteem. Because it is so hard to know ourselves, Aristotle believed that loving a friend is an integral part of gaining that emotional knowledge. May writes, 'We learn about ourselves from a loved one not so much because of what he tells us, but rather by observing our own reflections in him.'

This has been the author Candice Carty-Williams's experience of friendship too. In her bestselling novel *Queenie*, she explored the enduring support system you can find within it. And in her own life, friendship is where she's found a sense of belonging and a home. Her experience has been the opposite to some of my previous conversations: instead of a tendency to centre romantic love, Candice finds it easier to seek love in friendship. So I wanted to know why it has been easier for her to be vulnerable in friendships than in romantic relationships, what her friends bring to her life that no one else does, and how she continues to hold them close.

The power of friends who see the goodness in you, with Candice Carty-Williams

NL: When did friendship begin to play an important role in your life?

CCW: Today, if someone asks, 'Who is the love of your life?' I immediately think of friends, because friendship is the form of love I have allowed into my life. My childhood was difficult, and because of that I fear that people I get close to might leave. My dad was absent, and my mum had to figure out what it meant to be a mum and not just a friend. Then when I was twenty-five, two of my best friends passed away. I think a fear of abandonment has made me resistant of romantic love, but I haven't resisted love in friendship. It is the place where I learnt to let people in.

So far, my friends have treated me with more kindness than a romantic partner has. And it's so important to spend your life with people who not only see the goodness in you, but bring it out too. I know I need to get better at being open to a romantic relationship, but I feel that building and investing in healthy, loving, joyful friendships is just as important.

What have you learnt about love from your friendships?

Because I've never really seen family as a support group, when I met a group of friends at university it was the first time I could lean on a set of people who saw all the different sides of me. We had different dynamics and personalities, but they became a form of family I'd been longing for. They taught me love could be consistent and solid and steady, that it could make me feel safe. I know some people prioritize romantic love over friendship, but the truth is I love my friends more than I have loved any partner. They are the people who have shown me what it means to love and be loved. Friendship feels easy to me in a way romantic love doesn't.

A lot of people find it easier to be themselves with friends than in the early stages of a relationship. Why do you think that is?

I'm able to be more vulnerable with friends, because when I show them my true self it somehow feels less of a risk. There are so many societal expectations of what a romantic relationship should be: becoming 'boyfriend' or 'girlfriend', moving in together, marriage, children. That means, at some point, one of you will question whether you want to be together for a long time to do all those things. Which is why I'm bad at being my true self in romantic relationships. I think, what if I show you the parts of me that even I don't like and you just leave? I attach a fear of abandonment to the early stages, because I've experienced someone who is meant to love me leaving. But in friendships, I trust and understand that friends are going to be there, and that the love we share will be too.

Perhaps not having a label on friendship means it feels less like it could officially break. Of course a friendship can end too, but if it does, the break can be more of a slow drift.

There's also not the suggestion or societal pressure that you will move in or commit in a specific way. You do commit to each other, but on your own terms not someone else's. Not with labels or official markers. It's not like if you haven't gone on holiday together then your friendship isn't going to last. Whereas in a relationship, people around us – especially family, sometimes friends – ask about certain milestones: 'When are you guys going to move in?' or 'Have you said "I love you" yet?' Those expectations can make romantic love more difficult, in my experience.

What does it mean to you to be a good friend?

The first thing, I think, is to ask yourself that question. To me it's about demonstrating love, investing time, having an awareness of people – their history, their desires, what they need. And seeing and accepting the different facets of who they are. It's also about finding romance in your relationship. I do woo my friends. I tell them how amazing they are because I want them to feel good about themselves. When we end a phone call, I don't say, 'Love you, bye,' I say, 'I love you.' When we're apart, I tell them how much I miss them, and when we're together, how beautiful they look. I'm big on birthdays too, because I had a work friend who, after I'd had a horrible break-up, took on the role of my boyfriend on my birthday. She knew that no one else was going to plan anything, so she organized a day of nice things. We still do that for each other's birthdays: plan an itinerary of things and spend the day looking after the other person. Little rituals show someone that their friendship is important to you.

I know two of your friends died, one you spoke to every day. Did that make it harder for you to trust in the consistency of friendship?

Dan was my proper ride-or-die best friend. He was always there for me. He was the first person in my life who said, 'You can do anything.' Obviously I've let friends in since, but losing Dan is part of the reason I am avoidant of intimacy in romantic relationships. I think that's why I've always been the first to leave. I need to let go of that overarching feeling that people can leave me at any time, because I know that's not real. That fear is also what stops me asking for things from people I love. And in my friendships, I need to work on breaking out of my role as caregiver, because that's rooted in wanting to be needed. I've woven a big part of my identity through looking after people, and I know that part of love in friendship is asking for your needs to be met too.

What does real intimacy in friendship mean to you?

People see me as very strong, but I'm not. I'm vulnerable and I'm fragile, and intimacy is being able to show that to a friend, and them seeing me for who I am, in moments of joy and pain. It's about friends understanding I can be anxious and depressed, but also wild and shy and silly and fearful. When friends see all those parts of me, and guide me through them, gently and with time? That is real intimacy. And it goes both ways: a friend can call to say, 'Hey, sorry I'm not being very fun at the moment,' and I'll say, 'I don't require you to be fun. You're not a performing monkey. I'm here for the good and the bad and everything in between.' True friends see through any level of performance or denial or avoidance.

As your career has grown and you've become busier, have you had to find new ways to invest in that love?

When I was at university my phone was always in my hand. I was always on call for friends. Now, because of work and the demands of adult life, sometimes I can't be that person. But what's more important than replying to a message instantly is to give someone your absolute attention and focus when you do speak. I hope my friends know I have time for them, even if it can't always be the exact time they need me to be there. One thing I've learnt is that, just because I know how I feel about my friends, it doesn't mean they automatically know that. If I don't message for a few days, it's not because I don't care, it's because I'm a bit overwhelmed. Or sometimes because depression makes me feel I don't have anything interesting to say. That's something I'm working on: understanding how people see me, understanding myself, and vocalizing how I feel, rather than assuming people know. So if I feel depressed, rather than disappearing, I'll say, 'I'm feeling overwhelmed at the moment so I might go quiet for a bit.' The action is the same, but I'm communicating it. That's an important distinction.

We talk about needing to find self-worth on our own and not putting that on to a romantic partner. Do you think we can find self-worth through friendships too?

I would not be the person I am now without my friends. They point out my successes when sometimes I can't see them. They show me the good parts of who I am when I don't like myself. That sounds dramatic, but sometimes it is true. Again, it comes back to my childhood. My grandad is Indian and my nan is Black Jamaican Caribbean, and my mum and her sisters have straighter noses and different skin, pigmentation-wise. I have a cousin who looks like them; she has loose curls and light skin and a straight nose, and I don't look like that. Growing up, people would say, 'Your cousin is pretty, but you're smart.' (Now I'm older I think, why would you say that to a kid?) Then when I got to school they said I had behavioural issues and put me in the lowest sets. I thought, right, not only am I not pretty, which I've understood as the value that you have in this world, but I'm also not smart. When you're thinking those things until you're fifteen, there's no way that you're going to emerge as an adult who says, 'I am amazing.' Even when I was on the bestseller list, I couldn't really see what I'd achieved. So it's moving when friends encourage me to celebrate my successes.

Has having those friends cheering you on changed the way you see yourself?

They've allowed me to feel more confident in rooms I've had to walk into, to feel I have a place and a value. A huge part of that is being a black woman who's always been in white spaces, so finding a group of friends who are black women has been important. I can say, 'I had an argument with someone and they said X,' and no one says, 'You're overthinking it' or 'Maybe they didn't mean it like that.' They say, 'Yes, that's happened to us too. Let's talk about it.' That is something I've never had as a resource in my life before. Because if I said to my mum, 'This person said X and it felt like it was because I was different to them,' she would say, 'No, no, don't worry, Can, they probably didn't mean it, we're all just humans.' I think that was a problem, because I never understood that difference does exist, and it's fine to acknowledge that. So my friends taught me my feelings are valid. Now if someone speaks to me in a racialized way, I can vocalize that to those friends in a safe space. Of course I have different friends across every spectrum, but to be understood without having to explain everything all the time has been a precious thing.

What do you wish you'd known about love?

That friends will love you for who you are, not only because you give them something.

*

Speaking to Candice made me think Alain de Botton was right: it is a tragic misalignment, how we've relegated friendship to a lesser form of love. Because whether you are in a relationship or not, friends have access to parts of you that no one else does. How, then, do you pull friendship back to its rightful position in the hierarchy of love? I think with tiny rituals and reminders. For Candice, that's planning a birthday itinerary every year. For war reporter Janine di Giovanni, it's breakfast with a friend on Skype on Sunday mornings, from different countries. For me and Marisa, it's regular dates in Pizza Express, where we know the menu so well we don't have to waste any time looking at it. It's wearing the gold bracelet she once bought with the words 'May we always dance around the refrigerator light' engraved on the inside. She gave it to me when we lived just streets away and our lives were intertwined. Now that we don't live nearby, it's a reminder to find other ways to close the gap. A small symbol that means, *Let's keep on prioritizing each other*.

*

With friends, similarly to Candice, I'd experienced the rewarding joy of loving another human. But in romantic relationships, I'd spent little time thinking about what this might require. What it would feel like to combine two lives, two families. Or to see a partner clearly, to make space for them to change and grow, to encourage their dreams, accept their flaws and forgive their mistakes. How can we love someone in a way that brings out the best in them? How can we commit, not only to the whole of who they are today, but to who they could be in the future? I decided to put these questions to Heather Havrilesky, the author behind the acclaimed 'Ask Polly' column.

As an agony aunt, Heather has a beautifully worded answer to every problem in love. She told a reader looking for romantic love, 'You have to put on an artist's mind-set and get creative and paint a portrait of a life alone that's breathtaking.' She wrote to another who felt haunted by their affair: 'You made a mistake, but along the way you've been given an invitation to answer the lonely bleatings of your neglected soul.' Her words are ones I have often turned to for guidance, so I was pretty sure she'd be able to describe the crazy act of choosing to love someone without sugar-coating the process. Because it *is* crazy, if you think about it, to decide to commit to another person even though you have no clue who each of you will be in ten, twenty, thirty years' time. You make a pact to build a life with someone without knowing what that life will look like. Without knowing who will get sick or who will lose their job, whose sex drive will change or whose in-laws might need regular care. This is what we do when we begin a relationship: we commit to something unknowable. I wanted to ask Heather how we could possibly make this bet without knowing the odds, what she had learnt about the act of loving, and where she finds love today.

All love begins with imagination and fear, with Heather Havrilesky

NL: You once said that, while you get different kinds of letters, for the first few years you were drawn to questions about love. Why?

HH: I come to it from a kind of 'crawling off the battlefield and wanting to write about war' feeling. I dated a lot of people who kept me at arm's length. They were half-drawn in the relationship and I filled in the gaps. I made concessions and built my life around their personality and preferences. Then predictably, after about a year, I would knock them off the pedestal and be left to contend with the actual person underneath. That's why I dated people for exactly two years: in the second year I became annoyed by the human beneath the fantasies I'd built. That's not necessarily the partner's fault; you're the one who has created an imaginative fantasy around them.

How did you move away from that pattern?

I used to believe there was a scarcity of men, and the second I was single I needed to desperately grab someone otherwise I would be alone for ever. Then when I broke up with my final boyfriend, I realized that every time a relationship ended I'd find someone else within a year and get serious immediately. And so I said to myself, 'I'm not going to leap into a relationship with the first person that comes along.' I bought a house. I adopted a dog. I decided to figure out a way to be happy no matter what, because I couldn't depend on something as fragile as love to keep me happy. I was going to have kids or do all the things that I wanted to do, either way. Then my husband came along.

So you were thinking about who you wanted to be with, rather than just choosing whoever chose you?

Yes. By the time I met my husband I was also hell-bent on honesty. I no longer wanted to trick or lure a guy into sticking around; I wanted someone to see me and my flaws clearly, and either sign up for the whole or get lost! It seemed better to find out immediately that someone didn't like me, rather than in year two, so I stubbornly asserted my right to be a bit of a pushy, emotional person. My husband was delighted by that. He'd been married before, he had his own issues, and was very happy to bring them out in the open. Plus, I was thirty-four, I knew I wanted to have kids, and I didn't want to waste time with someone who wasn't demonstratively into me.

Although thirty-four isn't particularly old, I think the longer you end up waiting the more grateful you feel when you find someone who makes sense to you. It's easier to make a commitment when you've been through the wringer and you recognize when a relationship feels simple and good. You still have fights, but it changes the nature of how you get along with someone when you feel you are lucky to have them. It's harder to feel that way when you're younger and you haven't been in a bad relationship.

How did your relationship with your husband feel different?

He emailed me because I had written on my blog that I was single. Although I received a lot of emails, his was funny, not obsequious, and something about the tone of it made sense to me. Things were serious and magical from the beginning. Then, after three months, we both thought, we know we're in this, now what? Who did I just decide to spend my life with? Who is the day-to-day mundane person that I'm going to have to grapple with? Because you do have to get to know the mundane person after you get to know the mythical person created by your attraction, your love and your exuberance around the fact that you've found someone great. I think all love begins with imagination and fear. You make a bet with very little knowledge in the beginning.

One big difference was that we contended with who we were in real life more quickly, because we were all in from the beginning. When someone shows up completely, and you do too, it's a different experience. Firstly, you don't lose yourself. It's easy to do that when you're obsessed with someone because you're looking at them the whole time. But with a partner who's as invested as you are? You're more aware of your own failure to show up or to meet affection with affection. You also feel more self-conscious, because they are paying close attention to you compared to the partners who were inattentive.

What did falling in love with Bill teach you about building a relationship?

Bill and I spend a ton of time together, but we accept each other's limitations every day. Being in a good relationship requires that. There's always going to be stress on your day-to-day life, which makes it easy to push a partner away. To me, it's like you build a private religion with another person, and honesty and vulnerability have to be a part of it. You have to revisit what you each need and are afraid of. And tolerating someone else's vulnerability is a challenge if you're a tough person. I'm pretty tough, but I still have to encourage my husband to look at how he feels and unpack it, and then be patient with what he finds. He is seven years older than me and loves to complain about his back. I have terrible neck issues too, so I understand, but I don't complain. The problem is, if you say to yourself, 'I don't want to hear about your pain because I don't complain about mine,' then that's the death of love. You have to be tolerant and give the other person what they need. If you don't do that, it's easy for both of you to drift into your own worlds and to stop sharing yourselves. There is a callus that's always threatening to build up, and you have to break it down as a team somehow, again and again.

If wanting your partner to do things the way you would is the death of love, what's the opposite? How should you approach their differences?

Your partner is several different people, and you have different relationships with each of them. Some of them are great and some of them are annoying. Either way, you have to keep trying to take all the beauty and complexity that lie inside those many layers and versions of someone, then accept them and bring them out. That includes listening to them complain about their back hurting! Because to be in love is to recognize meaning in small, mundane moments. When someone grumbles about their back, that is part of your gift of their complex and gorgeous world. They are a character in the play of your life. And maybe moaning is how that character manages to keep despair at bay, and to exist. The weird little grumbly sounds you and your partner make to each other are their own strange poetry, and you have to try to approach those signifiers as rich, valuable and funny. It's not always easy. But the best definition of happiness is the ability to approach your life as this gorgeous, unfolding work of art that's always changing, and never quite what you expect it to be, and then seeing that it's more beautiful than anything that's supposedly perfect and pristine. So learning to love someone for all their faults and layers of weirdness is a way of learning to be alive, fulfilled and satisfied with the life that you have.

What advice would you give someone who hasn't met a partner when they hoped to, and is feeling exhausted by trying to find love?

When you're in the throes of obsession, there's a possibility that opens up every second you give up. And it's not giving up on ever finding a partner, or having a baby, or whatever it is that you want. It's giving up on trying to control what happens. When you're trying to manage your obsession around something you want really badly, it's soothing to try to let go of your sense that it is all up to you to make it happen. It's easy – as a person who works hard and is smart – to work, work, work at it. But stepping back and getting a little loose around it, and thinking, this is how it's supposed to be, can make you happier. You're living inside the romance of longing instead of inside the pain of it. It's also useful to recognize that intensity doesn't have to mean sadness, and longing doesn't have to mean desperation. Longing can actually be a generative stance that's lovely to feel.

But how do you find the tricky balance between active effort, hope and acceptance?

You do the things you need to do, but you try to do them in a slightly detached way, recognizing there's an element that is completely out of your control. All you're doing is showing up with the lightning rod and waiting, without waiting too hard. There's this dance of expectation and industry and letting go. It's hard to put language around it because it's *really* hard to wait for love. The best advice I have is to try on different positions. Giving up completely is a position that can help, and then absolutely believing that it's going to happen eventually is a position that can help too. Every day is a different picture where you have to tune into where you are and resist the urge to drape shame or sadness around the things you find when you look at your feelings. Resist that bad habit of thinking, I'm a failure as a woman, or I don't have some special womanly magic. I had that feeling when I had a baby. It was stupid. It was old shame.

So how can you ditch the shame and not let longing sap all the happiness from your life?

Part of feeling good through an intense period of longing is moving away from your old broken ways of experiencing intensity and towards one that is positive and thrilling. How do you take a sad story and live inside it without feeling crazy and sad? It can be helpful to go to the worst possible version of where you are and say, 'Well, what would I do if this didn't work out at all? What choices would I make if I knew ten years from now that nothing would ever come of this and I just would never meet someone, or never have a baby? Would I adopt? Would I travel? What would the best possible version of my life look like without the thing I am longing for?' I push my husband to do this all the time, to talk about the wild worst-case scenarios and possibilities in front of us. There's something heavy about that, but freeing too.

More and more, I go back to the idea that you need to save yourself. I used to hate that line, but showing up for yourself, having your own back and keeping yourself company through a hellish time becomes more important. You can still feel a tremendous amount of love and admiration for other people. You can still have everything that you want and be the person who saves herself. People tend to paint independence as an impoverished, compromised position, and when you love love a lot, like I do, it's hard not to fall into that. But the truth is that being in love, or loving someone and being *really* happy, includes a lot of self-possessed behaviour. It requires you to feel your way towards what you want, make your own decisions, and save yourself.

What do you wish you'd known about finding love?

I used to wish I knew you can only feel love when you feel worthy of love, and that includes doing things that make you feel good, like developing a career and becoming independent and having friends. But actually, I think what's more important is understanding your desires and your urges and your complexity, rejecting dominant narratives about how weak and needy and bad and broken you are, and defining for yourself what you are instead.

I still believe in love, maybe more than I ever have, and

if I have the chance I'm going to be looking for it at the old folks' home! But it doesn't blot out the sun the way it used to; it's one piece of a vibrant life. I understand it being at the centre of everything when you're having kids, in particular, and when you're young. But I always overvalued it and I'm learning not to now. I'm learning to value my imagination and my ability to create art more than being adored by someone or adoring them. I can still have connections to other people. My marriage is still a big part of my life. But I do think there's a joy in being alive that's not dependent on any person at all. And there's something permanent about recognizing that the defining energy of my life is now centred within me, not defined by anyone else.

*

What Heather taught me is that it's wise not to approach love – a fluid experience – from a fixed position. Because there will be times when we need or want to pour all the effort we can muster into a friendship or relationship. And there will be times, too, when love is just one thread in a tapestry of ambitions and hopes and discoveries.

She also reminded me that, as much as love involves consciousness, part of it requires us to close our eyes and jump without a plan. And the fact that we took that leap, without knowing that everything would work out? Perhaps that act of faith, of hope, might carry us through tougher times, when we look back and marvel at it, and think, how little we knew, how easily we could have found a reason not to jump. Perhaps we will feel grateful for this naive decision, which allowed us to make a hundred more. I think about this when I listen to my husband singing 'Hard-Headed Woman' by Cat Stevens in the shower, knowing that for one small move – a cancelled date, an ignored text, a hangover – we might never have met. What luck. Sometimes a gamble works out.

Although I had approached this conversation wondering how we might accept another person's flaws, Heather left me with a new intention: not only to make peace with these imperfections, but to cherish them. To see them as 'their own strange poetry'. Of course we are not saints; sometimes it's natural to feel annoyed when a loved one moans incessantly about their job, how tired they are or how much their back hurts. Just as I had learnt that a beautiful life contains joy and suffering, the people we love have amazing and frustrating layers. They will be mysterious and sexy and funny. And they will be boring and insecure and gross. They will repeat the same story four times, fart, get food stuck in their teeth, ask 'Have you seen my glasses?' multiple times a day or make a weird face when they orgasm. But Heather made me think that maybe these boring, insecure, gross bits are the things we might look back on fondly one day too. Maybe seeing them as funny or endearing, or beautiful pieces of a whole person, is what it means to love.

*

With Philippa Perry, I had explored how the stories of our past show up in our present. And how we might be able to use awareness to guide us through knee-jerk behaviours. But how can we remain in conversation with our past without letting it define us? I turned to the poet, author and broadcaster Lemn Sissay for the answer, because he has spent much of his life seeking a fragile balance between understanding his past and being solely steered by it.

In many of Lemn's poems, the greatest stories of love and heartbreak are born in family, and explore how that primary love – or a lack of it – shapes us. That's because family is something Lemn grew up without; he spent his teenage years in care homes after his foster parents cast him out when he was twelve years old, without explanation, and returned him to social services. As an adult, after winning redress from Wigan Council for his mistreatment as a child, he used his social services files to piece together his life story in a memoir, *My Name Is Why*. It was the process of writing it which made him realize that, through not having love when he was younger, he has been given the gift of understanding it as an adult. So I asked him: how did he find that gift? And what has it taught him about the value of love?

The ties that bind us, with Lemn Sissay

NL: How have you found a way to understand and accept your past, but not let your future be defined by it?

LS: It's a daily project. Some days I feel I've got nothing, some days I wake up and feel I've got everything. Some days I can let go of the losses, some days I feel they're crowding in on me, and they become stratas within the rock that I think I'll never dig through. That's just the way it is for all of us, ultimately.

I've spent a lot of time wondering how I could get over something or get around it or get past it or get through it, and I wonder whether those are the right metaphorical choices.

Because our past experiences are part of us, and to deny mine would be to deny who I am. It's what allows me to appreciate what I didn't have. All of us have unique stories and we seem to be looking to make them less unique. Or to deny them because we think that makes us 'normal'. Actually, it's OK if something painful happened to you. That's part of being human for a lot of us.

A dangerous trap is getting fixated on asking: why me? Because there is rarely an answer to that question, and it's an unhelpful one to live inside. How do you think we can pull back from self-pity when painful things happen to us?

Oh my God, yes. It's a very hard place to be. It's important that we feel sorry for ourselves, but that's different to a fixed point of self-pity. That's an emotional Groundhog Day, which can make it difficult to reach acceptance. So learning the difference between self-compassion and self-pity is one way we can be kinder to ourselves. Somebody said to me once, 'If you were your own best parent, what would you say to yourself?' Waking up that loving best parent within us is something we all need to do more. And if you can be kind to yourself, you can be kind to others. I find that when I'm not kind to myself, that becomes harder.

You told me that not having a certain form of love – family – when you were growing up gave you the gift of understanding love. How?

If I took away your breath, your heart would start to move faster. Your lungs would expand. Your legs would feel as if they were going to go from underneath you. It's only when you lose your breath that you realize how important it is, or when you are ill that you realize how important your physical self is. And similarly, it's only through experiencing an emotional deprivation that I started to understand how important love really is. For example, I stopped being touched when I was twelve, when I went into the care system. I realized that my grandmother used to touch me when I was a kid, on my face and my hands, and she did that because she'd stopped being touched as well, after her husband had died. She understood how important touch was, not because it was there, but because it wasn't. Similarly, from not having it early on in my life, I've learnt that the action of love is everything. It's physical touch, it's picking up the phone, it's going to see someone, it's saying what you believe or need to say, and it's doing those things again and again. Love consistently asks you to be answerable to it in actions.

A lot of people find it difficult to move forward when they have been denied a form of love. How do you not let the love you haven't had distract you from the love you do?

A question I get asked a lot is: why are you not bitter? Because for those who are deprived of love – and everybody is or will be deprived of it in some way or another – there are negative emotions that will try to fill that gap: guilt, anger, shame, bitterness, envy. I've found you have to clear space for love. One of the things I had to do was to stop drinking, which for me was a quiet self-harm. For someone else it might be something different, but it's important to ask: what is your thing that might be blocking love and leading you back to those negative emotions? Is it that you don't exercise and you think you should? Is it that you don't call people and you think you should? How can you make space in your life for love to thrive? Because if you don't, it won't.

When did you understand that was necessary?

I remember at the end of a big relationship I thought everything was the other person's fault, because she ended it. But a few months later, I realized she was right to leave. I didn't recognize the man who she'd been going out with. I thought I was the good guy. Actually I was behaving badly because I had not faced my issues.

She said to me, 'You've got to go on this journey on your own, because I'm done with being to blame.' And she was right, because when we don't face our shit, we play out our stories in relationships and make the other person the guilty party. To be honest, whatever's happened with my family, when it comes down to love and to me, I'm the source of the problem. Which is incredible, because I'm also the solution. I'm the only one who can change how I live from today onwards.

If your primary relationship with love is complicated, then when you're loved in relationships it often brings up those feelings. A lot of people think, I had a terrible relationship with my parents, I got away from them and now I'm OK. Not necessarily, because you're going to take your primary relationship with love with you wherever you go. You can't run away from that. Part of facing it, for me, was forgiving my foster parents. Once I forgave them I started to see their vulnerability. Before that, I was insecure around other people's vulnerability. And in relationships you do need it.

So, in a way, forgiving them was an act of self-love?

That's exactly what it was, but it had to be true forgiveness. I had no idea that I would feel good, I just knew I had to trust myself. That's the other thing forgiveness does: it allows you to trust yourself. I'm not asking other people to do that, I'm just saying I'm the last person I thought would be able to forgive, but, in doing so, a weight was lifted from my shoulders.

A lot of writers I've interviewed have talked about writing as an act of love: a way of being seen and forming connection. Do you see writing poetry as a form of love?

That's precisely it – in fact my psychotherapist said that writing poetry is an act of self-love, which allows me to feel a sense of purpose. It could be pottery, it could be painting, it could be running. Creativity is not the monopoly of artists. You could find it in your shopping habits or in how you design your front room or how you style your hair. I wish more people understood that, because then they could fully embrace its power and access that sense of self and love that I get when I've created something that matters. Sometimes poems feel like your children too. When they go out into an audience people may criticize them, but I think, well, that's my child, I don't care. I know where it's good, I know where it's bad, I know where it's got to develop. Poetry has also been my closest friend and my family. It holds me in mind. It is a flag in the mountainside of my journey. I can look back at poems I wrote when I was eighteen and they will tell me where I was, what I was feeling, what I was going through and who I was. In lieu of family, that's as close to being held in mind as I can get, which is a strong part of what love is.

Do you feel your experiences and the work you've done on yourself make you more attuned to the tiny details that make life beautiful?

Well, here's the gift: our experiences are bridges not ravines. They allow us to understand the world and its dysfunctions more. Why did we ever think that everything was perfect? Why did we ever think that loss wasn't part of what it is to be a human being? Why does it come as such a shock to us? Actually, the good and bad things that happen give us a great opportunity to connect with the world and to others.

What do you wish you'd known about love?

I'm talking to you from King's Cross station, and everybody here has got their unique story. But what we share is that every single person in the station, all of us, wants to love and be loved. When you understand that, you empathize with people. You understand that we're all part of something bigger.

*

After I hung up the phone to Lemn, I pictured the quietly spectacular scene he left me with. All those different people moving through King's Cross station, each with their own stories, their own private hopes and disappointments and yearnings, all connected by a desire to love and be loved.

When we see the world in this way, I think it makes us feel less alone. We realize that our private shame is universal, that our worst heartbreaks have been felt and survived before, and that, as Lemn said, 'our experiences are bridges not ravines', however painful they are.

*

Another way of feeling our shared humanity, I've found, is through stories. Although there are fairy-tale narratives I could blame for my fantasies in relationships, there are also stories that have brought a real form of love into my life. I'm not referring to books or novels about love, specifically, but rather to passages of writing that have the power to make you feel a little more alive. The paragraph that gives you a tingle of recognition. The lines that feel as if they are directly written for a deep, secret part of you, that you weren't necessarily even aware of until it was woken up by words.

Reading such a passage is, I think, a form of love. Like any relationship, that intrinsic recognition is a way of understanding and being understood, of seeing and being seen. The psychiatrist Gordon Livingston said that 'the fundamental requirement for any satisfying relationship is a reciprocal ability to see the world as others see it, to be able to put ourselves in someone else's shoes.' And that's what a truthful piece of writing does: by allowing us to access another person's reality, it shifts our mind into a higher gear of empathy.

This deep clicking into place doesn't happen often. But when it does? Those passages become a source of love for us to reach back for the next time we feel desperate or alone, like a float thrown out when you've lost the energy to carry on swimming. This is how I have felt reading Elizabeth Strout's books and watching Kenneth Lonergan's films. It's how I feel every time I read – and speak to – the writer Sarah Hepola too. Her words carry me back to a peaceful place inside myself where I know what really matters.

As well as writing a bestselling memoir about her alcoholism, *Blackout: Remembering the Things I Drank to Forget*, Sarah has explored the search for love through essays for Salon, the *New York Times*, NPR's *Fresh Air* and in a new book she is working on. Her writing reminds me that there are often lessons hiding in those moments where we don't get what we want in life, which is what I chose to dig further into with her in this conversation. How you can find meaning in absence, and resilience in loss, and agency in a life that you cannot control. I wanted to know how – and if – she made peace with not finding a romantic relationship exactly when she'd hoped to, and what that has taught her about how to appreciate the life she has today. Because while thousands of philosophers, writers and therapists have shared theories on how we can be more grateful and present in our lives, it's the simplest lesson to learn and the easiest to forget. Especially when our lives don't follow the straight line we expected them to.

The gifts of not getting what you want, with Sarah Hepola

NL: One problem I've been wrestling with is how to carry on living a full life when you don't get the exact form of love you wanted at a particular time. Have you found a way to not get distracted by what you don't get?

SH: I recently had two surgeries to remove a fibroid in my uterus, which was about the size of a grapefruit. And as part of that process I had to ask myself, if I didn't meet someone, would I have a child on my own? Ultimately I decided I didn't want to go down that path, but I did go through a period where I thought, this isn't fair. A lot of us have those moments of pointing to other people and saying, 'They got this, and I didn't.' But none of that matters in the end, because I know I've been lucky to have my life as it's unfolded. Once I let go of resentment, I was able to see that. So ultimately the diagnosis made me think, this is my life, what am I going to do with it? If you're lucky, you get that reminder: some choices you get to make, others you don't. So how are you going to navigate the choices you do have?

I'm beginning to think, as well as sadness we feel about not finding certain forms of love, it's the lack of control that makes those moments difficult. Maybe that's why the unknown feels unbearable. Because if I knew for certain something was or wasn't going to happen then it might be easier to manage. What have you learnt about how to live with not knowing?

I find the uncertainty unbearable too. There was someone I fell for recently, for the first time in a long time. When I knew it wasn't going to work, I wished somebody could just tell me that it was done so I could release myself. But I was also afraid to release myself, in case there was still hope. I ended up being stuck between two outcomes, and in some ways that is more difficult than knowing either way.

And sometimes the uncertainty fuels your longing for someone. In situations like that I've often wondered, if things worked out, would it have been easier to see the other person's flaws, rather than romanticizing what could have been in their absence?

Definitely. Recently, I reconnected with a man called Nick. In my thirties, I thought I was going to marry him. I had never experienced love like that and I held on to it for dear life for years. Eventually, I let go, he married someone else and we only stayed in minor contact. Then, out of nowhere, I got an email from him saying that a mutual friend of ours had died and I should come to New Orleans and stay with him. It turned out his second marriage had ended. And I did go. I got to do something that most people don't ever get to: I walked back into the past I wanted for myself and saw how poorly it would have fit. He was still a deeply lovable person, but I saw that he would not have been a good partner. Until then I hadn't understood how lucky you can be when somebody leaves you. It's a sign of youthful arrogance that we think we know what's right for us. The older I get, the more I realize the things I wanted were not necessarily the things that would've given me what I needed at the time.

I've had that feeling many times too, but only in retrospect. It's hard to see at the time. Did you find that, seeing Nick again in your forties, you were able to understand your relationship more clearly than you had in your thirties?

One of the things that originally drew me to him was his calmness. He never got rattled, whereas I felt like an exploding volcano. But when we reconnected I realized that was actually a deep ability to compartmentalize, which was always going to be a problem in love. I could see that a relationship between us would never work. That's been very good for me, because I think a lot of us live in the shadow of 'what ifs?': what if it had gone this way? What if he came back? What if she gave me another chance? Whereas I got the opportunity to understand, OK, I came out on the right side of this thing. My mistake was thinking that, because I loved him, it meant our relationship should last for ever, instead of understanding that it was just six months of extraordinary experience.

Has that experience helped you to see that there are strange gifts in those moments when we don't get what we want in love?

Absolutely. I do believe in the Buddhist idea that pain comes from a failure to see things as they really are. Obviously it's hard for me, the person who hasn't lost anyone, to say to someone that's in enormous pain, 'You're holding on to something that wasn't for you.' But the truth of this life is that there's a lot of pain in it. There's more loss and grief than we want to believe. How we make peace with that is the journey we're all trying to figure out.

Has that idea helped you see your search for love differently?

I wanted to meet a partner by my early forties, before I had a child, and that hasn't happened. Part of that is luck, part is circumstance, the rest is mystery. But one of the lessons I've had to learn is that, while many of my relationships didn't have the shape that I would've chosen, they were the shape that made sense for the connection I had with that person.

My parents have been married for fifty years, and maybe I will have longevity in a relationship like that, but my guess is that I will never grow that tree, and it's OK, because I'm going to grow a more varied garden. So I'm realizing that there isn't necessarily going to be one long love for me, but maybe a series of shorter love stories. Just as making peace with what I don't get is going to be a series of acceptances. Because life doesn't stop throwing you curveballs. There are people that find love and then their deepest grief is they don't get a second child. Or that their mother dies and isn't there to witness their adult life. My mother is still alive, so I haven't had to experience that loss yet. But I have a dear friend who has a beautiful house, a husband and two kids, and every moment of happiness in her life is undercut by the loss of her mother, when she was in her early twenties. She can't feel joy without feeling that loss. In a way, her loss is something that can help return me to the parts of life that I can overlook. Like having a mother and father who are still healthy into their late seventies. That is a gift I have to remember to find a deep gratitude for. If I don't, I'm missing something huge.

Have you learnt to see your relationship with your parents as a primary love story in your life, in a way that you didn't when you were younger?

They live ten minutes away so it's easy to take them for granted, but it's something I remind myself of all the time. As humans we have a default setting that's cranky and lazy and self-interested and slothful. The people I see that live good, meaningful lives have rigorous exercises to push back against that setting, whether through prayer, meditation, gratitude journals or running. We're creatures of wanting, but also of consciousness. So the way that we can push back on longing is to pay attention to what we have. I can see the fact I live in a house alone as a prison sentence. Or, like this morning, I can wake up and spend time with my beautiful cat and feel so grateful to be alive in the world.

For me, I think reading is a way to push back on that default setting.

Me too. It's an emotional realignment, like somebody's cracked my spine. If I get lonely, I reach for those pieces of writing that feed the soul. That can lead you back to the best in yourself, or articulate the things that you can't find words for. When you stumble on something you didn't know that somebody else felt too, you think, oh my gosh, I'm not the only one. That is a falling in love – it's the self recognized in someone else. A union of souls.

Are you now able to see that, whilst you still want a romantic relationship, it's not a permanent guarantee of happiness?

That part has absolutely sunk in. There is this idea that if you could just get someone to love you then you would be released from the low rattle of unhappiness. Then you find someone who loves you, and you *still* feel the rattle of unhappiness. Maybe there's nothing wrong with you. Maybe learning to tolerate that low rattle of unhappiness is part of what reminds you that you're alive.

As an adult I've watched friends marry and divorce. It's as if I was waiting in a long line, then everybody left the ride and said, 'That ride sucks.' But that helped me to understand that the romantic relationship I was yearning for was not going to fix the low rattle of unhappiness. The truth is it's hard not to have found a relationship and it's brave to go into a relationship and it's hard to find one and then to lose it. All of us, at some point, have to learn how to get our hearts broken.

What have been the gifts of not getting what you wanted?

For a lot of my life I've had the sense that I wasn't good enough or that I was better than everyone else – a back and forth between inferiority and superiority. Not getting what I want brings me back to a place in the middle, where I see I am no different to anybody else. It shows me that the things I flew past in the race to get what I didn't have were actually the gifts all along. And it makes me grateful that my life has unfolded in a way that previous generations of women could not have imagined. A lot of things are chance, but we also have choices and resources that, for a long time, women just didn't have. I don't even know that love was on the table for them in the way that you and I have been allowed to yearn for it.

That is definitely a privilege we have, but it also means we load a lot of expectation on to love.

Yes, which is why I have to correct on both sides: I have to be grateful that I'm not somebody that's been married off for a dowry, and I also have to do a fact check on my expectations of this world. How did I get so insatiable? Can I learn to ask for a little less from everything? I have been allowed to travel, to build a writing career, to have an unusual and fascinating romantic history. All of this I am grateful for, even though it has not led to the sustained love relationship and family that I wanted. In another lifetime, I think I would have been a great mother. But I also think that in this life I've been a great seeker. I didn't get everything that I wanted, but the things that I got were really great. And maybe not getting what you want allows you to see the beauty of what you have. Without that, it's too much of a smooth ride.

I'm interested to know if you approach being single now differently to when you were younger? Because for a while I thought that being single meant spending a lot of time alone. Then I realized that I didn't have to do that in order to prove that I could.

It was the same for me. I started travelling alone because I saw people travelling with their boyfriends, and I thought, being single isn't going to stop me. I'm going to go alone. It was a wonderful thing to do when I was twenty-five, to embrace the life I'd been given and find adventure, but somewhere along the way I lost the idea that I could go with other people too. I felt marooned by travelling alone, like I was in an orbit and I couldn't come back to Earth. I think we have to find a way to balance the messaging about being independent and self-reliant with the human desire to be connected, to love and be loved.

Some of that messaging is why I felt like a failure for wanting a romantic relationship. Now I think it's about separating the idea of 'I will only be happy if I have a partner' from wanting companionship. Because it's not the wanting love that's the problem, it's believing that you can only be happy in a relationship.

That's it. We're transitioning from a world where marriage and children were the default to one in which we're trying to allow space for different kinds of lifestyles. And rightly so. But everyone I've ever known wants to be connected to another human, in some way. I know now that I don't want to be alone and I don't have to be. What I can't control is what that companionship looks like, necessarily. I wanted a romantic partner, and that may or may not still happen, but either way, connection is still essential to my life and there are so many ways to fill that cup. The wisest among us uses all of them. I go through periods where my married or mother friends are not available, because they're raising children, but I've found other single friends who can go on trips with me. I've even found great guy friends through dating apps. We share our dating struggles and we give each other advice and I feel super-lucky to have them in my life.

What do you wish you'd known about love?

That the love of a partnership can be an incredibly important and transforming experience, but only one of many important and transforming experiences. As someone who has searched far and wide for somebody to love her, I feel I missed that the great love story of my life is really that I was born to two parents who love me, and that I never had to ask for their love. One of the tricks of this life is being grateful for the things that you are given. And boy, I can't think of anything – *anything* – being better for me in my life and my growth than having had that from the very beginning. I know other people don't have that love, and I don't know how to begin being grateful for getting it. I think that the search for love, as I understand a lot of my life and my work to be, is also the search to see that I already have it.

*

If we're lucky enough to have a loving parent, why do more of us not describe that relationship as the great love story of our lives? Too many, I think, take familial love for granted. I know I have. I've walked around Paperchase seeing Mother's Day cards as a stinging reminder of my struggle to become a mother, instead of feeling lucky that my own is still alive. I've wasted time with my parents in a restaurant checking my phone underneath the table, to see if a man who didn't really care about me had replied, missing the fact that the people I cared about most were sitting right in front of me.

As well as a reminder not to overlook this grounding form of love, speaking to Sarah made me think about the choices we get to make and the ones we don't, and the fact that very few – if any – of us will get everything we want when we want it. I think her answers are an invitation to ask: who are *all* the people who add joy to our lives? Whose voice on the other end of the phone reminds us to have faith? Whose company reminds us of our best qualities when we've forgotten them? Who makes us laugh when we're on the edge of tears? And then: how can we hold on to these people? This, surely, is the most important choice we *do* have every day.

Looking Out

'The lack of love in my life was not a reality but
a poverty of imagination and a carelessly narrow
use of an essential word.'
(Krista Tippett, Becoming Wise)

Last year my mum called while I was getting ready for work. I was already late, and as she spoke about her plans for the week ahead – her Pilates class, the friends she was having round for dinner, the recipes she was considering – I absent-mindedly asked short questions, holding the phone in one hand while fishing around my drawer for two matching socks with the other. At first a familiar feeling rose up in me, a combination of distraction and frustration and stress; a reminder that I didn't have time to talk. But then, a second feeling: a sudden awareness of the fleeting beauty of this phone call. The latter only appeared because, a few days before, I'd interviewed a woman who'd lost her mother, who said what she missed most was sharing the tiny, seemingly pointless details of each other's lives. Like which *Gogglebox* star was her mum's current favourite, or which plants in her garden were flowering that week, or which member of Take That was the most 'handsome'. It was only because of that conversation that I sat down on the edge of the bed and really listened to my mum's voice: the way she shortened Pilates to 'lattes'; how she said,

'I'll give you a tip . . .' every time she talked me through a recipe. Instead of waiting for the right moment to interrupt, soon I wanted to tightly bind this conversation to memory. 'And what are you making for pudding?' I asked, knowing then that, since I was already late, five more minutes would not make a difference. I wanted my mum to keep on talking, to always be there on the other end of the phone, updating me on the state of Karl and Susan's marriage in *Neighbours*, or asking who we should invite for Christmas this year even though it was February.

Do we notice these subtle opportunities for love which are woven through our daily lives? I think more often we miss them, as I nearly did. It shouldn't take a story of loss to make me appreciate a Tuesday morning phone call with my mum, but I've found there are few epiphanies in life that lead to an automatic change of habit. Even when we learn a lesson, it's likely we forget it and have to learn it again. Even when we recognize a mistake, we make the same one a few more times before fully ditching the pattern. This is certainly the way I learnt – and am still learning – that a meaningful life is built on many different forms of love. Not from a seismic turning point, but through a collection of small reminders that nudge me closer to the truth, like a lost boat at sea suddenly steered in the right direction by the wind.

I used to think love was the feeling hanging between me and my mum on that phone call, a mix of what I felt for her and what she felt for me. But now I understand that love was the act of switching the way I responded to the moment; it existed in both the intention and the choice to consciously focus on it. When you understand love in this way – as an action, not a feeling – it's easier to see why it's unhelpful to view the absence of one form as a complete lack of it. The best description I've found of this error is from psychoanalyst and philosopher Erich Fromm, who compares the attitude 'to that of the man who wants to paint but who, instead of learning the art, claims that he has to just wait for the right object, and that he will paint beautifully when he finds it'. Love, by his definition, is 'a power which produces love'. It is not the object you're painting, but the process of learning to paint. It's not admiring flowers from afar, it's the act of nurturing them so they don't die. It's an 'attitude', a 'power of the soul' or an 'orientation of character which determines the relatedness of a person to the world as a whole'.

But how do you commit to actively practising love for people and the world without getting distracted by longing for a form of it you *don't* have? I think you plumb the depths of who you are until you find a purpose in life that excites you. You take all the efforts you've been pouring into longing, and instead use them to dig deeper for the love that's already there, hiding right in front of you, so that you can grow it. This doesn't mean pretending that you don't want to meet a partner – or have a child or make new friends or find whatever love it is that you're searching for; it means being brave enough to hope for what you want, but wise enough to know that life is not one love story, but many. It means trying to build love with a partner – if you want one – but also in purposeful solitude, in creating something that others connect to, in a stranger's kind words, in friendship, in family, and in the sometimes-bright-sometimes-grey sky that's always been there, all your life. It means understanding, too, that all these forms of love are not given or acquired; they are learnt and earned.

I received another reminder of this on my thirtieth birthday, which, at the time, seemed a significant milestone. I'd always hoped to have a boyfriend to bring to the party. Or at least a date. By this birthday, though, I understood romantic love was not something that would pick or choose me after years of patiently waiting. It was something I had to try to create opportunities for, with hope. So I'd finally downloaded a dating app, filled my diary full of Wednesday-night dates and assumed my open-hearted enthusiasm would pay off. I kept a spare space on my invite list, just in case.

By the time my party arrived, I still didn't have a date or a boyfriend. (That's the thing about finding romantic love: sometimes you put in the effort and sustain hope and it still doesn't happen. So it's useful to understand this isn't a reflection on who you are, like a bad grade given on your personality. No matter how hard you try, you also need a little luck.)

Unexpectedly, this particular birthday turned out to be a night full of romance. Friends and family sang and laughed and danced and wrote Happy Birthday messages on the giant cardboard cut-out of me as a toddler that my parents had blown up into a lifesize version. As I watched them, I saw the love in my mum's big heart, in my dad's gentle kindness, in my brother's deep understanding. It was in my friendships too: in one friend's sensitivity, in another's faith. It was in the new experiences I had shared with colleagues and journalism college friends, as I forged a career that meant something to me for the first time, and in the old history I shared with university flatmates, whose hugs still felt like home. Seeing these people sitting side by side, who saw all the versions of me – and I them – reminded me that we were each responsible for tiny pieces of each other's hearts and happiness. It wasn't only that this night made me realize life was full of different types of love, but that the capacity to love exists inside each of us – and our task is to tap into it. Instead of waiting for love, I could choose it. I could notice and listen and pay better attention to the people already in my life. I saw then that my search for love had been distracting me from the very thing I was looking for. Instead of asking, 'Will I ever find love?' I needed to ask a better question: 'How could I love better?' The first part of finding love had been to look inside myself. The second was to practise looking out.

Taking the journey inwards had still been important, because when you don't understand or value yourself it's more difficult to generate love for other people. It made me see, too, that I had never really loved the men I'd dated and idealized in my twenties. I had not been invested in helping them grow, or in seeing the whole of who they were, because I was more interested in how I looked in their perception of me. It was a half-hearted version of love, rooted in ego. I resolved to give it up.

The search for any kind of love, I now believe, is a continual process of looking in and out. Looking inwards to understand yourself, to be curious about your needs and desires and gifts and flaws, to develop generosity and self-compassion. Then looking outwards to use the power those things give you to love other people, and the life you are living too. What I had learnt is that you don't really find love at all; you create it, by understanding that you are part of something bigger. A small speck of colour vital to a picture of life.

How do we sustain love?

'The story of human intimacy is one of
constantly allowing ourselves to see those we
love most deeply in a new, more fractured light.
Look hard. Risk that.'
(Cheryl Strayed, Tiny Beautiful Things*)*

The Honeymoon Phase

'We are the treasure itself: fathoms deep, in the
world we have made and made again.'
(Dani Shapiro, Hourglass*)*

There are few completely flawless nights in a life; the evening
Dan and I first kissed was one of them. There were chips and
negronis under a cool summer sky, fairy lights in the trees.
Afterwards, we stood on a pavement outside a restaurant in
Canonbury and he said, 'I'm going to kiss you now,' which
sounds awkward, but somehow wasn't. I had spent years
accepting that online dates were often dull interviews with an
aftertaste of disappointment. But then, there we were. Two
not-quite-strangers kissing on the pavement.

What we didn't know then was that four years later we
would be sitting in the back seat of an Uber in the *exact* same
spot. We would be married. We would be tired. We would
be holding hands in the back of a Toyota Prius that had collected us from UCLH hospital, where a doctor had removed
from my womb a ten-week foetus that we had given a name
to. Sore from the surgery, I winced every time the driver went
over a bump or turned a sharp corner. Dan squeezed my hand
and said nothing, because there was nothing to say. When the
car stopped at the traffic lights by the pavement where we first
kissed, I looked out of the window while Foreigner's 'I Want

to Know What Love Is' played from the radio. I remembered the bouncy, giggly people we were that night, playing conversational striptease and not wanting the date to end. Now we were deflated and silent, longing for the car journey to end. We were supposed to be flying to Mauritius on our honeymoon the next day, but the doctors said we couldn't travel. I had to have the operation to remove the baby first.

When we planned the trip to Mauritius, I thought – as well as an excuse for an expensive holiday – a honeymoon was an opportunity to celebrate a commitment. It is only later I discover that the etymology of the word comes from the Old English 'hony moone' and may have a more cynical meaning. The word 'hony' refers to the 'indefinite period of tenderness and pleasure experienced by a newly-wed couple'. 'Moone', meanwhile, hints at the inevitable waning of that tenderness, like a phase of the moon. After we were forced to cancel our honeymoon, it seemed as if we fast-forwarded into a darker, thornier patch of our lives together. Had those tender, easy times already slipped away from us, like a fleeting phase of the moon?

Here I will say this: I know I am still a beginner in long-term love, and there will be bigger tests than struggling to get pregnant after a miscarriage. But the year that followed that long taxi ride back from the hospital made me reflect on what I have learnt about trying to sustain love when life doesn't go to plan. Because a relationship isn't a course you can study for and then complete. Instead, it is a decision you make every day to build something meaningful with another person. Doing that takes awareness and understanding – of yourself and each other; and it takes effort and a belief that you can survive what life takes away from you and find a way back to one another when it threatens to prise you apart. I thought I knew this. But when life took something from me – from us – for a while I forgot it all. I was too busy looking back, at what had been lost, and forward, at what I could not will into existence: a pregnancy. It felt like my life was a picture and my loss was the frame; everything I did hung in the context of what I didn't have.

Six months, six periods and six more heartbreaks passed. (Because when you are trying and failing to get pregnant, that's what a period becomes – a monthly missive that breaks your heart into a mess, like a raw egg smashed on the floor.)

All the things we usually enjoyed doing together were suddenly framed in loss too. We woke up on Saturday mornings to the sound of the neighbour's baby crying in the flat above. We walked through Clissold Park in the golden five o'clock sunshine and all I could see were the couples pushing their prams past us, the little girl riding a bright blue bike with a basket and shouting, 'Daddy, look at me!' Even when we went to a friend's child-free dinner party, someone played that Foreigner song. Was Dan, like I was, instantly back in that Toyota Prius? I didn't ask, because if he wasn't, I didn't want to take him there. And so, for the first time in our relationship, there were unsaid things.

Another three months slipped by. There were six pregnancy announcements from friends. Three babies were born; two girls, one boy. And I still carried all the unused baby names on a list in my phone's Google notes. I couldn't explain to Dan how the sadness of not conceiving every month was tangled up with the miscarriage, because I didn't understand it myself. And I couldn't explain to anyone why such a short period of time – particularly in the world of fertility – felt agonizingly long to me. It was as if a sadness played inside me like a piece of music I couldn't switch off.

Every month when I had to say, 'Nope! Not pregnant!', I thought about the joy in Dan's eyes when we'd watched our baby's heart beating inside my womb on the screen – a look I had never seen before or since, so raw and pure. I hated being the messenger of our mutual disappointments.

After so many years of sharing the minutiae of our days, it felt strange that there were parts of our journey to conceive that only I knew. I wanted Dan to know all the times I anxiously examined my knickers in the work loos, trying to spot a drop of blood that might end a love story. I wanted him to know about the woman in the bed opposite me in the hospital, after I came around from the anaesthetic, who was quietly crying and had the saddest face I had ever seen, which I still thought about sometimes at night. I wanted him to know the clues I scrutinized my body for in the shower every month (dark nipples? swollen breasts? bloated stomach?); how I totted them all up and made an impossible decision: whether to risk revealing to him that I was hopeful. I wanted him to know it all – but I didn't want to have to tell him.

Around this time, I reread a line by relationship coach Susan Quilliam: 'Love often goes wrong because of a lack of self-reflection and understanding.' In order to be a good partner, she suggested, you have to understand what you need and fear, the insecurities that disguise themselves in other emotions. To do that, I had to first figure out something I had been reluctant to admit to myself. I thought I was frustrated at the biological inequality of our situation, at the fact that my body had to be operated on and Dan's didn't. But underneath my irritation was a sense of shame, a feeling that the miscarriage and subsequent struggle to conceive was my fault. Our test results had shown Dan's sperm was healthy, but one of my fallopian tubes was blocked because of complications with the surgery, so the doctor recommended I have another operation before we could start IVF. When we got this news, I felt my body was letting us both down.

This feeling of shame was sharpened every time I watched Dan hold a baby, or make a toddler laugh. One of the first things people notice about Dan is that children gravitate towards him. As well as being a primary schoolteacher, he is the kind of person that ends up showing friends' children how to moonwalk while the rest of the adults sit at the table. Or who comes home with a framed note, which says, 'Dan, you are my favourite teacher. I will miss you. From Alice,' with each letter written in a different-coloured crayon. Each time I watched him connect so easily with children, when I witnessed the joy they brought him and he brought them, it was painful to think that I might be the one to deny him fatherhood. In this way his personality, the essence of who he was, only deepened my sense of failure. Sometimes in his face I saw our loss reflected back at me, and so I did not want to look into it.

It would've been easier to let this unsaid thing stack up with all the rest, but I told him everything one night, over pizza, including how I worried what the worst-case scenario of this fertility journey might do to us as a couple. Could we survive all the treacherous unknowns: the rounds of IVF that might fail, the pieces of ourselves we might have to give up along the way? In response he took my hand and said, 'We will make it even if we don't make it.'

Although identifying and sharing my vulnerability was a

turning point, I realized then that Dan could not carry my longing for me. He would, if I asked him to, but that wasn't the answer. To some extent, we each must carry our own sadness and I was the only person who could forgive my body and learn to be at peace inside it. I began to take responsibility for my own feelings. And we decided to take our individual journeys, together.

It would be a neat lie to say that I then learnt to turn down the volume on my sadness. It was still there every day, the quiet tune of a life we never got to live, and weren't sure, just yet, if we ever would. I heard it when I walked past the 'lost child point' at Leicester Square tube every weekday morning, and when I turned on Netflix at night and saw three icons on the screen: Dan. Natasha. Children. It got louder when a man selling touristy beaded bracelets approached us on holiday and innocently asked, 'Are you married?' 'Yes,' we said. 'Children?' We shook our heads, and I thought, how casually this question is tossed about, this small word that can mask a chasm.

What I did learn is not to try to silence the sadness, but to focus more on living. Because love is rarely a pristine story. There will be shiny pavement kisses and painfully slow taxi rides. There will be orgasms and diarrhoea, promotions and debt, tricky relatives and attractive strangers and claustrophobic, mundane days; and we have to find a way to keep connecting with those we love – and trying to understand ourselves – through *all* of it. We have to rebuild the relationships we value again and again, even when our hearts or egos are wounded (perhaps especially then).

It took me a year to realize that our honeymoon wasn't a cancelled holiday to a luxury hotel in Mauritius. It was twelve months of trying and hoping together. This would always be the year in which a life was taken from us and we failed to create another. But at the bottom of this hole in our lives we dug up something else. It wasn't shiny and light, like a beginning. No. What we had instead was a hard-won, heavy intimacy. A tender love born from a shared experience, in the empty space where our baby never was. It's true, of course, to say that we were no longer those light-hearted people we were the night we first kissed. But those versions still live somewhere inside us, along with a dozen more. Now there are so many different selves to discover and recognize in each other. What a challenge – what a gift.

To celebrate our one-year wedding anniversary, the following summer we flew to Puglia. On this holiday I began to wonder if, like the stars at night, I could see the beautiful parts of our lives more clearly against the dark backdrop of a difficult year. There were days when I imagined what the holiday might have been like had we had a six-month-old baby in our arms, as we were due to. But there were days, too, when I understood that the tender joy in front of me would not have existed if our other life had. I noticed and took a mental photograph of those moments – the morning Dan was swimming in the sea, when I shouted 'Wave!' as one rolled towards him from behind, and he just waved his hand, and I laughed because it was silly. The afternoon we drank too much at lunch and went for a nap in the cool, air-conditioned bedroom, where we slipped in and out of sleep, holding hands, bodies sticky from sun cream, his big heart beating against my back. I realized that whoever came up with the definition for the word 'hony moone' got it wrong. The tenderness of love does not wane over time – it deepens. The fleeting parts are tiny pockets of time like these, which we must do our best to pay attention to.

The day before I sat down to write this, my friend Helena sent me a postcard of a painting called *Ad Astra* (*To the Stars*). When I looked it up, I found it can be part of a phrase meaning 'to the stars through hardships', sometimes thought to originate from the line 'there is no easy way from the Earth to the stars.' As I stuck it to the wall above my desk with Blu-Tack, Dan came in. We talked for a few minutes, then he said, 'I was thinking that, if we ever have a girl, her middle name could be . . .' Then he said the name we gave to the baby we'd lost, which I won't write here, because it is a piece of the story just for us. And I knew it then, so clearly: that, although at times that year I had felt alone, I never really had been.

*

By the time we celebrated the end of that first year of marriage, I saw love very differently. The warm feeling swelling in my chest had expanded into something deeper and darker and bottomless. Our relationship had become something new too: a living thing, separate to us, that we had both made a pact to keep alive. Now it was like a plant – we couldn't just pour a whole watering can on it once and hope that it survived for ever. Instead, we had to take turns to water it, frequently, in order to nourish its roots. As it grew, it would change shape. And if we neglected it for too long, it would wilt and die.

The next question, then, is what do we need to do to sustain love? That year I had learnt a little about how to find a way back to a partner in the middle of a painful experience, but what about the boring, busy days in between the peaks and troughs of our lives? How do we carry on loving our friends, siblings, children and partners – and ourselves – as best we can, even when other areas of life (work, health, money) demand more attention? Because building a good relationship requires dozens of people, not just two. And as Ayisha Malik told me earlier, we need different people in our life to see different parts of who we are. Just as we talk about working on our romantic partnerships, we need to talk about the effort and inevitable complexities that come with trying to love *all* the people in our lives.

I use the word 'sustain' because it means to strengthen and support, and also to suffer. At first, I thought this word was too negative to describe any loving relationship. But as I began to speak to people about the challenges of long-term love – change; assumptions; complacency; time; fear of loss – I saw that few relationships – if any – can escape struggle entirely. Fumbling through these struggles together, forgiving each other when we slip up, then trying again, and again after that – this is how love evolves. It's also how we evolve within it. This is the process this section of the book will explore, and I wanted to begin by looking at the reality of romance.

*

I used to envy people who fell in love at first sight, because Dan and I didn't. We took a couple of months – at least – to get to know each other, and a couple more after that to commit to a relationship. We were both guarded. We both held back. Perhaps we were both a little afraid too. For all those reasons, the early months of dating felt like trying to blow up a balloon that wouldn't inflate, and our love story bears little resemblance to the ones I grew up idealizing, where attraction was instant and urgent. It did, however, turn out to be my most romantic relationship: a slow-burn love story, no less poignant for its undramatic beginnings on a dating app. It introduced me to the beauty of knowing the whole version of someone, rather than your fantasy of who they are. And the quiet sturdiness of real love, which, like anything meaningful in life, requires effort. But what does that effort look like? And where do we find *real* romance in a long-term relationship? I turned to author Roxane Gay for answers to these questions, in the hope that by redefining what romance really means, we can make sure we don't neglect it.

Roxane is an essayist, professor, opinion writer and the author of bestselling books *Bad Feminist*, *Hunger* and *Difficult Women*, among others. She's also a romantic, who was for a long time in love with the idea of love. I decided to interview her after reading a piece about Valentine's Day in the *Guardian*, in which she wrote, 'I created elaborate fictions for my relationships – fictions that allowed me to believe that what any given paramour and I shared looked a lot like love. I would say, "I love you" as if the words were currency, as if they could force the objects of my affection to genuinely reciprocate those feelings.' It was reassuring to know that even one of our wisest intellectuals and writers could fall into the trap of idealizing an unrealistic notion of love, as I had done, and to read that, through a mix of age and experience, Roxane learnt to recognize the difference between the idea of love and the reality. I wanted to find out how she learnt that lesson, and what romance looks like in her relationship with author and podcast host Debbie Millman, who she was engaged to when we spoke, and married in 2020.

Redefining romance, with Roxane Gay

NL: What are the differences between the idea you had of love when you were younger, and what you understand real love to be now?

RG: The main difference is that I understand a lot of the mythology around love is just that – it's mythology. Growing up, I read and watched a lot of romantic comedies and dramas, which generally give you a grand sense of love and romance, not necessarily a realistic one. Now, rather than that instantaneous flash of new love we often see in stories, I am more interested in the love that deepens over time.

Everybody's relationship to love is different. Sometimes it is great; sometimes it isn't. New love is always exciting, but what happens after the newness of a relationship fades or dims is more beautiful to me. It's something that grows, where there is patience and humour, where you can be furious with someone and still love them. I appreciate that now, especially because I'm older and I'm in a functional relationship. It has certainly shown me that you can have a spark and excitement and romance with someone who's also going to be there in the morning when you haven't brushed your teeth.

Now I find joy in loving my partner as much as I enjoy being loved by her. And I don't think we talk enough about what it means to truly be loved, and to be able to reciprocate that.

And what does being loved mean to you?

Feeling cared for at all times, being truly seen, being accepted for who I am – the good and the bad – and being held to a high standard. I love that my partner has expectations of me, and I always try to rise to that occasion. It's also about believing your partner when they articulate where they're at emotionally, instead of trying to talk them out of their feelings. You have to accept their feelings as they are, even when they see things differently to you.

For me, the most beautiful thing about long-term love is understanding that a person has become necessary to your life. My life doesn't make sense without my partner in it and I feel as necessary to her life as she is to mine. And also – it sounds obvious but it's important – we make each other laugh every day. Enjoying each other's company is a big part of love. I use my parents as a model: they've been married for forty-seven years and they still laugh, they still go on dates. Even when they bicker, they're still friends. They have their ups and downs, for sure, but at the end of the day, they like and respect each other. That is the constant.

Is there anything that has surprised you about the reality of love, compared to the fantasy of it you had when you were younger?

The most surprising thing is that when you find the right person, it's not a lot of work. People often say, 'Oh, love takes a lot of work,' but I've found it's an effort that doesn't feel like work – it's just maintenance. What I love, and what has been unexpected, is that in a good relationship loving someone can be easy. Of course we all have moments when we don't necessarily like our partner, but in a good relationship that is a temporary feeling. It doesn't affect the fact that you love them. Now, whenever my partner and I have disagreements they never last long, because we've realized that the discomfort of not speaking, or of not getting along, is more trouble than trying to work through the actual problem together.

Do you think you can do that now because you're older and you've learnt from relationships in the past? Or is it because this particular relationship works?

We're both at the right time in our lives to make the relationship work. We are finally mature enough. We're both in therapy, separately, and when I met her I was as ready as I've ever been to be in a good relationship and to be a good partner. But I do think it's that she's the right person too. She's very patient. She has a good sense of humour. She knew who I was before we got together – because she had read my memoir – which meant she had a good sense of at least one version of who I was. That closed a lot of the potential distance between us. And so, frankly, a lot of it is luck. We got lucky.

I never used to believe in soulmates. Now I think my fiancée is absolutely my soulmate. I feel I've known her a hundred years and yet every day there's still more to get to know about her. I love that potential, the unknown that can exist in the familiar.

Why did you decide that you wanted to get married?

Commitment is important. Do you need the piece of paper? Not necessarily, but I do think marriage is more than that, and it's a strange reflex to minimize the commitment to just 'a piece of paper'. For me, marriage is about saying, 'Yes, we've already committed, but now we're going to make vows to each other in front of our friends and our family, and they're going to hold us accountable for those vows. We're going to hold each other accountable for them too. We're going to try to stay together, no matter what. We're going to stick it out. We're not going to run away when it gets too hard or too scary, and we're going to try to always see the best in each other: today, tomorrow and twenty years from now.' The fact that you're willing to do that with someone? To commit to really trying to make it work? I think that's a very sexy, lovely thing. Sometimes it doesn't work out and there's nothing wrong with that. But marrying someone means that you're going to give it a go anyway.

I think when you decide to get married you also look ahead and understand there will be challenges to sustaining long-term love. What do you see as the biggest challenges?

The biggest challenge is recognizing that new isn't always better. Often people get distracted and think, oh, look at that sexy person. I want that. Or, this person intrigues me intellectually. Instead of thinking they could be a good friend, they consider having a fling with them, because people tend to be more interested in the new than the steady. But I've learnt you can absolutely find newness in an older relationship, too, if you're open to it. And frankly, that's one of the most exciting things about being in love. I don't want to get to know someone new, I'll tell you that for sure. I'm old and I am done. I have had it with trying to figure out someone's new quirks. I want the quirks I already know!

You have a rich life outside of your marriage – with your work, your friendships and with yourself. Do those things strengthen your relationship?

Oh, without a doubt. This is the first time I've been in a position to truly be in a relationship and not expect it to be my whole world, or to fix all of my emotional needs. I have a reasonably good career, I have very good friends and I have my family. I love that my partner complements all of those things, and that I get to include her in them. But because I have a rich life separate from the relationship, she doesn't have to fix everything and be everything for me.

As well as learning about ourselves through spending time alone, I think we can continue to do so in a relationship too. What have you learnt about yourself inside this relationship?

I have learnt what my capacity to love is, what I want and don't want, and that it's OK to share my boundaries, my desires and my needs. So yes, this relationship is definitely a journey of self-growth as well as growing together. But I am not fully formed; I still struggle with articulating my needs. Intellectually, I know that this relationship is a safe place to be open about who I am, what I want and what I need. But often my partner does have to drag those things out of me. I know that's not the most enjoyable thing, but she's willing to do it, and hopefully sooner rather than later I'll get to a place where she doesn't have to. Believing that I deserve love is a work in progress for me. I try to believe it every day, and on the days when I don't, I try not to be too hard on myself. I'm able to do that because I know our love is steady. I know my partner is going to love me, whether I believe I deserve it or not.

You've described yourself as a romantic. Have you found that to be a hindrance or a help in a long-term relationship?

It's a help, as long as there's true love beneath it. It can't just be romance for the sake of romance. I love doing romantic things for and with my partner, and every day she does something romantic, like leaving little Post-it notes with messages and hearts on everywhere. One day they're in my suitcase, another day they're in my toothbrush drawer. Those sweet words are always a surprise. Often, we think romance has to be a room full of roses, but sometimes it's a Post-it note. Sometimes it's picking your partner up from work and taking them to a special place to relax. Sometimes it's taking out the trash before they get home. Romance is about finding ways to show someone they are appreciated.

Perhaps I am romantic because I don't like being taken for granted and so I don't ever want someone I'm with to feel that way either. Inevitably, at some point in the course of a relationship, one of you will take the other for granted. That is just the way it goes. But when that happens, I want it to be an aberration, and not the norm.

What do you wish you'd known about love?

If it's a true, solid love, then it can withstand difficulty. It can withstand you being human and being flawed and being unhappy or having a problem with your partner. I wish I had known that love doesn't disappear when you aren't quiet and perfect.

*

Roxane was not the first person I've interviewed who had been surprised by the ease of real love. Journalist Christina

Patterson said, 'I wish I'd known that love wasn't like climbing Everest.' And Ariel Levy told me, 'I always thought that love was supposed to be fraught and painful and complicated, a kind of battle. I wish I'd known that it can be really easy.' Their answers reminded me of something written in my Great-Uncle Ken's order of service at his funeral, about his marriage: 'Ken and Annette were extremely lucky to remain totally in love from the moment they met. Ken said it was the easiest thing he ever had to do.' When I read those lines, at first I thought they contradicted a lot of what I'd learnt about love being something that requires constant work and renewal. Now I realize that what these answers point to is that, although you have to work at a relationship, you shouldn't have to work at convincing someone to love you. Either they do or they don't. The loving and being-loved part should be easy.

And, as Roxane pointed out, sometimes even the 'work' of relationships doesn't feel like work at all – actually, it's just maintenance. A series of daily decisions we make in order not to take the people we love for granted. For Roxane, that might be a Post-it note. For my friend Sarah, it's her husband putting toothpaste on her toothbrush so when she gets to the bathroom it's waiting for her on the side of the basin. For you, it could be someone bringing your favourite chocolate bar back from the newsagent's for no reason, or folding and putting away the clean underwear you've left on the drying rack all week. Now I see that these small gestures aren't just maintenance, but a form of romance too. Tiny, everyday details that quietly say, 'I love you.'

*

There were two lessons that stood out in my conversation with Roxane. The first was about accepting and believing your partner's feelings when they are different from your own, rather than trying to talk them out of them. The second was that you can still find newness in a long-term relationship.

I wanted to understand the challenges of continuing to learn those lessons, not just at the beginning of a marriage or relationship, but after decades together. Is it unrealistic to expect to find newness after so many years? And how does it feel when someone you've known for half your life changes, and expresses feelings that differ greatly from your own? Having only been in a relationship for six years, I could not answer these questions myself. So I talked to one of my favourite writers – illustrator and author of the graphic memoir *Good Talk*, Mira Jacob – about what she has learnt from sustaining love through two decades of marriage. Mira has been married to her husband for just over twenty years, and they now live in Brooklyn together with their son, who is twelve.

Happily, speaking to Mira convinced me that getting to know someone *is* a never-ending story: a partner can still be a mystery to you, even after years of knowing them. And by accepting that, instead of resisting it, you can fall in love with them again and again. What she helped me to see was that long-term love offers everything I had assumed was reserved for the early years: mystery, eroticism and even romance, if you pay enough attention.

The unknowable corners of someone you love, with Mira Jacob

NL: You wrote in Vogue *that when you fell in love with your husband you 'couldn't hopscotch over the vulnerable parts of falling in love'. Why did you find that part so difficult?*

M J: We learn to keep our jagged bits inside for fear of appearing unattractive. I always thought there was a part of your messiness you saved for yourself, that no one else would ever see. It's enormously humbling to realize how many times and ways my partner will pierce that. I can pretend I have all sorts of things together, but when I am at my most broken, he is still the person I turn to.

After so many years together, what have you learnt about how to make love last?

No marriage is perfect, but if you try to forgive each other for the necessary bumps that come with being two people trying to live together, that goes a long way. There are clumsy things we do in the act of trying to love each other – not all of them feel great; some of them are hurtful – but in our marriage there's a lot of forgiveness for all the silly fuck-ups we make along the way. We make plenty. We will continue to make plenty!

People sometimes talk about long-term love as a comfortable companionship. I'm only six years into my relationship, but I have found the opposite to be true: the deep romance in some ways gets more intense over time. Do you feel the same? And does romance mean something different to you after two decades together?

I think the reason people view older love as safe companionship is because we are scared to look honestly at its frailty. If we were to admit how fragile it is, it would be terrifying, because we have leveraged so much of our lives into it. Whereas with a new love, you're aware of every fracture and place that it could go wrong, but the stakes aren't as high yet. This is my way of telling you that I very much believe passion still exists in older love, because those fault lines still exist too. It's a comfort to tell ourselves they don't, but of course they do.

What always surprises me, when I talk to a friend whose relationship of fifteen or twenty years has ended, is how quickly things can go wrong. They might say, 'Things haven't been good for ten years,' but sometimes it's actually only the last few months that were hard. When I hear stories like that I think, wait, what? Shouldn't it be that, if you spent ten years investing in something, it should take at least ten years to dismantle it? Or ten years of mistakes before it ends? But that's not how it works. So it always feels somewhat treacherous to keep going. I know that seems like a negative thing, but I find that fragility to be a positive part of love.

How does understanding the fragility of long-term relationships make them more passionate?

When I feel that frailty, there's a scary part to it that ensures I don't take love for granted. The other day I was on a train and I realized that I'd met my partner twenty years ago to the day. Suddenly I thought, oh my God, what if we don't get twenty more years? (Which is a high likelihood, frankly; this life is not as long as we would like it to be.) I carried on thinking, what if that's not in the cards for us? What if one of us leaves the planet? I felt a sense of urgency to be with him. I knew in that moment that the twenty years I've spent with him have gone by more quickly than two years would have with the wrong person. Partly because there's a way in which he always feels new to me. Just when I think, I know this guy really well, he changes: a new part of him emerges that I hadn't known before. Figuring out who he is now is deeply interesting to me.

So making room for both of you to change can be a source of passion, as well as a challenge in a long-term relationship?

Yes, and I wish I had known that change happens consistently and constantly in a relationship. There are times in my marriage when he has felt like a stranger to me, and I've thought, who are you? Those moments can be lonely, but they're not evidence you're in the wrong marriage – they just mean that you're going through a tough moment of change. In one way, I wish I'd known that when I was younger. In another, I'm glad I didn't, because it has been a delight to be surprised by the changes in each other. The truth is you don't ever really choose a person, because they change, and your lives do too. So when you're choosing a partner what you're really choosing is how a person weathers change. You're choosing how *you* weather change with and alongside them.

Like you, your partner is always work in progress. As someone who loves them, your job is to keep knowing them, to keep being curious. One of the things I'm proud of in my marriage is how curious I am about my partner and how curious he is about me. When a day ends, there's no one that I want to tell things to the way I want to tell them to him.

In the early stages of a relationship you naturally ask questions about each other, because you're getting to know the other person. But as time passes some people can stop making a conscious effort to ask who their partner is, and then, if they've changed, that might feel threatening.

For sure. It is scary to have somebody you are counting on become a different person. You have to catch up. You feel the strain of that. You want to judge it. But we all have our unknowable corners. The interesting thing about marriage is you commit to the idea of getting to know those corners, and of really looking at them when they develop into a different thing. That, to me, is what a marriage is: showing up to do the work of re-seeing someone again and again.

I do feel my partner is committed to the idea of my growth. Every time I've had a new project come up, or something I'm scared of trying, he always says, 'You can do it. You can figure it out.' And inherent in his confidence in me is an understanding that doing that new thing will change me.

As well as change, what are the other challenges you've faced together?

It's a hard time to be an interracial couple in America. My partner and I are two different colours and races, and we have a mixed-race child, so we are having two different experiences of the world. He grew up in New Mexico, like I did, so because I was Indian and he was Jewish we both knew what it was to be a minority. But now we are in New York I don't think he lives with the same level of fear of what's happening. If there is a fear, it's for me and his son, not for him. It's like one of us is in a rainstorm while the other is under an awning, and our love has to span that gap.

How do you overcome feelings of frustration about your different experiences and sustain intimacy through them?

The only thing we've been able to do in this moment is to keep talking (it's easy to stop talking when your experiences of the world are vastly different). I've also had to realize that sometimes I'm just going to be furious because I have a lot to be furious about. When I was younger, I felt bad about that – the idea that 'my' race issues made things harder for us. But honestly, *my* race issues aren't the ones driving my country to madness right now, and they're not what has hurt us most as a couple – whiteness is. And if he chose to be with me, he chose the life of living through this with me, of not getting tired of it or giving up or pretending it's something I should fix for us.

Also, some things are easier than people would have you believe: I'm still attracted to him, I still want to be right next to him, I still want to share a life with him. The harder part is exposing and locating a vulnerability in yourself that you know the other person will never have to shoulder – and not resenting them for that. Talking, bridging that distance and trying to make yourself known stops the wall between you from solidifying.

Becoming parents can be a tough adjustment in a long-term relationship too. How did having your son change your relationship?

For me, it was physical and animal-like at the beginning. I knew that we could give our son formula, which is what I did when I went to work, but I wanted to breastfeed, to have my body next to my baby's body. Because of that, I was the one that got up in the night and my sense of time and space completely altered. Once my son was born, I saw the world through his eyes and his needs. At first, that made me furious with my partner. I thought, who are you, this adult person who operates with an enormous level of freedom? How do you walk out the door and not think about this as much as I do? Whether you are a biological parent or not, I think there is a primary parent for some reason, who thinks, it is on me to make this work. And when you do that? It isolates you. It puts you in a relationship with the child, and then you have to find your way back to your partner. You have to acknowledge the rage and say to them, 'I'm pissed that I lost my sense of self and you somehow retained yours.' You have to address it and move through it. But now our son is twelve we both feel the same pressure. We are both the people who will always look out for him in the way no one else will.

Although my partner and I had to shift to accommodate someone else in our relationship, the cool thing is seeing the person you fell in love with horizon in someone else. Seeing the parts of my partner that I am taken with arrive in our son, and understanding that strange chemistry of nature, and how that has worked to reveal these things to me? It's unbelievable. You make space for a new person, but that new person is comprised of many of the things that you love about the person who's already there.

We've spoken a lot about sustaining emotional intimacy, but how do you make sure you stay physically connected after so many years together?

I think of sex as the dream life of a marriage; it tells you things that you don't know or can't admit in your waking hours. I'm of the firm belief that our bodies often know things before our minds are ready to process them, and, in that way, sex becomes a kind of subconscious language, a way to make sense of a part of you that can't be put into words, much like art or music. What I love most is that there's a kind of bottom-line truth to it, an essence that can't be made into anything other than what it is. You know if you're connecting, and you know if you're going through the motions and holding yourself back.

While we do put emotional intimacy on a pedestal sometimes, I think it's easier to fall out of the habit of having sex than the habit of talking, and so perhaps we need to put just as much — if not more — effort into that too.

Completely. I get scared when I haven't had sex with my part-ner for too long, the same way I get scared if I haven't written in a long time. I feel estranged from a vital part of myself. And I get scared of the idea of doing it again, because I think, what if I don't love it as much as I used to? There's a ner-vousness around it, until it becomes this incredibly weighted thing. My shortcut around that whole quagmire – which I can go into so easily – is to keep doing it regularly. Because then every time doesn't matter as much. It's like, yes, we're doing it again, great! How was it this time? Sometimes it's amazing and there's a preciousness around it. Sometimes it's as rou-tine as washing a T-shirt. And I like to be open to the idea that sex can have numerous outcomes. There's not one kind of sex you have with a partner.

You definitely have to work at it, though, and by that I

don't mean sprinkle rose petals around the house. I mean: shut your brain off and just go for it. We have to stay in constant conversation with someone we love, and sex is a different way to have a conversation with them. Which is why I think it's exciting when you've been with someone for ever and then you suddenly have a different kind of sex than you've ever had before. You think, what just happened? I thought I knew you.

What do you wish you'd known about love?

I used to worry about presenting myself in a certain light because I didn't want to give up the mystery of who I was and lose someone's interest. I didn't know that there are always new things you will learn about your partner and they will always be a mystery. They hold worlds and worlds inside of them that are inaccessible to you at certain points but can be accessed at others. And that's tremendously gratifying.

We have so many lives folded within this one life. We have so many secrets and longings and stages and alternate parts of our personality; our partners live with all of that. My partner and I will be sitting together, and he'll tell me a story from his life, or something he was thinking, that will be new and vitally interesting to me. I didn't know that was how love worked. I thought it was a book you read and finished, and once you got through it you knew the story. But you never know the story. There's always a new chapter.

*

My questions about whether or not you can ever fully know someone (you can't), and whether newness can appear in love after decades (it can), had been answered. But this conversation left me with another clue: 'the subconscious language of sex' – what our bodies can tell us that perhaps our minds can't quite yet. Although trying to conceive had turned sex into a more complicated issue in my own relationship, I knew, as Mira described it as the dream life of a marriage, that if I wanted to truly understand how to sustain love, I could not shy away from it.

*

Like emotional intimacy, good sex, I think, requires great vulnerability. Each time we put our body beside someone else's and decide to fully let go, we show them a little more of who we are. We show them our desires, even those we worry might seem strange or shameful to someone else. It is a conversation, another way of seeing and being seen. Except there are fewer words to hide behind. No way of knowing exactly how things will unfold, or how your bodies will react when you touch each other this time or the next. If you are physically able to and in a monogamous relationship, it's also one of the few things you do with a partner that you do with no one else. That is what sex is to me: a mysterious portal into another part of Dan, through which he can access another part of me.

Of course, since we've been together our sex life has been through different phases: the hot urgency of the first few years; the less frequent but more exploratory sex when we knew each other better, when we were less afraid to test boundaries and more willing to be honest about exactly what we wanted. Then there were the more functional times that served their purpose: the clumsy days when we were out of sync, the nights where one of our minds was somewhere else. There have been times, too, when I worried my libido was waning, because I didn't crave sex as automatically as I used to. At that point I equated a good sex life with spontaneous desire. And so I looked back enviably at the body I inhabited for the first three years of our relationship, which was turned on as easily as a switch.

It wasn't until we started trying to conceive again, after the miscarriage, that I learnt to rethink my understanding of desire entirely. I won't lie: having sex when you're trying to get pregnant can be as mundane a task as hanging up wet washing. You know it has to be done there and then, however tired you are, or the washing will smell damp . . . or you will miss the fertile window. It also becomes a more loaded act. What was once a way for me and Dan to connect and enjoy each other soon turned into something more complex: a potential doorway to everything we longed for. Sex could give us a baby or repeatedly disappoint us, and even when it did, we had to do it again and again and again. Not out of pleasure, but out of necessity. By this point, doctors told us we should try to do it every other day.

Sometimes, particularly in the early months after the surgery, I felt so disconnected from my body that I had no interest in pleasure at all. Reaching the finishing line of sex – and as quickly as possible – was the only goal. Occasionally we masturbated first to speed things along. Other times we laughed at how functional things had become. Surprisingly, finding humour in those moments was a new flavour of intimacy. Not an erotic or mysterious one, but something intensely honest. Even on a rainy Monday at 5.45 a.m., before Dan left for work, if I was ovulating, we had sex for each other. We showed up: two people with a shared dream, committing to something neither of us particularly wanted to do, trying to be kind and generous to one another while we attempted it anyway.

But the strangest thing about those months was that, even when sex felt like a chore for both of us, sometimes, a few minutes in, I would change my mind. Unexpectedly and suddenly, I craved the sex I was already having. This didn't just happen once or twice, but repeatedly, and more frequently, the longer we kept *having* to have sex. It was the first time I understood that spontaneous desire for sex beforehand was not directly related to the quality of my pleasure during it. And this was the revelation that led me to the work of Emily Nagoski.

A sex educator and bestselling author of *Come As You Are*, Emily uses science and psychology to debunk myths around sex. She challenges us to rethink what a 'normal' sex life looks like (there's no such thing). She questions assumptions that have been made about women's bodies (particularly by men). And she shows us that it is often the risk of failure that interferes with people's ability to enjoy the sex they're having. The part of Emily's work that transformed my attitude to sex looks at the two different types of sex drive: spontaneous desire (out-of-the-blue interest in wanting sex) and responsive desire (which emerges in response to, rather than in anticipation of, erotic stimulation). She explains that, although responsive desire is healthy and normal, often when we think about what defines good sex our minds jump to the wrong question: how much sex do I want and how often do I automatically want it? In fact, as Emily and I discuss below, it's only when we let go of the myth that spontaneous desire is the sole measure of a good sex life that we can begin to ask a better question: what does thrilling sex really mean to *you*?

The science of sex, with Emily Nagoski

NL: Is there a scientific reason why, in the early stages of a relationship, we often want sex more urgently and frequently?

EN: Not everyone does. People vary enormously. But yes, the common experience is that in the hot, early stage of a relationship the attachment mechanism in our brain drives the chemical process. It makes us want to bond with another person to secure the attachment, and one of the ways we do that is through sex. When we're falling in love and easily motivated to want sex, that's because our brains think, what else can I do to feel closer to this person? Ooh, sex is one way to do that.

Is that why, as an attachment to a partner becomes more secure, some people don't want sex as frequently?

Yes, that's the ironic thing: when a connection is secure your brain doesn't need to reinforce the attachment. But even when you're in a secure, long-term relationship, if the attachment is threatened, that drive to connect can return. For example, once a year my sister's husband (a high-school music teacher at the time) used to go to Europe for ten days with his choir. My sister would stay at home feeling an emotion she called 'homesick', and when he returned she would feel motivated to have sex, because the attachment had been tested. She missed him, and sex repaired the attachment threat. Even though they've been together for twenty years, the temporary distance created a stronger desire. The same thing happens in unstable relationships: if you're always worried your partner is going to leave, you may feel sexually motivated in that unstable connection, because your body's trying to use sex as a way to stabilize the relationship. This is at the core of why desire is bullshit. I would love people to stop putting desire at the centre of their definition of sexual well-being, because all it means is that you're motivated to engage in sex – regardless of what the motivation is – and often that motivation may be slightly twisted, or not good for you.

The way our culture often talks about pleasure – for example you should have sex a certain number of times a week – can make people feel like a failure for not having it 'enough'. Whereas what you're saying is perhaps if you're not constantly craving sex, it could be a sign that you have a strong, secure relationship?

Yes! One of the most exciting pieces of research I've seen in the last five years is by Peggy Kleinplatz in Canada, about optimal sexual experiences. Researchers interviewed dozens of people who self-identify as having extraordinary sex lives, of many different relationship structures, including those who've been together for decades. They asked, 'This great sex you're having, what's it like?' From their answers the researchers developed a list of the characteristics of extraordinary, optimal sex and published them in a book, *Magnificent Sex*. You know what's not on that list? Spontaneous, out-of-the-blue desire for sex. Neither is frequency. And yet we have these cultural scripts about sex that prioritize those things.

So what are the characteristics of extraordinary sex that Kleinplatz found we should be prioritizing?

1) Being completely present in the moment, embodied, focused and absorbed. 2) Connection, alignment, being in sync. 3) Deep sexual and erotic intimacy. 4) Extraordinary communication and deep empathy. 5) Being genuine, authentic and transparent. 6) Vulnerability and surrender. 7) Exploration, interpersonal risk-taking and fun. 8) Transcendence and transformation.

Going back to the example you used of your sister and her husband . . . do you think that one way couples in long-term relationships can increase desire is to find safe opportunities to introduce distance into the relationship?

Yes. In Kleinplatz's research the phrase that came up was 'just safe enough'. For some people 'just safe enough' is turning on the lights or experimenting with a new position. For others, it's going to a swingers' club and having sex in front of another person. But this is not about clichéd sex tips; it is the emotional risk that's important. It is the vulnerability, the authenticity. It's daring to accept your partner fully for who they are and what they desire, and to be accepted by your partner for everything you are and desire too. It is far harder than lingerie and porn, but it is more rewarding. Pleasure doesn't have to be a priority all the time, but if there are times when you decide that it does matter to you both, and you can find the courage to explore those places in each other, then your entire relationship transforms. You can feel more connected to each other – and even to your own humanity.

Why, then, do we fixate on spontaneous desire as a measure of a good sexual relationship?

I've wondered this a lot and I don't have a science-based answer. I think it's partly to do with desire being an optimal state for capitalism. You have to continue wanting things so you continue consuming, so you continue stimulating the economy. There's a baseline sense that being constantly full of desire is the appropriate state to be in, which is bizarre, because isn't desire just dissatisfaction for what we currently have? Why is that the goal?

So if someone comes to you and feels she doesn't have spontaneous desire, but wants to work towards fulfilling her and her partner's responsive desire in a relationship, what advice would you give?

A big part of the process is understanding that responsive desire is normal – it's not a symptom of anything. One of the reasons people may resist letting go of the myth that spontaneous desire is necessary is because we all like to feel wanted. It can be disappointing for people to accept that what actually happens is you put sex on your calendar. You wear your favourite underwear, you get childcare (if you can), you carry up the last of the laundry, you get into bed, you wait for your partner to show up, and they show up. You let your skin touch your partner's skin and your body goes, oh, right. I like this. I really like this person. That's normal. That's what sex looks like in a long-term relationship, where people sustain a strong sexual connection over decades.

People want sex to be hot like it was when they were falling in love, when they couldn't wait to get their hands on each other. But when they think scheduling sex sounds boring, I remind them of the effort and anticipation they used to put into having sex. Even in the early stages, you didn't just show up; you thought about it all the time. You prepared your body and you chose an outfit, and, in the process, you got excited. You did things to woo and court each other – it didn't just happen. And you need to put an equivalent effort into creating sexual experiences and impressing each other in a long-term relationship, even if the anticipation comes from a different place.

You're right that what we often look back on as spontaneous desire was really a series of calculated decisions and efforts.

Yes, and the difference is that, early on in a relationship, it's easy to prioritize sex and feel motivated. But ten years down the road? Your bodies have changed, you might have kids, you're more tired, there might be some emotional gunk building up between you. If that's the context, you have to work through your feelings about all that other stuff first, before you can get to each other sexually.

For some people, saying, 'I don't spontaneously want sex as much, shall we start scheduling it?' can be difficult. You're acknowledging a change in your relationship (even if, as you said before, that could be a positive one). Why can that conversation feel so loaded?

The idea of initiating a plan for sex is so fraught. We're all fragile and fearful of rejection, and it requires great vulnerability to say, 'If we showed up for sex at three o'clock on Saturday, I'd be glad to be there. I'd put my body in the bed.' To ask for that is to risk being turned down. And our identity is tied to our success as sexual people. Some heterosexual men, in particular, are taught to believe that the only way they can access love and be fully accepted is by putting their penis in a vagina. So if their partner says no, they're not just saying no to sex, they're saying no to their partner's whole personhood. Sex itself is not a drive, but connection is, and we don't grant men access to other channels for giving and receiving love. If a man in a heterosexual relationship can recognize that there are other ways he can give and receive love, that would take pressure off of sex. It wouldn't be as much of an obligation for the woman, because she wouldn't feel she was rejecting his entire humanity just by saying, 'I'm too tired for sex.' That has nothing to do with his humanity, she's just exhausted.

Thinking about taking the pressure off sex, do you feel we aim too much for orgasm, and that by focusing more on pleasure, for both partners, that can be freeing?

For some people orgasm is important and they don't feel satisfied if they don't have one, and that's fine. But others feel they have to orgasm or they're a failure, and that's a different dynamic. For those people I do recommend letting go of orgasm entirely as a goal. Because when you take orgasm off the table it makes pleasure your goal, and you can't fail as long as you're having fun. It's often the risk of failure that hinders pleasure.

Before this interview, I asked my female friends about their biggest problems in sex. The two most common answers were: 1) I feel I'm bad at sex because I am out of the habit of doing it and I don't easily get turned on, and 2) I can't get out of my own head to let go and enjoy it. What would your advice be for those problems?

The biggest thing is learning what's 'normal'. If people are defining being good at sex as conforming to the culturally constructed aspirational sexual ideals, they are bad at it. The problem is that the standard is utter nonsense and has nothing to do with how people actually work. We have to stop beating ourselves up for falling short of an arbitrary destructive standard and instead begin assessing our sexual well-being on our own terms. But it's very difficult. It's much easier to get out of your own head, which you can do through mindfulness.

But, scientifically, why is it easier to get turned on when your mind is in that calm, more restful place?

The part in your brain that controls sexual response is called the dual control mechanism. It has an accelerator that notices any sex-related stimulus: everything you see, hear, smell, touch, taste, think, believe or imagine. It sends the signal to turn you on. At the same time, because it's a dual control, there's also a brake. If the brake notices a reason not to be turned on, a potential threat, it sends the turn-off signal. So becoming aroused is a dual process of turning on the on switch and eliminating the stuff that hits the brakes. When you're chattering in your mind and worrying about your sexuality, how your boobs are falling or the cellulite on your thighs, all those thoughts hit the brake, not the accelerator. It's only when you let go of everything around you, and in your mind, that it frees up the brakes so the accelerator can do its job.

The way we talk about sex often focuses on how to get turned on and hit the accelerator, but perhaps we should be learning more about how to switch off the brake?

Yes, articles about handcuffs and lube and role play focus on how to get turned on. But actually, when people are struggling, it's usually not because there's not enough stimulation to the accelerator, it's because there's too much to the brake. Young women in particular are more likely to orgasm six months into a relationship than the first time they're sexual with someone. Obviously the first time you're with someone they don't know how to touch you, but also, your inner monitor is paying attention to the other person's concerns and expectations. All that stuff hits the brakes and distracts you from pleasurable sensations. Whereas six months down the road, your body can let that stuff go, it can trust your partner, and your partner has learnt to touch you in a way that feels good.

Is that why desire for sex changes over time? Because the brakes are stronger at different points in your life, depending on what else is going on?

Yes, your brain responds to changes over your lifespan. It is normal for desire to be low shortly after a child joins your family. You're sleep-deprived, you're exhausted, and if you're a birth parent, the whole meaning of your body has changed. Of course you don't feel like sex! The same shift happens if you're caring for an elderly parent. And in a way, worrying about why you're not interested in sex during those times can hit the brakes too; judging sex is a great way to shut down sex. So the more you can relax and recognize it's normal for desire and sexual connection to ebb and flow in a relationship, the more freely you can move out of those phases where sex fades, and back into a phase where it returns.

What do you wish you'd known about sex and desire?

The neuroscience of pleasure. The simple way to think about it is if you're in a sexy state of mind and your partner tickles you, it could feel good and lead to other things. But if that same person tickles you when you're pissed off at them, you might want to punch them in the face. It's the same sensation with the same partner, but your brain interprets it differently because the context is different. So in order to know what pleasure feels like in your body, it's not just about saying, 'Touch me here. Don't touch me that way.' It's about creating a context that allows your brain to interpret a sensation – any sensation – as pleasurable.

*

After I put down the phone to Emily, I reflected on the unstable relationships in my past. Her words made sense, because in many of the interactions where I felt insecure, or as if they could end at any moment, I was always motivated to have sex. I wish I'd known then that urgent desire isn't always a sign of a deep, chemical connection to another person, but perhaps a sign that the relationship isn't offering any security. Isn't that an unhelpful fact of life, that insecurity can trick us into craving sex with someone who cares for us so little?

On the upside, Emily helped me to see that the potential for erotic connection doesn't disappear over time – it expands. I reread the words she used to sum up good sex:

vulnerability, surrender, exploration, risk-taking, transcendence . . . all words that describe the way in which Dan and I physically connect now, but didn't in the early years of our relationship, when we held back more often. Perhaps, as well as being something that means we have to work harder at sex, the trust that comes with security is what can give us the courage to expose ourselves completely.

There are still times when I will be motivated to have sex out of the blue. And that feeling of spontaneous desire is a welcome one; a reminder that my mind can lead my body. But since speaking to Emily, I also know that being motivated to have sex automatically is not the only 'normal' form of desire. Actually, nearly all of us will have to anticipate and plan sex at some point, to show up and make it happen. Maybe there will be months when I feel disconnected from my body again; maybe I will feel too tired; maybe I will even ask myself if it's worth trying to reach out to Dan when he seems far away, if we've neglected each other for too long. But in those moments, I will try to remember that – like anything good in life you want to prioritize – we have to *try* at sex. And that won't always be easy. Sometimes it might disappear from our life completely and we'll have to be brave enough to raise that with our partner in order to bring it back. Sometimes it won't matter at all for a while, which is OK too. It certainly won't be transcendent every time. But when it is? When we feel the release of compressed energy in our body, a mixture of acceptance, tenderness and lust; the indescribable feeling of being deeply in tune with another person in a way that we don't fully understand? I think that is a kind of magic.

*

Emily had showed me that emotional distance could lead to good sex, so I hoped to discover how it could benefit other aspects of a relationship too. And why, without it, intimacy becomes more challenging. Why, for example, once we know someone more intimately, is it easier to overlook them? And why does closeness often lead us to take out our frustrations on our partners? Or to find them more irritating than our friends when they let dirty plates pile up in the sink, or when they borrow then misplace our phone chargers? To explore this, with relationship coach Susan Quilliam, I delved into one of the biggest challenges we face in love: the balance between distance and security.

Susan has been helping couples with their relationships for over thirty years, has written twenty-two books (published in thirty-three countries and twenty-four languages) and has also developed and taught courses on love at the School of Life. After three decades of listening to couples' problems, she understands how the parts of a relationship that feel most comfortable (security and togetherness) can often be the root of the most painful (unkindness and resentment). It was her words that led to a turning point in my relationship, when I realized that I had to take responsibility for my own feelings in order to sustain love – for myself and for Dan. It is a simple, obvious lesson, but here Susan digs into it more deeply, showing us why the closeness that begins as a boon of a relationship can soon become its burden.

During our conversation, I was reminded of this quote by the poet Rainer Maria Rilke: 'Once the realization is accepted that even between the closest human beings infinite distances continue to exist, a wonderful living side by side can grow up, if they succeed in loving the distance between them which makes it possible for each to see the other whole and against a wide sky.' Like Rilke, Susan helped me to understand that distance in a relationship is not a threat; it is a door to a more rewarding connection.

The importance of separateness in love, with Susan Quilliam

NL: What is the most common reason that love goes wrong?

SQ: A lack of self-reflection and self-understanding. A lot of people think all you need to do to find a romantic relationship is to find a partner and, actually, the first step isn't that – it's to understand what you need and want. I always guide people away from defining what they want in a partner to defining what they want in a partnership, because they can be very different.

You see clients who are struggling with the challenges of sustaining love. What are the common mistakes couples make?

This is going to sound like a cliché – once I've said it I will expand on it because it's complicated – but what people lose in a long-term relationship is kindness. They lose it for a number of reasons: because once you've got close to somebody, they can much more easily push your buttons than a stranger can, and vice versa. You're unlikely to throw a temper tantrum if a friend does something that irritates you. But with somebody you love and who loves you, often it's easier to shout than it is to step back and think, no, I ought to treat my partner almost as if they were a stranger. I should be kind and keep a little distance.

The technical term for this in therapeutic circles is that couples get 'enmeshed' – they get so close that they start treating each other badly because it feels like a betrayal when they don't feel the same about something. The initial stage of falling in love is about finding similarity, but as the relationship progresses, and you start trying to individuate, a partner might say, 'Hold on, you disagree with me? That must mean you don't love me, because you never disagreed in the beginning.' You can either react to the threat of difference by nagging each other all the time, or by shutting down, having no connection at all and putting your attention on work or children or elsewhere. A constant problem for couples I see is that balance between keeping the connection while also keeping sufficient distance, so that you can be kind to one another. Whereas other things can vary, this underlies most of the problems I've seen.

It sounds like what you're saying is that the security of the relationship is also its enemy? Because the safety net of being together allows you to treat a partner unkindly, whereas in the beginning stage of a relationship, where there's no security, we make more effort to be kind?

Exactly. We get seduced by the fact that, in the beginning, we are completely kind and try to please our partner. Therefore, when that starts to fail, because we feel secure enough to fail at it, we don't understand why.

When you first meet, you're two independent people moving towards being part of a couple, which is wonderful. But there is a double danger: 1) of becoming too dependent, or 2) trying to run the relationship as two completely independent people. The clinical psychologist David Schnarch describes the delicate balance you need as 'interdependence' – a balance between you where your lives are intertwined, but they're not so intertwined that you lose your own identity and the elements that brought you together in the first place. There will always be times when you come together and connect, and times during even the best relationships when there is distance between you. You have to be grown up about it and say, 'Right, we'll work at coming back together, but we're not going to panic, because we trust each other.'

Once you get to a stage in a relationship where you feel secure, how can you stop yourself from getting irritated and treating your partner unkindly?

The first step is the ability to self-reflect, which a remarkable number of people don't have in a relationship. They can be wonderful when they're analysing a project at work, but ask them to reflect on what's happening in their relationship and they flinch. They say, 'No, it should be spontaneous.'

The second step is self-regulation. Notice you are being mean and calm yourself down before speaking to your partner. Once I've got a couple or individual doing that, the rest often falls into place. I also challenge the statement, 'He or she made me feel X or Y' – for example, 'She makes me feel angry' or 'He makes me feel like a failure.' Actually, your partner can't *make* you angry, because you have the ability to control your emotions. As soon as you rely totally on your partner to make you happy, you run into trouble. Because your partner has no hope of fulfilling that expectation; no one person can ever meet all your needs.

If someone is self-reflecting and self-regulating, what are the next steps?

I reteach communication (because at that point it's probably got a bit mean) and negotiation, which allows a couple to see that in most situations, apart from ultimate deal-breakers (for example whether or not you want kids), you can both get what you want in a relationship. Then it's also the ability to take responsibility for your own feelings. To keep yourself together. To be mature and balanced. To not just think, right, you're going to have to put up with every single flicker of emotion I have.

I'm not saying we should be able to do this a hundred per cent of the time; we're not robots. It's about getting into the habit of thinking, I can feel myself getting angry. It's fine to have this feeling, and it's important, because it's telling me something. But what should I do with the feeling: do I snap at my partner? Do I walk away and slam the door? Do I lash out verbally? And crucially, do I lose the sense of 'we' rather than 'I'? Or, instead, can that person think about how both parties are viewing the situation, and say, 'Look, I'm feeling angry at the moment. I need to find a way to calm down and then I can listen to you, I can reflect on myself, I can start taking responsibility and we can have a conversation which includes both of us'?

Why do you think some people lean so far into togetherness that they become enmeshed, and then find it difficult to allow space within the relationship?

If we're very lucky, as a child we're safe and supported. We need to be compliant with what's happening around us, but we're looked after, we're cared for, we get attention. And often when we find a partner, we're searching for the force of love we got as children: total security and validity. In the end no other human being can give us that particular love we had from our parents. But some people try to, so they get closer and closer. They ask for more and they give more, and then it becomes dependence.

Thinking about the parent–child relationship, there is a time when we are wholly dependent on our parents, and then as teenagers or adults we have to detach and see them as separate individuals. Does that mirror what we need to do in a romantic relationship?

That's a good parallel: all human beings need to individually be able to survive alone, emotionally. Often when we begin to individuate from our parents successfully and live alone, we start to see the gaps: we no longer get validation from our parents; we realize nobody's going to look after us completely. And some people transfer those needs solely on to a partner. I've dealt with couples where both partners rely on each other completely, for everything, and they therefore become vulnerable or the relationship becomes toxic. Falling in love is wonderful, but you need to pull back from that initial stage of enmeshment to get to a point where you allow your partner to be a separate human being, so that you don't twist yourself out of shape to meet their needs. But equally, I think it's a toxic sign when people become too independent – if you look at couples in that situation, there are usually big problems underneath: a fear or a lack of trust, an avoidance of intimacy. They're not revealing themselves, they're not confiding in each other.

Do you think we argue less in the beginning of a relationship, because we don't feel secure enough to say what we really mean yet?

It is that, but at the beginning it's also about focus. Your attention is on all the ways your new partner understands you. That powerful feeling can distract you, or encourage you to overlook issues you disagree about. You both collude in doing that. If you're on the fourth or fifth date, and one of you goes back to the other's flat and it's a tip, it might not feel like a big deal in that moment. Perhaps you're too busy thinking about when – or if – you will move into the bedroom. But over time, as you become not only more secure but also less focused on the things that brought you together, you start to think, well, would this mess be a real problem if we lived together? While the big things – like your political values – are likely to come up early, these small niggles only become important later on. They can start to dominate, and if you're trying to regain interdependence rather than dependence, you will often begin to stress the differences as a way of saying, 'Look, I'm an individual. I am not you. Don't ask me to agree with you on everything. I need some personal space or identity.'

But in a positive way, should we see the fact that we are able to voice our frustrations as a sign that we are being our whole selves in a relationship?

The healthiest couples are those who can argue without feeling threatened, come back together quickly after an argument and see the conversation in context. Arguing itself is not the problem, it's the attitude to arguing that can be the real issue. In a healthy fight about who is tidy and who isn't, one person might say, 'You know what? You're allowed to be untidy. I'm allowed to be tidy. How are we going to find a practical solution? I don't mind you being untidy, but please don't be unhygienic.' And the person who leaves their coffee mugs all over the place says, 'OK, I accept that in my office I can do that, but I promise not to leave mugs around so long that they grow mould on top.' The distinction is that both people are working together and making compromises – there's a devotion to 'we' instead of just 'me'. But if what you are really saying in an argument is 'Do it my way' and 'No, do it my way', then it can damage a relationship in the long term.

On the one hand you're saying that it's important to retain a sense of 'I' and not 'we', but in arguments you have to go back to the 'we' to understand it's no longer only your needs that are a factor.

That's an important point because there is a contradiction. Every relationship – not just intimate ones – is an unconscious negotiation around that balance between 'I' and 'we'. Sometimes both or one of you needs to say 'I'. But if you're only ever saying 'I', then you don't have a relationship. On the other hand, if you're only ever saying 'we', you're enmeshed or you're codependent. All the time you're balancing this out, and when something big in your life changes – if you have children, for example – you have to renegotiate that again. It's about being close, but not so close that you treat each other badly. It's the ability to take responsibility for your own feelings, to step back and treat your partner with respect and kindness. If you can do that, and your partner can reciprocate, then you can get back on track.

What do you wish you'd known about love?

That it is infinitely harder and infinitely more glorious than I'd ever imagined.

*

Susan pointed out a useful contradiction in love: if you lose a sense of yourself as an individual it can damage a relationship, but if you can't accept that your needs and wants are not the only story, then it will be difficult to understand your partner's perspective. That's why it's useful to think as both 'I' and 'we', to live together and apart, to trust the distance between you as individuals and learn to share your life with another person too.

All of this, I think, comes back to a word I never used to associate with love: responsibility. Maybe I'd never considered it before because I'd been too focused on being loved, rather than loving someone, and what that might require. Responsibility is at the root of many of the valuable lessons Susan shared: be as kind to your partner as you would to a stranger. Don't rely on them to meet all your needs (or to make you happy). See arguments in context. Don't expect them to put up with every flicker of emotion that you feel. Sift through your own feelings first.

My earlier attempts at love had been a falling – a rushing, crazy, forceful feeling that took control of me, overshadowed everything else. I was not answerable to it, or accountable to it; I was lost in its drama. So at first I did not understand what the psychoanalyst Erich Fromm meant when he said that love is 'a "standing in", not a "falling for"'. But this, I think, is the process Susan describes: standing in love. Developing the emotional maturity it takes to remain steady, to hold your balance, to have control over your position. To give the person you love the gift of spaciousness. To not lean wholly on them, but to stand beside them.

*

When I was a teenager, I believed that if you loved someone intensely enough then that love would keep you together, no matter what life threw at you. It was a romantic view, but not a realistic one, and when I interviewed *New York Times* Modern Love editor Daniel Jones he summed up why: 'Many relationships and long-term marriages fall apart because one person says, "I don't feel in love with you any more." The idea that that is the reason to end a relationship? There's got to be more than that, because feelings alone are not enough to sustain a relationship.' The truth is, there are going to be times when you don't feel 'in love' with your partner, or when you wonder if someone else might make you happier. It's useful to know and accept that, instead of thinking it means there is something wrong.

So when, I wondered, did we begin to load so many expectations on to love – that it could conquer all, for example, or that one person could complete us? Why do we expect love to make us happy all the time, and is it realistic to expect lifelong monogamy? Because if we are going to think honestly about love, that means confronting the uncomfortable facets of it too: infidelity, doubt, and the ways that we can hurt each other. To explore these questions, I talked to one of the most prominent and respected thinkers on modern relationships: author, podcast host, speaker and couples therapist Esther Perel.

When it comes to changing the conversation around intimacy, Esther is incomparable. For over three decades she has explored its nuances through her international best-sellers (*Mating in Captivity* and *The State of Affairs: Rethinking Infidelity*), her anonymous couples therapy sessions podcast (*Where Should We Begin?*), her TED talks (watched by millions) and her therapy practice in New York. As I discovered on our Skype call, Esther is tough but compassionate. A pragmatic romantic who skewers clichés and confronts the messiness that comes with two humans trying to connect, she reminds us, always, of the redeeming power of love – as long as we approach it with truth.

The expectations we place on love, with Esther Perel

NL: Do you think that part of our reliance on love and intimacy today is about feeling that we are special? Because I think we like to feel that we are the only person who could make our partner happy, so if someone cheats or leaves, that damages our ego.

EP: We have this romantic ideal that we will find 'The One', a soulmate, a one and only. And in this romantic union, we believe that we are also 'The One' for our partner. We believe we are unique, irreplaceable and indispensable. When this grand ambition of love is shattered by something like infidelity, I think it's fair to expect the ego to be bruised.

On top of this, we are isolated. In the US, in the last twenty years, studies suggest we have lost between 30 and 60 per cent of our social connections. That means people who we share significant pieces of our lives with – neighbours, friends, siblings – and all this loss of social categories has been siphoned into the marital relationship. We now look for our romantic partner to give us what a whole village used to provide. We saddle them with all those expectations. So, you bet, if and when that person betrays us, we feel like we have lost everything we had.

If we were living in a more communal structure, with more than one person around us who is important to us, who we matter to and who matters to us, we would be no less hurt by betrayal, but we wouldn't feel like we had lost our entire identity. That's the difference. I don't think that infidelity ever does not hurt. It hurts badly. But saying, 'My whole life is a lie, my whole life is a fraud, I no longer know who I am' – that's a different scale.

Do you think, then, if before we got to the point of the affair we didn't put our reliance on one person in the same way, we could have a better chance of avoiding one?

No, I don't think that. These things may correlate but that does not mean there is a cause and an effect. I think by design, yes, we are putting tremendous expectations on our intimate relationships these days. But the better marriages are better than ever before, it's just fewer are as good. When a marriage is good today it's more egalitarian, more satisfactory, more rounded, holistic – there's no comparison. The good marriages of today are better than any marriages of the past. But there are not that many who get there.

You said earlier that today we often believe we deserve to be happy all the time. Do you think the pursuit of happiness has put the pressure on committed relationships?

Happiness is not a pursuit these days, it's a mandate. You have to be happy. And you are entitled, in the name of your happiness, to do all kinds of things. So people are constantly asking, 'Is my marriage good enough? Could it be better? Maybe I don't have to deal with this, I'll find myself someone else.' The consumer mentality of 'I can do better' . . . You know 'good enough' is not in vogue any more, it's all about the best. So you don't just leave because you're really unhappy, you leave because you believe you could be happier.

How do you tell the difference between a couple who should work on their relationship and the couples for whom sadly it's too late?

Thirty-four years of couples therapy. There is a certain intuition you do develop after decades of working. That doesn't mean I know, and that doesn't mean I'm right. But if I have any sense that one person still has a foot in, still has a deep attachment, still cares deeply and will help the other person fight for their marriage, then I will help them do all kinds of things to fight for it. But I don't know that it is wise to help them to engage in fighting when I know that the other person ultimately will not come back. It's almost cruel.

What kind of things would you help somebody do when they're trying to fight for their marriage?

For example, this man yesterday, he hurt his partner badly and he had to sit there and feel the force of a passionate woman who feels scorned. That is the woman he was missing all those years – she's now, in a way, fighting for him. And it's rage, but it's passionate rage. Then he says, 'I'm going to repair it, I'm going to fight for us, I'm going to help us get back together.' And in the beginning, that means an ability to really acknowledge how hurtful he has been, and not being so ashamed that he can't be responsible. Because the first inclination is to say, 'Let's move over this, we've decided to stay together, let's not talk about this any more, it's past, it's behind us.' Well it's absolutely not, she's just beginning the nightmare – his has ended, hers has just started. I will work on how he can show up for her and make her feel really special, because her value has diminished. So what are the things he can do to give back her sense of value?

With another guy, I made him write a love letter in which he came clean on a lot of things. More than she even knew or asked for. And I said, 'I want you to get on a plane and go across the country to hand-deliver the letter to her. Because she doesn't expect to see you until next week. So show up. Show up! Show her she matters. Show her your relationship matters. And demonstrate it.' There are no set answers for these kinds of things, but the intent has to be clear. And that means demonstrating someone's importance to you.

What do you think the couples who are able to move past an affair have in common?

There are many things that make them succeed. But, in the reverse, I can tell you one ingredient that you know will prevent the success: when the person who betrayed and lied and deceived has very little empathy. That is a real giveaway of something that can't heal. And the same thing is true on the other end: if the person who was betrayed has no ability to engage with the curiosity to understand what the affair was about. When the only way they can think about the affair was how it hurt them, it's a challenging dynamic. The curiosity of the betrayed is secondary, but it's equally important. Basically, to succeed you need each person to bring a degree of empathy and interest and deep desire to understand about the experience of the other.

What do you think couples can do to sustain that deep understanding of each other?

I do think couples should have a little annual summit. Their review. I'm big on rituals. If you tell me, 'I care about my partner,' then my second question is, 'How do you show it?' The fact that you feel it isn't enough. What do you do to let the other person know and yourself that that's the case? If you let it go, that is the neglect. For some people it's a weekend away every six weeks, for some it's beautiful letters every once in a while, for others it's showing up at a most unexpected moment and surprising the other, or doing the thing they hate doing because the other one cares about it. It's all these things that really say to the other person: you matter to me. And I'll go out of my way to show you, to tell you.

After thirty-four years of couple counselling, do you think marriage still has value as an institution?

Yes, but it's not the only model. When it comes to marriage we have a rather monolithic model and there can't be a one-size-fits-all. We have reinvented family many times. We have nuclear families, extended families, blended families, single-parent families, accordion families, gay families . . . we have really allowed for a rich variation of family models, but we have not done the same when it comes to coupling.

I think people want a couple – nothing has changed about that – but they need more of a variation as to different forms of couplings, relationships and relational contracts. We have opportunities today that never existed before. When in history did a person at fifty-five have the opportunity to marry for the first time and have a whole new family and have children? Our longevity and our flexibility have offered us new options and I think that we're going to see more new relationship models.

Europe is filled with people who have long-term contracts without marriage [from civil solidarity pacts in France (PACS) to civil partnerships in the UK]. People have commitment ceremonies, but they don't go through the traditional, legal piece of marriage. In the US, where there is very little social welfare, marriage is also a sort of welfare state too. People really want you to marry here because then the state won't have to help you with anything. It's not about monogamy.

And also people are marrying later, which changes things?

People are marrying later, marriage has changed and, like every other institution, it will survive if it can be adaptable and flexible. Every system in nature, every living organism in evolutionary history, either adapts or it dies. So marriage has adapted throughout history: the marriage of farmers on the land is not the same as the marriage of the industrial age, which is not the same as the marriage of entrepreneurs, which is not the same as the marriage of the 40 per cent of American couples where women outearn men. That is a whole new picture. That is a change in marriage because that is a change in the power structure, and marriage is a power structure like any other organization.

You often talk about the fact that we don't address infidelity until it happens. So do you feel at an early stage in our relationships we need to sit down and be honest about what it means to us? Whether it includes sexting, an emotional affair or sending flirtatious emails, for example?

Yes. So you asked me before, 'Do people have to share everything? Do they have to share their fantasies and all of that?' And you also asked, 'Is marriage obsolete?' I think that a lot of people do not have some of the conversations that are very important to have. That doesn't mean they become contracts, but they are conversations. The openness of your relationship depends on the openness of your conversations. If you don't talk about any of these things ever, you basically invite the concealment because you start to say, 'I can't talk about that, this will upset him or her, this would create problems, this would lead to tension.' And you make an assumption that that is not part of your communicative space.

An adult relationship is one in which people negotiate disclosure, intimacy, openness, what is together, what is apart. Some couples live in completely overlapping circles where everything is shared and there is very little individual space. That's their model. Other couples live in a much more differentiated style and they have a small overlap. They share some very important things, but they have an entire world of their own. Both models can be equally fertile but it is totally clear that, in the aftermath of an affair, one of the most common sentences you're going to hear – not with everybody – is 'we are having conversations that we haven't had in decades'. And you wonder: what have you been talking about all these years? Somehow, in an affair, the dam is broken. There is nothing to lose, and people actually open up, and you know for the first time they have conversations about the quality of their sexual relationship, about all kinds of things they haven't wanted to discuss because they wanted to avoid conflict.

You've been with your husband for over three decades. How have your studies changed the way you approach your own relationship?

I think we talk. Obviously there's no taboo subject for us about this, and the myriad things that happen in long-term relationships. We are well aware that, around us, half of other couples are no longer together, and after thirty-five years it's almost like a relic! When you say you've been together for thirty-five years people almost want to clap. But longevity is not the only marker of success. You know, I think we have invested in our relationship and we apply our understanding to it. We understand that you need renewal, you need new experiences, you need adventure. You need to do new things that are outside of the comfort zone. *You* don't need to, but for us that is an important piece – a relationship that grows and stays fresh. Part of what brings that is the creation of new experiences. We apply what we see and learn from working with people, from research and data. We say, 'We should do this, this is important.' And occasionally we say, 'Do we really have to?' And then we say, 'Yes, we actually do,' in the same way as, 'Do we have to go to the gym?' We can afford not to go for a week or two, but afterwards we're going to feel it.

And have we ever regretted it when we've gone, or when we did something that was good for us, that showed that we were putting effort into us? No, never.

What do you wish you'd known about love?

What would I say to my younger self? Keep your feet well planted. You know it's not just about who you find, it's also who you're going to be. Love is not a state of enthusiasm. It's a verb. It implies action, demonstration, ritual, practices, communication, expression. It's the ability to take responsibility of one's own behaviour. Responsibility is freedom.

Sometimes it's amazing, this thing called love. One day you just think, I've had it, I'm out of here, I'm so done with you, I can't take another minute of this. The next morning you wake up and you squeeze the person and say, 'I'm glad I'm waking up with you.' It's this bizarre thing, it just comes and goes, and it's really complicated. So invest in it. Learn about relationships, don't just read about everything else. Because you learn how to be in a relationship – it's not a given.

The Seasons of Friendship

'The friend who holds your hand and
says the wrong thing is made of dearer stuff
than the one who stays away.'
(*Barbara Kingsolver,* High
Tide in Tucson)

One month after Dan and I got back from Puglia, I received two WhatsApp messages from friends. The first, a picture of a schoolfriend with the baby she'd just given birth to. The second, a photo of a university friend's twelve-week baby scan. Both made me wince, the latter particularly. It looked so similar to the picture I had of our own blurry black and white baby scan, which promised a world and never delivered. When I first opened it, I thought I was about to vomit. This sounds dramatic, I know. It seemed silly and unexpected to me at the time too. Because I was truly happy for my friends, and I knew there was no scarcity of babies. Other people conceiving did not affect whether I would, or could. Yet each time I opened a picture of a baby or a pregnancy announcement on my phone, it sucked composure out of me. Not only because friends were conceiving easily when it had already been a year since our first pregnancy, or holding babies who were the age ours would have been. But because I felt guilty that I could not summon up the pure joy for their news that I longed to. In response to the second message I replied, 'Amazing news!xx' which looked forced and strained on the screen. To the first, for a few days, I didn't even reply. And so, my sadness robbed our friendships of authenticity in these moments, which we would never get to do again.

These feelings made me ask uncomfortable questions: could I still find a way to be around pregnant friends or those with babies? And if I could never have children, and my friends' lives revolved around theirs, would I need to branch out and make new friends too? When I was struggling to answer them, I wrote to Philippa Perry for advice. First she conceded that babies do change friendships, just as not having a baby when you want one changes them too. 'Sad as it is,' she replied, 'it's inevitable that some people fall away at these times. Sometimes you will reconnect later, sometimes the drifting apart remains. But because you love your friends and want to remain close to them, I think you will find a way through all this with the messiness of misunderstandings and make-ups. You will keep communicating, and it might be painful at times, but if friends know where you are at, and you know they know, you will be able to enjoy their children more.' She also reminded me that, although when we are younger we often confide every-thing to one person, as we get older one friend cannot hold all we need to share. So in order to feel understood, we have to tell different things to different friends. She put it this way: 'People with shared history are very precious indeed, and yet new friends become old friends in time too.' I noted down two lessons: 1) New friends soon develop their own history; and 2) even when life experiences divide old friends, there is a way to keep connecting, just as long as you're willing to try.

I am reminded of the second lesson when I visit my

university friend Jen. When we were eighteen and lived two doors apart in halls, our lives were intertwined. I remember the brand of her eyeliner (Benefit Bad Gal), the sound of her GHD straighteners flattening her hair, her Pilot boob tubes, her warmth. When we got our first jobs in London, two streets away from each other, I remember her shirts and cufflinks, her BlackBerry, the exact sound of her heels clipping the pavement. Whether we were commuting together, spending lunch breaks in Patisserie Valerie, emailing all day or sitting around the kitchen table after work, our daily conversations were the space in which I learnt to fully be myself around another person. Once, Jen pointed out how much I needed to be in control, which I only remembered last year, sitting in a group therapy session, where I realized that, even then, she had seen pieces of me that I only understood a decade later. If you had told me then that we would only see each other a handful of times a year, I would probably have assumed the friendship had failed. It wasn't until my late twenties I understood that sometimes old friendships evolve like plants whose roots outgrow their pots: they are still alive, still growing, but they need more space to survive. More room to allow new people and experiences in too.

The same year I receive those pregnancy announcements over WhatsApp, Jen and I spend a precious afternoon at her house together, with her baby. Soon her two sons return from school. It is then I feel the bittersweet depths of long-term friendship. First, I watch her in action, a wonderful mother to these three children, and wonder whether I will ever be a mother myself. Then I look into her children's faces and realize that I do not know them. It is an odd feeling, to realize these three people at the centre of her life are strangers to me, as I am to them; a reminder of the gaps in our know-ledge of each other that exist today. All the times, perhaps, that I forgot to send a card, or a gift. But what's strange and unexpected is the surge of love I feel for her children in this moment. I do not know them, but I know I want them to be happy, to feel loved, to be safe in the world, because they come from a woman I share a history with. I understand then that old friends do not always need to be the centre of each other's worlds to continue to love each other.

To sustain friendships – old and new – I think we have to learn when to accept distance, and when to fight to repair it. By this point I have watched friends lose parents, divorce, give birth, deal with family trauma, begin and end relation-ships, wrestle through periods of depression . . . and we are only in the middle stretch of our lives. That none of our lives are static means the friendships which are part of my everyday life today might be the ones that drift further away tomorrow, just as the ones that currently work from a distance might become closer again if life unexpectedly throws us together. Although we might think we choose our friends at school, at college, at work, or wherever we meet them, one day we will leave behind the places which we shared. The clothes we swapped will no longer fit. The conversations we bonded over about which men we fancied at university will be replaced by ones about dwindling sex drives, and how to care for a sick parent. So if we give up on a friendship *every* time our lives are out of sync? At the end of our lives, we might find we don't have many left.

Inevitably, there are some friendships that do slip away completely. In others, there might be months or years when we have to give each other space to disappear; and maybe that is a form of love too. Understanding this helps me to cut myself some slack in the weeks when I am unable to attend a first birthday party or visit a friend's new baby without slipping into sadness. I even allow myself to bow out, when I really need to, knowing those who love me will understand that my absence doesn't mean I don't love them back.

Now I think of friendship as a thread that tethers us to another person. There are years when, if we pull on it too much, tug for more of the thread than the other person is able to give at that point in their life, then it will become tight and strained and tense. It might even snap. But if we can loosen our grip a little, let it slacken in the middle, it will give both friends space to move closer and further apart. We won't necessarily feel its presence every day, but it'll still be there when we need to find a way back to each other.

No meaningful relationship can be consistently easy. Even the closest friends will neglect or misinterpret each other, say the wrong thing, feel rejected by change when different life stages pull them apart. The question, then, is not how to avoid these painful missteps, but how to keep trying to tell the truth to each other, regardless. After all, as Susie Orbach tells me in the interview ahead, 'Part of growing up is learning about disappointment and giving up grandiosity and not seeing yourself as the centre of the world. Because you're the centre of *your* world, but you're not the centre of *the* world.' This is something I had forgotten while trying to conceive. It wasn't until I picked up the phone at the end of the year that I realized I had been missing my friends' struggles: the loneliness of motherhood, or a disintegrating relationship. I had been so lost in my own reality that I had not pulled back from it for long enough to see anyone else's.

It's true, of course, that we need friends who we live life closely alongside. But I think there is a case to be made for keeping the more distant friendships ticking along too, even when they remind us of the everyday intimacies that have been lost. Because life takes people from us all the time. The husband or wife we share everything with might leave the world before we do. The friends we see every week could relocate to new cities, maybe even new countries. Colleagues move on to new jobs. Kids leave home. Parents die too young. When any – or all – of these things happen, we might be grateful that we tolerated the mundanity of a WhatsApp group and diary dates; all the little gestures that sustained our friendships when we needed them less, so they survive to hold us when we need them more. That shouldn't be the only motivation to make an effort – after all, it's a selfish one – but it's useful to remember, every now and again, when we're sleep-deprived or overworked and the easier option is to let friendships fade. Because one day, when we're walking in a park with a friend who can access an older version of us, and we find something silly to laugh about together in the April sunlight, it might save us, or them, in some small way.

Today, as much as I treasure newer friendships which are – in this season of my life – present and active, I also see the distance in older ones as a reminder of their strength. Because when you feel the force of closeness between you, *despite* the distance? When you – or they – make a little gesture that reminds you that you still understand each other from afar? It is like a beam of light from you to them. I notice this after crying over my period in the shower one morning, when I open my drawer and put on some socks Marisa bought me with the words 'go go go' stitched on, and I feel she is spurring me on into the day. And when Jen writes to me out of the blue to say, 'I just wanted to let you know that I *know* you are going to be a mum. Have faith in my faith.' And again, when I send her an early cover of this book and she texts back, 'This colour reminds me of an old lipstick of yours.' A tiny echo of a shared history, of being known.

For all of us, there will be times when distance drifts into a friendship and it might seem easier to withdraw. Perhaps because, if we decide to give up entirely, we have more control. It's much harder to hold our nerve, to trust in the love between us, to accept the gaps in our knowledge of each other creeping in and then continue to make the effort anyway. But when we do, the greatest gift: to find that it's still there, love, shining between us, despite everything.

*

In the first section of this book, with Candice Carty-Williams we explored the romance of female friendship. But in order to treat this form of love with as much reverence as it deserves, I knew that, just as with romantic love, I needed to address the messier parts of friendship too. Which brings us to envy.

I didn't know how to show my uncomfortable feelings to my friends, or even if I should. But I knew that Susie Orbach would have the answers. A psychotherapist who has spent more than forty years digging into clients' inner worlds – including, famously, Princess Diana's – Susie has been described by the *New York Times* as 'probably the most famous psychotherapist to have set up couch in Britain since Sigmund Freud'. In her work as a psychoanalyst and in her books (from *Bodies* to *Fat*

Is a Feminist Issue to *In Therapy*), Susie cuts to the heart of our fears and desires, our insecurities, hopes and the truths that we might already be processing but not yet know ourselves. It was her work on envy, specifically in *Between Women: Love, Envy and Competition in Women's Friendships* (which she co-wrote with her friend Luise Eichenbaum), that convinced me to call her up for an honest discussion about the complications of friendship love. Our conversation does not sentimentalize it. Instead, it explores the duality of friendships: their bitterness and their sweetness.

Understanding envy in friendship, with Susie Orbach

NL: In friendships, as we go through different life phases, we can feel rejected or abandoned as those relationships change. How can we nurture our friendships through those conflicts?

SO: There are many differences that can be tricky to handle in friendships: if one of you has a lot of 'success' at work and another doesn't, for example. Or the children issue, which can be a great divide. Sometimes you go through the pain of a big change and the friendship turns around; other times it won't, and that'll be a hurtful loss. You can be close to somebody and then their new friend or relationship or job can make you feel excluded, which means you withdraw. You might phone or text your friend less, and before long you're no longer inside their life. In those cases, you've got to work out if they're a person you want in your life, and if they are, you have to reach out to them to kick-start the relationship again.

These challenges will always appear, because change can feel threatening when we know someone very well, just as it can be in a romantic relationship. But if a friendship is strong, you allow each other space to develop in novel and unexpected ways, rather than clinging to the old versions of who you once were. Sometimes that will require you to say to a friend, 'Actually, I don't feel that way about X any more,' rather than letting them make assumptions about your character today based on your shared past. Love, whether in friendship or romantic relationships, goes wrong when we forget to tell people who we are and forget to ask who they are. Both friends have a responsibility to continue to learn and accept who the other is in the present.

We can envy a friend even when we are happy for them. How can we accept and move through those feelings?

The envy is just a starting point – what we are really feeling is more complex. There is the specific envy for somebody having what you want (I'd love to be successful or have a baby or a great holiday, for example) but, on a more profound level, I believe what envy lets us know is that women often feel embarrassed or ashamed about their own emotional needs and desires. That's been schooled into us for hundreds of years. For that reason, envy becomes part of how women understand themselves: they can project on to others the things that they want, because actually activating their own longings feels impermissible. For example, even though young women are now taught to be ambitious, that doesn't mean the internal psychological architecture to go after what they want is there. There is still a complex set of internal taboos that induce shame around wanting. So the envy you project on to others is a sign of what you want but can't get for yourself.

It is a signpost to your longing, rather than literal envy for the other. It's showing you what you want.

That's interesting, because envy is an uncomfortable emotion. Why do we find it easier to feel envy rather than face up to what we want for ourselves?

Our desires have become so hidden and forbidden that we're not even aware of them on a conscious level. You could argue that, because people want to be rich or famous, those wants are visible. But materialistic desires often don't relate to ordinary needs for connection and understanding, or the need to be seen, recognized, cherished and heard. In a way, the desire for fame or success is a cover, which then obfuscates the fact that people don't really know how to accept or admit more fundamental desires. On the surface you might crave status, or the right type of car, when really what you are afraid to want is to be valued for being you. And so we measure ourselves in relation to our friends or colleagues instead.

Why is it unhelpful to keep our envy private?

Because it festers. It doesn't allow you to understand that behind the envy is something that could be productive. Say we're friends, and I envy your capacity to do something. If I could ask myself, 'What is it that she has that I'm not able to enact for myself?' then instead of feeling stranded and envious, maybe I could tell you I'm feeling inadequate in X, Y and Z departments, and I could get help. That's difficult to do. It's also useful, because there are always going to be times when you're out of sync with friends, and that's going to hurt if you have been in sync for great periods of your life. Once those words are out, the thing that is gorgeous about friends is that – more often than not – they do want to help. People want to give. They don't want to deprive.

If you're on the other side, and you are the one who is envied, how can you receive that emotion from your friend? Because that can be uncomfortable too.

If people say something to me, I reply, 'Yes, I was really lucky.' Because it's true, a lot of life is chance – what family or social class or area you're born into – and it's helpful to acknowledge that.

When I was trying to conceive after miscarrying, it was difficult to be around friends who were pregnant or who didn't seem to understand, even though I didn't expect them to. Do you think it's sometimes necessary to pull back from friendships when we feel this way?

For some people being around friends who have what they want can give them hope, and for others it is too painful. I understand, because when I had a miscarriage I was devastated that people didn't know how to be there for me. I'm not talking about my very close friends, who were of course wonderful, but people I considered good friends who didn't ring me. Who didn't know what to do. It's a form of incompetence, of not knowing how to say, 'I'm so very sorry.' For me, avoiding people didn't help, but I understand why it would for others. And that's perfectly legitimate, as long as you are aware of what you're doing and why.

Are there some times when we have to allow distance into our friendships? Or do we just have to work harder in those moments to bridge them?

In some cases, you will be distant for a period. If your friend is a new mother, unless her experience is unusual, she will be preoccupied with her baby – how many hours they sleep, how much weight they've put on, how they feed – and that can make a friend without children feel she is being abandoned. The reverse can happen too: after one woman I know had a baby at thirty-seven, her friend said, 'I don't want to see you with your baby, and I don't want to know about your baby.'

It's true that when you're in one of those life shifts you don't notice what happens to others as much. But you get better at that as you get older, I think. You learn to understand that one friend's problem doesn't take precedence; they can both coexist as difficult situations. It can be harder to see that when you're young, because you're experiencing certain changes for the first time and facing the enormous hurdles of creating your identity in the world. Of course, you might also make new friends who are in a similar situation to you. For example, when you become a parent you still love your old friends, but because it's bloody tedious, sometimes you want to be with people who also have a baby so you can do the mundane parts together. That doesn't mean you're going to be friends for ever; I'm not lifelong friends with the mums I met at the school gates. And yet they were very important and lovely in those circumstances.

Then there are also people you go off as you change and grow, perhaps because your interests, politics or emotions don't converge enough when you're not stoned or struggling together. I don't think that we should be ashamed about that either.

To allow space for those phases, should we be working on introducing separateness and self-reliance into our friendships, as well as dependence, just as we would in a romantic relationship? And to understand that our friends can't fulfil all our needs?

Exactly. I think separated attachments are what we should be aiming for in friendships: when two friends are separate but connected, so they can each feel whole in themselves. It's about resisting the dated world of competition, and learning to admit to our own individual feelings, however ugly. It's about acknowledging that our experiences in the world are different from each other's, rather than only seeking to find similarities. A lot of the negative feelings we have been discussing appear in friendships because women desire space in the world to self-develop, to want what they want, to find their autonomy. And they can actually work towards those things while loving and supporting each other, rather than competing for them. They can support each other's choices (to become a mother or not; to prioritize work or not) and empathize with the differences in their situations (if they are single or in a couple, for example). When friends do that, they can see each other for who they are and feel secure in their relationship at the same time.

If that's what we should be aiming for, how can we work on being both separate from and connected to our friends?

Our culture makes it difficult, because everybody's supposed to be oh so happy all the bloody time, and that isn't
who we are – we have multiple feelings. To me it's about
giving up the fantasy that everything is OK or great all the
time, so that we can find a more authentic, complex way of
talking about how we feel. We have to stop pretending that
our lives are perfect. Then it would be easier for us to say,
'I'm happy for you, but I found this really difficult because
I'm having a tough time.' At the moment, I think the ersatz
nature of how we're supposed to conduct ourselves means
that, when it comes to intimate friends, it's hard for there
to be space to share the whole variety of emotions. And you
have to do that in order to be both separate and attached.
It's important to understand that friendships contain hope,
grief, love, disappointment, conflict, pleasure and so much
more.

*Do you think that our lives being more visible on social media has
aggravated the problem of competition in friendship?*

It must do, because the anonymizing makes it less real. A
physical encounter with somebody can smash through projec-
tions, because you realize that a person is actually generous,
or thoughtful. Or you discover they have their own fears and
vulnerabilities. Whereas you can't really tell that from an
Instagram post, because it's a construction.

What do you wish you'd known about love?

There are so many different types of love. There's love for
friendship, love for children, love across the generations,

romantic love, love of work, love of cooking. I wish I'd known how big that word is, how capacious it is, how many different expressions it can have, and how many ordinary graces people can give to each other.

*

A shared past, Susie taught me, can be both a beautiful and frustrating thing. It means old friends have a nostalgic language to fall back on, memories that allow them to access different versions of each other, which someone new might not be able to. But it also means that, as we change, our friends won't necessarily understand that we are not who we were last month, last year, or a decade ago. And we can't expect them to. It is up to us to tell our friends who we are, and to be curious about who they are today too.

At times, that ongoing conversation might include sharing painful things. Saying, 'I'm proud you are achieving so much in your career, but sometimes that reminds me I'm struggling with mine.' Or, 'It's amazing to see you content in your relationship, but often I feel there's no room in your life for me any more.' Or, in my case, 'I love seeing pictures of your baby, but they also remind me how sad I am about not being pregnant.' Because Susie made me realize that my envy was not only rooted in wanting what others had. Really it grew from a fear of being left behind, and of loneliness.

This honesty in friendship might also involve recognizing when we have been incredibly lucky, and reaching out to the friend who is in a tougher season of their lives. This won't just happen. We have to *make* it happen, with patience, effort and without ego. If we can, perhaps we will see the miracle of friendship: its ability to remind us that we are not alone, even when our lives seem to separate us.

*

When I entered my thirties, I started noticing the gaps in my knowledge of my friends, as I had at Jen's house. Fifteen years ago I knew the contents of their bedside drawers, which deodorant they used, which CDs in their car were too scratched to play without skipping. Now they had children I did not know, whose ages I sometimes lost track of. Songs on their iPhone I didn't recognize and partners I was only familiar with in a polite, surface-level way. These pieces of knowledge slipped away from friendships so gradually and subtly I barely noticed, until they were no longer there.

As I had learnt from Susie, though, separateness is part of growing up. So I wanted to know, what does retaining intimacy look like when you're no longer living in the same flat, in the same city, with the same priorities? And why can being honest with our friends, who often know us most intimately, feel like such a vulnerable act? To find the answers, I spoke to author, journalist and podcast host Dolly Alderton.

In her *Sunday Times* bestselling memoir *Everything I Know About Love*, Dolly turned her female friendships into a love story that thousands of us recognized ourselves in. It captured what so few books have: the intense intimacy that exists between two friends who commit to loving each other. She is also someone who explores the depths of friendship, not only in her work, but in her life – whether she is writing a newspaper column or sitting across from you in a restaurant. Who better to call for an honest discussion on the challenges and rewards of retaining and sustaining love in our friendships?

The beauty of vulnerability in friendship, with Dolly Alderton

NL: After I read your memoir part of me felt sad, because I recognized that magical time in my twenties when friendships were romantic and intense, but I was no longer in that period of my life. In my thirties, friendships have changed — some friends have kids, others have sick parents, others have moved away. I wondered if you too have noticed a shift in your friendships between the time you wrote the book and now?

DA: Definitely. I was twenty-eight when I wrote that book, and at events afterwards often women in their thirties, forties, fifties or sixties would put up their hands and say, 'We believe that you believe what you're saying about this vow of utmost devotion you've made to the women in your life. But when you're twenty-eight and none of you have children and you all live three buses maximum away from each other, it's an easy promise to make.' Very quickly, when you leave your twenties, there are constant obstacles thrown in the way of your friendships, which make maintaining that bond and vulnerability with each other more challenging. Phoebe Waller-Bridge spoke about how you spend your twenties figuring out who you are, and so by the time you've carved out an identity you share less with each other, because the stakes are higher. I think that's true, you do spend your twenties trying to work out what your job is, what your politics are, what part of the world you want to live in; and you do that with a band of brothers or sisters. You create an identity patchwork in a group, as well as on your own. Then when you get to your thirties, you have to declare who you are in a permanent way. It's either, 'I'm someone who is going to live in the suburbs' or 'I want to be a stay-at-home mother' or 'I want to retrain and start a new career.' Your identity hardens. You have to defend this edifice of who you are, because it's too late in the game to change it. Once you declare that, it can feel more dangerous to say, 'I don't know if I should have married that man' or 'I don't know if my job makes me happy.' To admit that in an authentic, vulnerable connection with someone close to you is scary in a way that it's not in your twenties, when everything is in flux. For all those reasons, letting people in and allowing yourself to be unsure or vulnerable becomes harder. It's more of a potential threat.

Is another reason it gets harder, the practical change of not being in each other's lives every day? Because in your twenties you don't have to make the effort to tell friends things – they witness them. Whereas as you grow older it's harder to keep friends updated on the events in your life. For example, I realized recently that, although my university friends and I used to be incredibly close, I don't know their children, and they don't know Dan in the way that I know their husbands, who they met when we were younger. There are huge parts of each other's lives now that we have not witnessed.

Exactly. You go from those years when the details of your lives are so entwined that you know the exact food that makes the other person flatulent, to those periods when you only see each other a handful of times a year. The children thing is interesting because there's a cultural narrative that divides women in their thirties who have kids and women who don't. And my relationships with my closest friends who have children have changed the most dramatically. Even if, culturally, in an academic switched-on way, we don't think that raising a family is the most important thing a woman can do with her life, that idea is still so embedded and entrenched within us. For so long that's what a woman's great achievement was in this period of her life. And because that idea is hard to fight, a lot of women I know who are single or childless – or both – and are navigating a friendship with a woman who has children, have at some point said to me, 'I feel she doesn't think my life is as important as hers.' What's difficult is, because motherhood is so sanctified, and it is such an extraordinary shift physically, psychologically, domestically and professionally in a woman's life, the line we're always given is, 'People without children can't imagine what it's like.' If my friend has had that experience, it's my duty as someone who loves her to try really hard to extend my empathy as much as I can and stretch my imagination, because that's what this woman deserves; she's going through the most insane experience of her life. The problem is, that courtesy is rarely extended to women who don't have children.

I think that's where the imbalance and the frustrations can be, because it feels like we allow metamorphosis for women with children, but we're not as good at understanding the people who don't have kids, and the enormous changes and adjustments and fears that are part of their daily lives. That's the thing that becomes difficult, when giving space for change within female friendships when some people start having kids and some don't: childless or child-free women have to give so much time and respect and sensitivity for the changes that mothers are going through, and often that's not paid back.

There were definitely points, when we were struggling to conceive, that I had to withdraw from certain friendships with parents. But when I did speak to those friends afterwards, I realized that, even if their lives appeared to be everything I wanted on the surface, they in fact had struggles of their own that I had not been there to listen to.

And you can be forgiven for that, because the archetypal story that we're told of heterosexual womanhood is that you get married, you have babies, and then your problems have gone. That is a detrimental myth for so many people. I was talking to a married woman with two children who, from the outside, has everything I want. I think she could tell that, on a low level, I have felt anxiety and panic about whether or not I will meet someone and have a family. She said to me, 'Live and enjoy that beautiful life of yours for what it is right now. Because it's so precious, and you have no idea how much I yearn for a time where I can wake up and write for five hours undisturbed.' As trite as it sounds, I think the key is that, when women start having children, it's sometimes very painful and stressful and claustrophobic and boring and lonely. And what is also a fundamental truth is that it is incredibly painful, stressful, claustrophobic, boring and lonely to not have a family when you want one. Neither experience is more painful or more difficult than the other. Once we free ourselves from asking who we feel most sorry for, or who has made the best choice, and just allow those pains to coexist? I think that is the key to intimacy in your friendships.

I'm starting to think you go through some seasons in your life when your friendships overlap and some when they don't. So perhaps, as well as being more vulnerable with our old friends, we also need to gravitate towards new people when our lives are thrown together?

Definitely, and the main difference between where I am now and when I wrote my memoir is I used to be a girl who was terrified of being abandoned and being lost and alone and not being loved. I think because your twenties are a fraught time, you spend a decade adjusting to the fact that you're parentless. I spent those years creating a surrogate family within my friendships, and that meant that I could go out and have a wild, risky and exciting time, both creatively and romantically, because I always had that unit to return to. And that is not your friends' job.

Now I'm more relaxed about how often friends and I speak or meet up, or how much time they spend with their partner as opposed to with me. I've sunk into the safe, precious solidness of their love for me, and I know that, although it will take work, it is also a love that will be there for ever. True friendship is about taking it easy on each other, knowing that life has tides that take you to various places, and that you'll find a way back to each other at different points.

In a way, just like in romantic love, in friendships you have to accept that the other person is not responsible for you. But allowing distance into those relationships does require you to let go of one version of a friendship. With that loss, I wonder, are there other things we gain?

You do start feeling the longevity of your friendships in an incredibly moving way. It moves me that the girls that I was at university with, who at one point felt like recent friends, are now people who have known me since I was a teenager.

Reflecting on that as an incredible acquisition – even if it has had to change as we've grown older – feels like you're gaining something, rather than losing something. In my thirties I had a break-up and I texted the girls the following day to say, 'We broke up last night and I feel awful.' My friends had obviously split into a sub WhatsApp group to be like, right, who's free tonight? Like an emotional A & E. Three of them told me to go to a cocktail bar. They got there before I arrived and, when I came to the table, they had a cold vodka Martini waiting for me. I said hello and burst into tears. It was so moving that the first time I cried over a boy sixteen years ago, the same people were there to advise and to love me. It was different advice. We were all different people. But the love had remained. That becomes more profound, the older you get.

What do you wish you'd known about love and friendship?

What we learn about friendship when we're young is that, if everything stays the same, then everything's great. That's a difficult mindset to get out of when you reach adulthood, a time when things are going to change so much, all the time. Actually, that change is not only a sign that life is going well, it's an unavoidable fact: everything is constantly in flux.

I wish I could go back to my 25-year-old self and reassure her that the format of a friendship is going to change many times over the course of a lifetime – and that's normal. I resisted change in a way that must have been stressful for my friends. I probably put pressure on them to remain a certain version of themselves, and for our friendship to remain in a certain dynamic, because, for me, something being constant meant that it was successful. Now, so little would faze me about a friendship: someone saying that they're moving to the other side of the world, someone saying they're getting married, someone saying they're getting divorced, someone telling me they're pregnant. I cannot think of anything that would threaten my faith in my close friendships. And that's such a nicer place to be.

*

'All companionship,' Rilke wrote, 'can consist in only the strengthening of two neighbouring solitudes.' I see now that his words apply as much to friendships as they do to romantic relationships. In both, I had learnt, we cannot expect another person to shoulder all of our needs. We can cry on them. We can share our lives and fears and underwear with them. But in order to experience the joy of these relationships, we have to make space for each other's separateness.

In this messy, humbling process, as Dolly pointed out, there are likely to be gains as well as losses. The everyday experiences we shared as teens or twentysomethings might be replaced by something less consistent yet no less powerful: a knowledge of each other so deep that it can withstand distance, and space, and time.

To delight in it, though, when life gets harder – as it often does – we have to find a way to truthfully share our vulnerability, even when that feels like a risk. This is how we continue to reach each other. And, perhaps, it is only once we trust in the sturdiness of our friendships that we can fully appreciate the richness of their layers. The lives that change. The love that remains. How it continues to hold us.

*

As much as I longed to be a mother, I still thought about how parenthood might put new challenges on love. The sleepless nights during which Dan and I might not share a bed, or the hour-long phone calls to friends that might be more difficult to concentrate on with a crying baby in my lap. The things I might have to give up – aimless Sunday walks; spontaneous drinks with friends; regular sex; reading in bed – and how my sense of self might be eroded, or at least altered, in the process. I wanted to ask, if we choose to become parents, how do we make sure there is still room for love in purposeful work, friendship and romance? What pieces of ourselves could – and should – we protect, and which would we need to give up? I decided to put these questions to the novelist Diana Evans.

In her writing, particularly in her beautiful novel *Ordinary People*, Diana explores the impact of domesticity on women's lives and sense of self. From interviewing her once before, I knew that retaining her identity – as a woman, as a friend, as a writer – was something she fought for in her personal life too, even after becoming a parent to two children. This hadn't been easy, but she knew it was important to her, and so she protected it. I wanted to find out how.

Though she is honest about its mundane parts, Diana speaks movingly about the intensity of parental love, and how it differs from loving a partner or friend or parent. She also considers the humanity, not just of children, but of the parents who care for them.

Our conversation was the first time I accepted the multiplicity of parenthood: the boredom and the beauty of it, the relentless sacrifices and the transforming gifts. It was also the first time I allowed myself to hope that I could one day be a good mother to another human, even if I resented some of the things I might need to give up in order to bring them into the world.

How parenthood changes love, with Diana Evans

NL: I know that retaining a sense of self and carving out space for work is important to you. What have been the challenges of doing that as a parent?

DE: For me that's one of the biggest challenges of motherhood: trying to maintain your sense of self, identity and independence in the face of this person that came from you, and who changes the dimensions of your life. At times I felt like I was gasping for air, trying to exist as myself aside from all the demands of parenthood. The biggest adjustment is that your life no longer only belongs to you. I used to say that writing was the most important thing in my life, and I believed that categorically. But once I had children, I couldn't say that any more. Gradually that line shifted to: actually, they're the most important thing, and how do I negotiate that? How do I make that work alongside my need to express myself as a whole, lone person? That's been difficult, but my writing has helped, because it allows a space that requires solitude.

Did your children become the most important thing automatically when they were born? Or was understanding that a slower process?

It was a slow reckoning. For a long time after I had children I still believed that my writing was paramount. It took a while to fully accept and admit to myself that it wasn't any more. That life stops in the face of the needs of your child, and they become the centre of your moment, and of the universe. For example, if one of my children is ill everything goes up in the air, however deeply I'm entrenched in writing.

I think the intense love we have for our children is what makes it possible for us to withstand the work of parenting. Without that, it wouldn't be possible – at least not for me. That's something I realized when I had young children: parenthood is so hard that, if you didn't love your children so deeply, you might just walk away. But it's also love that constantly redeems you and brings you back to the moment, because your children can melt you in the midst of deep dissatisfaction. You see a smile, or you see them being wholly themselves, and those moments contain so much joy. Suddenly everything is in balance again. I remember my son saying to me once, about age three, 'I'm your son, you're my moon,' and I felt that then.

Was that intense love instant?

It was immediate for me. The love completely enfolds you and envelops you. It's almost a living thing that you can feel, which colours the world and creates this magical mist around you. Especially in the first two or three weeks of becoming a mother, there's a magical feeling in the air that is created by a human being that has come from you. I know it's not like that for everyone, but that's how it felt for me: immediate, unconditional, and as visceral as a physical thing. It was as if the child was the embodiment of love.

As somebody who hasn't experienced parenting yet, it seems to be such an act of service. You do absolutely everything for your baby and, in the beginning, that love is not reciprocated in the obvious ways – you don't get conversation, for example, or expressed gratitude. But nearly everything you do is devoted to keeping them alive.

What you get back is the sense of purpose that that gives you. Their complete dependence on you is a huge responsibility, but it gives purpose to everything you do. It makes you feel essential in the world.

Now that your daughter is sixteen and your son is ten, you're a long way from that initial stage. How does parental love change when your children grow and form their own opinions?

It does evolve as the child develops their own personality, but I think that fundamental nugget of love doesn't change, and that's what keeps you connected to them. In the beginning motherhood is very physical and when they're older it becomes more emotional. When my kids were babies somebody said to me that it gets harder the older they get. I wanted it to get easier rather than more difficult, because I found it so challenging, but now I understand what they meant. Especially when children become teenagers, there's emotional labour in terms of supporting them in becoming a functioning human being with the ability to express themselves fully. To a certain extent, that is your responsibility.

There's a line in Barbara Kingsolver's *The Poisonwood Bible*, where she talks about this idea that every time you look at your child as they're growing, you see the same person through different stages of their life. You see the eight-week-old and the five-year-old and the ten-year-old and the fifteen-year-old, so the love you have for them evolves through a multiplicity of emotion and memory. That's exactly what it feels like to me: when I look at my sixteen-year-old daughter, I see memories of her as a baby and as a toddler and as a six-year-old, et cetera. In just one glance, I recollect her in a multidimensional way. There's a richness of feeling in the connection you have with someone who came from you, which is always evolving.

Because they came from you, can that make it difficult when you recognize parts of yourself in them that you are frustrated by? Or perhaps when they do something that reminds you of an unresolved issue from your past?

That is something I worry about: what I pass on to them, and what I have tried to avoid passing on to them but nevertheless have, simply because of who I am and my constant proximity to them. There's still judgement around doing everything perfectly, and when they're a baby you can maybe pretend to be that saintly mother, but the older they get the more difficult that becomes. Eventually you realize that you have to be you. There's no other way you can be when you're raising and living with someone, trying to pay the bills and trying to live your life, all at the same time. You have to let go of that image you have been trying to aspire towards in your parenting. You have to let yourself be who you are. When my daughter was thirteen I let go of the guilt that comes with other people's judgement, because I realized that was an unconstructive way to think. There are lots of books that focus on how a parent might mess up their kid, but there's not enough acknowledgement of the astronomical impact a child has on an adult too. An adult is also a human being with feelings and emotions, and that's something children aren't made aware of as much. Of course I know the parent is the caregiver, but I think there could be a greater acknowledgement of the humanity of the parent, and the idea that we can't be anything that we're not, no matter how much we try. We have to accept ourselves in order to be good parents.

It sounds exhausting!

Yes, it is, but I love being a parent. I really do.

Perhaps because we rarely hear people speak about parenthood in the way you do, the decision to become a mother can be a loaded and frightening choice, especially when you understand that there are parts of your life you will have to give up. How did you approach that choice? Particularly as you never know what it's like to be a parent until you become one.

Even though it's become an intrinsic part of my life, I've tried to maintain a sense of self, so that there's enough of me left on the other side to continue as a fulfilled individual. That is constantly brought into jeopardy, and I think for lots of women their sense of self does tail off. Some reach a point when the children are old enough to leave home and there's an emptiness, a sense that something essential has been taken away. I'm always aware that I'm trying to avoid that circumstance. My life has become centred around the children in terms of my timetable and daily schedule, and I will miss the sense of order, structure and punctuation that their lives give me. But I'm hoping there'll be enough at the other side to fulfil me, and I'm sure there will be.

On the whole, being a parent has required huge sacrifices and it's also enriched my life. It probably happened at the right time, when I was thirty-three and almost ready. When I first became pregnant I was frightened that I wasn't ready, but I'd just done my MA and finished my first book, and there was space in my life. I didn't know what that space could be for, but I sensed it. It was a sign, looking back on it, that I was ready. It was only the fright that made me think I wasn't.

I think what people relate to in your writing is your honesty about the duality of parenthood, and how, although there is one part of it that is a deep, intense love, there is another that is mundane and difficult. Do you think it is hard for women to say, 'There are parts of being a parent that I dislike'?

Women are ready to talk about that in private, but it's often relegated to 'women's talk'. Even in friendships, women can be reticent about admitting the full extent of their difficulties. There's a sense of competition, which is created by society and the judgement on women that they're supposed to do motherhood in the right way, or to feel a particular way. But in my close friendships we connect most deeply when we share how those things feel: that sense of being erased, and of our identity being eroded – not just by motherhood, but by marriage and long-term relationships. When women allow themselves to have those conversations and express their complexity with honesty, I think they save each other. They saved me lots of times.

Has maintaining those friendships been a challenge, given the demands placed on you as a parent, a partner and a writer?

Yes, it has. There isn't much space left for friendships when you're trying to keep a relationship going, looking after a child, and trying to keep your work and sense of professional identity going. Even logistically, you don't have time. I used to talk to my friends on the phone for hours, but you reach a point where you don't have time to do that any more. Even meeting up is difficult – you have different schedules, people move away. At the same time, the friendships I have with women who I've known since I was a child are the most precious relationships. There's a purity to them, because they're not connected to my romantic life or my life as a parent. Those types of friendships create a space where you're free to be the person that you are, or the person that you thought you were, or the person that you want to be. You can fully witness each other changing. And there's something reassuring about the fact that, no matter how distant you might have become from yourself, no matter how much your relationship or your career has changed you, you can still connect with a person who knew you when you were a teenager. An old friendship is one of those things that helps you remember who you are in the world, and that's so valuable.

We've talked about how parenthood has changed your relationship to yourself, your children, your work and your friends, but I am also interested to know how it's changed your romantic relationship?

Long-term companionship is a warm thing to have in one's life, but it has definitely been compromised as a result of my work and my mothering. I always feel like I haven't given enough to that companionship, but I value it so much at the same time. In a good way, becoming parents has given us a common focus, which means we're always linked in a sense of purpose. It has been wonderful to create something together, to watch it grow and blossom, and to share a sense of fascination and wonder at who our children are going to become. But that changes romantic love, because it gets in the way. Parenting and writing are all-consuming, and I've struggled to make enough time and emotional and spiritual space for my relationship as well. I don't know how people manage to do all three things to equal effect. At times, I found it hard to share what was left of me, after the children, with my partner. But parenthood also intensifies the love you feel for your partner, because you see all the possibilities of their personality pouring out into the way that they communicate with your child. That's a wonderful thing, when you see the goodness of someone you love, and you watch them pouring that goodness into your child. So, as well as creating distance, parenthood has formed an eternal cord between us.

What's the most important thing you've learnt about parental love?

I've learnt that the most important thing to give to children is love. Because in my childhood, I wasn't very aware that I was loved, or that I was valued, and so it's always been important to me that my children know that they are deeply loved.

*

When Diana described seeing her children in a multidimensional way, I knew exactly what she meant, even though at the time I was not a parent. It was the same feeling I have sometimes when I look at my younger brother, Oliver. In his face, all at once, I see the chubby toddler squinting in the sunlight on a beach; the smiley kid with a bowl cut in a backwards cap; the teenager playing guitar in the garage; and the twenty-something dancing to 'Born in the USA' in our parents' kitchen. I've witnessed all thirty-four years of his life; he's witnessed all but two of my thirty-six. This means that, in our conversations, I feel all the layers of the people we used to be. As the writer Jeffrey Kluger puts it in *The Sibling Effect*, 'From the time they are born, our brothers and sisters are our collaborators and co-conspirators, our role models and cautionary tales . . . Our spouses arrive comparatively late in our lives; our parents eventually leave us. Our siblings may be the only people we'll ever know who truly qualify as partners for life.'

As my 'partner for life', my brother has expanded my view of intimacy. Because our love exists in a strange, unspoken knowledge of each other, one that doesn't require us to share everything in order to stay close. He is not the person I called to dissect a break-up, I doubt he would want to share any relationship problems with me, and neither of us has any inclination to discuss the other's sex life. And yet, even without these details, there is a way in which he knows me better than anyone else. Sometimes intimacy *is* exposing every corner of yourself to another person. But sometimes, it is built on experiences, not words: the camps we built together out of bedsheets, or the songs we recorded together in the garage. The tense family car journeys we endured side by side in the back seat of my mum's Saab, or the nights we slept in bunk beds, talking for hours underneath the plastic glow-in-the-dark stars we'd stuck to the ceiling. It was in all these early moments that I learnt how to share my life with someone. It was with Oliver that I first learnt how to fight – over teddies and Lego; for our parents' attention – and how to reconcile without holding a grudge. I learnt, too, how to make another person laugh, and how much humour matters. Without knowing it, growing up side by side, we were learning how to love.

In many of these conversations I have asked: how do you join your complicated life with another person's complicated life, and not lose yourself along the way? But next I wanted to know: what happens if your lives have been joined together from the very beginning? How do you carry on loving each other long after you've moved out of the home you grew up in? And how do you respect and enjoy both the history you share and the new people you've become? I turned to journalist Poorna Bell to answer these questions, because I knew that her relationship with her older sister, Priya, was a great source of love in her life.

Poorna and Priya have maintained their bond across different countries – Priya lives in Barcelona, Poorna in London – and through difficult life experiences: when Poorna's husband Rob died by suicide, her sister was the person who knew what she needed. How have they stayed so close? Through effort, annual sisters' holidays, regular contact, and by paying attention to how they each change and evolve as adults. For me, Poorna's answers were not only valuable in the context of sibling relationships, but in the way they remind us that consciousness is at the core of connection. And that love is not inevitable, even in families. We still have to choose to keep it alive.

The challenges and comfort of the sibling bond, with Poorna Bell

NL: How do you think a sibling relationship differs from a friendship?

PB: As siblings, we automatically have a deep interest in each other's lives, like friends do. There are things Priya and I are jointly interested in that we unite around and provide advice on. We're each other's ride or die. We're there for each other absolutely. But where the sibling bond is trickier than friendship is when you slip back into your default teenage mode. You say things too sharply, or assume you know how your sibling is going to react, because you have a certain idea of who they are. The challenge is that you both change at various points in your life, so your idea of who your sibling is might not necessarily reflect the person they are any more. (For example, Priya used to be quieter when we were younger, and now she is bolder, more forthright and more passionate.) Because you have known each other for so long, there are also patterns of behaviour that have locked in at formative ages, which determine how you behave with each other. You may not even be aware of them consciously.

What are the patterns that you can slip back into with your sister?

I am four years younger than Priya, which might not sound much, but when you're a kid or teenager it can be a huge difference maturity-wise. When we were young I was quite needy around her. I still can be. And when I was a teenager, I created a narrative in which I was the naughty one. Everything I did was either wrong or not good enough, and Priya was the golden child who could do no wrong. Now that I'm a grown-up, I know that wasn't the reality; it was just my perception of things. I know that Priya is my comrade, not the competition. But that narrative – of feeling slightly left behind, or not matching up to the type of person my sister was – does flare up from time to time. Not because of anything anyone has done. It's just an intangible feeling that I haven't been considered in the family plans. Or that I'm an afterthought, because I'm the second child and everyone assumes I'll be happy to go along with whatever they want to do. That's not true, but because it's an area of sensitivity for me, it's a place I have to catch myself from going to. That's the childlike pattern that, unfortunately, I think a lot of us have and can go back to very quickly when it comes to our family.

As I've been speaking to people about romantic love and friendship, this issue of continuing to learn who somebody is keeps coming up, because we all change, and being wedded to an older version of somebody can create conflict in love. How do you and Priya continually get to know each other as adults? Has that been a conscious effort?

The reason my relationship with Priya continues to evolve is because we've noticed that we each have to be an active participant. But it doesn't feel like effort, because we communicate in some shape or form every day. It's not like a friend you might catch up with once a month, when you have to pour your entire life into two or three hours. Priya and I understand what is going on in each other's lives because of the day-to-day communication we have. That doesn't mean we don't have misunderstandings, but it means we have a shorthand to each other. I don't have to ask her a thousand questions to try to get to the bottom of how she's feeling about something, because there is a part of her that is already known and understood by me. The same is true the other way round. She knows who I am and how I might be feeling about something.

Friends often come in and out of your life at certain points, whereas, if you're lucky enough to have a close relationship with a sibling, you know in some way they'll always be there, because your lives are tied together. Do you think that can also allow you to neglect that relationship, or take it for granted? Or be too harsh to each other?

With Priya, of course one source of conflict is saying something more harshly than you would to a mate, but I also think the relationship is more easily recoverable than a friendship. If one of us is being a bit harsh, Priya and I can say to each other, 'You are being a little too sharp.' Having someone point that out to you is helpful, because friendships can drift apart if people avoid conflict. People will lose a friend rather than say something that the other person might not want to hear. But with siblings, you don't have that luxury of deciding to avoid the other person for ever. Of course some siblings are estranged, so that's different. But if you have a strong relationship, there's just more rough and tumble when it comes to the words that you use with each other, because you know that it's easier to repair. Certainly with Priya, reconciliation often feels effortless in a way it doesn't with anyone else.

I know Priya was with you when you received the news about your husband's death. Was your sibling relationship a source of solace during that time?

She was there when I found out over the phone that my husband Rob had taken his life in New Zealand. From that moment I needed someone to look out for me and to protect me. Up until that point that had been Rob. But Priya made me feel like I had a warrior on my side. I needed someone who would understand me and be in my corner without trying to fix things – and she was that person. I didn't know what I needed in that moment, and she knew. It's not the same as a romantic partner, of course, and I'd be lying if I said that it has replaced that need, because it hasn't. My sister also has her own family, and they are that person for each other. But I know how lucky I am to have someone who, unequivocally, will be on my side, no matter what, as much as they can be.

The experiences we've had – her becoming a mother, me losing Rob – are vastly different from each other. Neither of us can understand them because we haven't been through what the other has. But we are still able to understand each other through them. We still know what the other needs.

That's an important difference: that you don't need to understand the experience as long as you understand each other through it. I've felt that way too. When everything falls apart in my life, no matter the experience, there's a feeling of being loved by my brother that I'm always sure of which makes me stronger.

Yes. The way Priya and I describe it is that our family is a solar system and we draw strength from being in each other's orbit. When we spend time in each other's company, our batteries have been filled up a little, and when we're apart, there's this little part of us that's missing. When I'm with Priya I'm able to be myself in a way that I'm not necessarily in other aspects of my life. It makes me feel super-connected to who I am: what I'm like as a person now, but also where I came from. We can make each other laugh and be silly and revert back to the children we were. We can also be brutally honest with each other as adults, in a way I don't think you necessarily can with friends. With a sibling, because of that honesty, you know that when they are on your side it comes from a very pure place. If you were doing something that was bad for you, or you were in the wrong, your sibling would probably tell you. That sometimes means they can tell truths you are not ready to hear. But it also means that, when they do back you up, you are probably in the right. And to have that support in your arsenal when it comes to tackling life is a powerful thing.

Has becoming an aunt brought a different form of love into your life?

Yes. I didn't have any expectations beforehand about how I would feel, but when I held my niece Leela for the first time, I remember thinking how infinitely precious and fragile she was, how I would die for her and do anything to protect her. My niece is not my biological child, but there is still a bond there that runs through our family, that I feel very connected to. Now she's about to turn six she is one of the sweetest human beings, but I felt that love for her before I knew what she was going to be like as a person. That felt very primal, and it was connected to the bond I have with Priya. It's another form of love entirely.

What do you wish you'd known about sustaining sibling love?

My relationship with Priya is strong because we are now very good at communicating. In our teens and twenties there were assumptions I made about our relationship, about who my sister was, without actually getting to know her as a person. Of course you'll always have certain dynamics within a family that are sometimes hard to navigate, but communicating what you need and understanding why a person might be feeling a certain way is still worth doing, even if it's your sibling and you think you already know them inside out.

The Work of Re-seeing

'Love is the quality of attention we pay to things.'
(J. D. McClatchy, Love Speaks Its Name*)*

One Sunday Dan washes up while I chop onions. There is only the sound of 6 Music on the radio, a saucepan of water simmering on the hob. The easy intimacy that exists in the absence of words. Then he lends me ski goggles to stop the onions from making me cry. 'Try putting a teaspoon in your mouth too,' he suggests, and I do. The sight of me chopping onions in ski goggles with a spoon in my mouth must be a ridiculous one, because he laughs, and I laugh, and soon we can't stop. But underneath the silliness, I feel the swelling of a sweet, sorrowful knowledge: these are the moments one of us will miss the most, one day, when the other dies. These ordinary afternoons.

This is what I now believe is part of the work of sustaining love: first, to create and make space for moments like these. And then? To notice them. To feel their fragility and their preciousness and their newness, even when they seem familiar. It is helpful, I had learnt, to understand love as a practice, a continuous revealing of oneself, and a vast force that exists and shifts between you and another person. But I think, to grapple with the big subjects, we must begin with little details. And love *is* small things too: the squeeze of a hand, an unexpected note on the kitchen counter, a text that says 'I'm so sorry for your loss', a song recommended, an insecurity shared, a detail you'd told someone years ago remembered – that the furry skin on peaches gives you goosebumps, say, or that you don't like milk because when you were at primary school you sat next to a boy on the bus who always had a milk moustache, and for some reason it made you queasy.

It is easy to notice someone when they are not there, when their absence makes you crave their return. It is harder to pay attention to someone when they are right in front of you, every day, their life so closely intertwined with yours that – if you're not careful – you can forget to see them in context of their separateness to you. Just as you can't take in the full beauty of a vast painting if you stand too close to it.

It is possible to practise using that muscle of noticing, though, until it becomes easier to pay attention to the parts of love that all of us can overlook. Until you remember to build those moments from scratch, with spontaneity and kindness. Until you stop skim-reading your friend or lover or family member, and instead read them more closely, as a never-ending story. A story whose plot you cannot control, or rewrite, or ever fully finish.

Then again, once you pay better attention you might feel the sharper edges of intimacy more keenly too: both of your inadequacies, your missteps, the small resentments you collect and stow away, then use as weapons in a fight at a later date. There are moments too, however rare, when I look at Dan and feel a flash of rage that makes me forget all the love between us. Like the night we go to our friends' house for a Burns supper. We are both drunk; he is drunker. We have cut down on alcohol for the last six months – the hormone specialist's recommendation – and so decide this is a 'fuck it' night, when we will drink whisky, eat haggis, forget the high-protein diet and accept the inevitable hangover the next day. It is supposed to be fun. Except it isn't. For no obvious reason, we start to grate on each other. Dan is getting louder, talking over people, entertaining the room. Everyone else finds him funny; I feel he is showing off and being offensive. A woman – single – sits down next to him who I know he would find attractive. He knows I would know this too. So even if he does not flirt with her, our shared knowledge of this fact sharpens the edge between us. On another day, I wouldn't care who sat next to him. I wouldn't care if he was being an exhibition-ist, and I would be laughing too. We would catch each other's eyes across the room, and he would wink, and I would smile, and it would be a telepathic 'I love you'. But some strange cocktail of hormones and alcohol and pettiness, and the strain of a life governed by longing, means that tonight the tension between us is tightly coiled. We drink more, we annoy each other more, I want to go home, he doesn't yet. And when we finally do, we have the biggest fight ever – about nothing, about everything. In the thick of his drunkenness, he swears at me, and in the midst of mine, I hate him. I want to hurt him and so I do; I use against him a painful memory from his past he had shared with me in a vulnerable moment. (A reminder that intimacy sometimes allows us to hurt the most the people we know the best.)

The next morning, tentatively and tenderly, we climb down from our anger and find a way back to each other. The tension between us melts like an ice cube on a hot day. We talk about what was really happening in our argument and show each other our version of it. Because after a fight, as the author Sandra Newman told me, it's important that you're not left with a discrepancy between what you each think is real. 'I think that's a lot of what makes a relationship work in the long run,' she said, 'if you can understand each other's perception of reality and not dismiss it. If you are able to be honest about it, even when it's not flattering to you, rather than just keeping that knowledge for yourself.'

Through all of these small moments – the joyful familiar Sunday afternoons and the painful drunken fights – we have a choice. In the joyful ones, will we overlook the beauty, or will we be consciously present? And in the painful ones, will we decide it's easier to shut the conversation down than to dig for the uncomfortable truths? Or will we find a way back to a loving place? (Even if that is the morning after.) I think these are the questions we have to ask if we want to sustain any kind of relationship. Not because, if we do, we will reach a state of love. But because the love is in the act itself: the noticing, the forgiving, the reflecting, the *trying*.

And part of the trying is finding ways to show up. During this period I turn Esther Perel's words over in my head: 'If you tell me, "I care about my partner," then my second question is, "How do you show it?" The fact that you feel it isn't enough.' This sentence is what reminds me to make my mum Ottolenghi's blueberry birthday cake even though I am a nervous baker, to send Dan a letter in the post when we have to live apart for a month in the first coronavirus lockdown, and to send my schoolfriend Caroline a book for no reason other than I think she would enjoy reading it to her daughter. It is a constant reminder that intention is not enough, and that even if our friends and family and partners know that we love them, sometimes they deserve a little evidence.

After all, the people we love are a constellation. In loving them, it is our privilege to see and bring out all the different worlds and colours and depths within them, just as they have the potential to do the same for us in return. This reciprocity is at the heart of love – a balance of giving and receiving, of seeing and being seen, of asking and answering, of thinking always as 'I' and 'we'. Perhaps what all of this comes back to, then, is finding the courage and consciousness and curiosity to do 'the work of re-seeing', as Mira Jacob described it. To stay conscious enough to see the smallest moments of our lives in all their shining detail. To stay curious enough to see all the versions of another person, then re-see them when they change over time. And most of all, to fully understand and see all the versions of ourselves, so that we might find the courage to show them to another human, in the light, and trust that they will love us for all of them.

How can we survive losing love?

*'The heart that breaks open can contain
the whole universe.'*

(Joanna Macy)

The Loss of the Imagined Future

'The unborn, whether they're named or not,
whether or not they're acknowledged, have a way
of insisting: a way of making their presence felt.'
(Hilary Mantel, Giving Up the Ghost)

When we return from our Italian summer holiday I see an acupuncturist who thinks I haven't fully accepted the emotional impact of my miscarriage. It's been nearly a year, and although I'm aware I haven't moved on completely, it's startling to hear someone say I have made so little progress. 'Do you feel like you might cry at any time?' she asks. And I do – it's as if a sadness sits just below the surface. 'Are you having vivid dreams?' I am, often gory and bloody ones, full of images of dead foetuses and misshapen wombs. In a recent one my baby had been too small – as tiny as a fly – and when I drained the water out of the bath it drowned down the plughole. Before it did, I frantically tried to cup it in my hands, but it was too small – I couldn't see it, I couldn't save it. I didn't tell the acupuncturist about my bloody dreams. I just said, 'They've been a little intense.'

After the appointment, although I knew there was truth in her words, I felt irritated, my chest tight. I called my friend Marisa. 'Why can I not stop thinking about this? I've done the work. I've acknowledged my sadness. Why does she still think I am stuck inside the early stages of grief?' Marisa did what good friends sometimes do: she took my side and made me feel better, even though my frustration at the acupuncturist was misplaced. But that night I remembered a lesson I'd learnt at a couples therapy class the year before: pay attention to the moments in which you feel irritated, because hidden in your anger are often clues to the deeper story.

When it comes to heartbreak, an ocean of suffering is often squashed into a short, sharp sentence. 'I think I should move out'; 'I'm not in the right place for a relationship'; 'There's been an accident'; 'We found a lump.' Or, in my case, 'I'm sorry, there's no heartbeat.' The shock ending is delivered in a few seconds, but the sadness chooses its own timeline – you lose a future in a moment, and then you are left to mourn it at a pace you can't control. That's what I lost when a doctor showed me a motionless shape on a screen: not only a baby – or a foetus to some – but a picture of our future, which had already formed in my mind. Who they might have been, the life they might have lived. In five words, a world was taken.

Other than Dan, the first person to know I was pregnant was the man who served me coffee in the Pret near work. Even though he knew my order, every morning he would ask, 'Black Americano?' and I would reply, 'Yes please!' So when one morning I replied, 'No, decaf Americano please!' I caught him off guard. 'You're pregnant?' he asked, not in an intrusive way, but like someone who had automatically said what they were thinking out loud. I said, 'Too early to say!' which was code for yes, but I haven't told anyone yet. He nodded and we both smiled. Even as Dan and I began to share our news with those we loved, the consistency with which the barista always asked, 'Decaf Americano?' made me smile each morning. It was a happy secret between two people who barely knew each other. This was the mood of my first months of pregnancy: a precious excitement I carried around with me, sometimes private, sometimes shared, always there.

I imagined we were having a girl. Although I knew it was just a feeling, I daydreamt about the type of human she might be. Would she be good at cooking and keeping plants alive like her dad? Would she have his dark hair and dark eyes? She would surely be short, like both her parents. Perhaps she would be as gentle as her uncle, as romantic as her mother, as much fun as her grandmother, who was already so excited to meet her. We would teach her to swim, to sing, to ride a bike, to dance around the kitchen, to forgive herself, to read the same stories my dad read to me. We would smell her head, kiss her cheek, stroke her forehead when she was sick. We would tell her how many times we'd dreamt of her. How we'd longed for her to live, how wanted she was, how loved. And so a thousand small dreams stacked up into an imagined future that was a fantasy, and yet real to me.

A lot of people who have shared their stories of heartbreak with me have lost their vision of a future too. One mourns the fact that her late mother will never meet her children or witness her wedding day. Another shares the story of her friend who died, and the holiday they booked but never got to go on. One woman opens up about the dreams that evaporated with her divorce: all the Christmas mornings she and her ex would never spend together with their kids; the family home she thought they would grow old in and now have to sell. How do you mourn the loss of a future you never really had? I think about this question most nights, as I try to understand how this particular loss gutted me.

My body, like my mind, had refused to let go, so I had surgery to remove the foetus. For the first weeks afterwards, I walked around feeling that my stomach was a pumpkin with its insides carved out, and I was the only one who knew it was hollow. It was winter outside, and inside my body too. One of the worst parts of heartbreak, I think, is waking up each morning and remembering. For a second upon first waking there is a bright moment where you forget and outrun the sadness. But then another second passes and the memory catches up, so you just lie there, not wanting to get out of bed, not wanting to face the day that contains your loss. It seemed there was no part of me that my baby hadn't occupied, so there was nowhere inside myself I could go where I could be free from the memory of it, or the life I imagined we'd share. I knew the future I had hoped for was no longer possible. Still, I longed for it.

Friends and family offered condolences, but I was distant, removed, somewhere else. The most comforting words came from my father-in-law, who wrote inside a card, 'It's OK to howl at the moon.' Less comforting was the well-meaning woman who told me she believed all babies who died did so for a reason. All that day I fantasized about slapping her until her cheek was pink – and these dark thoughts scared me. Other people told me how common miscarriages were, which was meant to be reassuring. But if it was so common, I wondered, why did I feel so alone?

There were moments of morbid humour to my heartbreak too. I laughed when a pregnant cat suddenly started visiting our garden. 'Are you kidding me?' I asked it. I laughed again when a young builder wolf-whistled and said, 'Nice arse!' to me as I walked home. It was before I'd had the baby removed, and it seemed ridiculous to be catcalled when my body contained life and death – my living heart and my baby's dead one – all at once. I was not annoyed; I was grateful for the dark comedy. I only hoped that he never had to make the lonely walk to Boots to buy the extra-large sanitary towels for his partner as Dan had done the night before.

I knew, by then, that I had to let go of the future I'd lost, but everywhere there were reminders, small but painful ones, like wasp stings. I tidied the shelves and found a photo of our baby's scan tucked inside a book. I put my hand into a coat pocket and felt the pebble my mum gave me when the foetus was the same size. In a kitchen drawer, the positive pregnancy test. On my phone, a BabyCentre alert that said, 'Your baby is about the size of an apple.' I deleted the app, and put everything else in a small wooden box in the back of our wardrobe – all the traces of a different life that was not ours.

When I sift through these memories after my acupuncturist appointment, I see there are three parts to the deeper story of my sadness: the loss itself, the loneliness that accompanied it, and the shame – a feeling that I should have moved on by now. I'd interviewed women who had lost children, who had given birth to stillborn babies or survived years and years of IVF. It seemed pathetic that I could not loosen my grip on a loss that was so small by comparison.

To someone who cannot understand why a miscarriage can be a painful loss, I would say: imagine for the first time in your life you are not alone inside your own body. While it's curious to think about the parts that grow inside you – arms, legs, feet, hands – about how the amount of blood in the body increases by 40 to 50 per cent as your heart beats faster to pump it through, I think what changes you for ever is the sense that there is suddenly another life in your inner world.

When that second heart stops beating it forces you to confront what we all know but try to avoid: death. You can no longer look away from it. You can no longer deny it. It is within you and from then on always will be; this understanding that all of our hearts will one day stop beating, just as your baby's did. In the space of a few months – or in some cases longer – women who miscarry experience inside them the bookends of our existence: the beginning of life and the end of it. I would not describe that experience as a small one. I know for some women it can be. But it wasn't for me.

All losses have their own private complications, and, whether we acknowledge them or not, their lasting consequences will show up somewhere – in the next relationship, in a drunken fight, in a panic attack, in jealousy. That's why we should honour the heartbreaks that matter deeply to us, however insignificant we fear they might seem to anyone else. The bigger challenge, I think, is how to carry those losses inside us without letting them distract us too much from our lives. I had to accept my miscarriage was meaningful to me, but I also had to let go of the future I'd planned for in order to live fully in the life that I am lucky to have. The real life that's happening now, here, today. As Dr Lucy Kalanithi would later tell me, 'It's worthwhile to realize that we are still ourselves, that there is an essential self that's still there, separate to the future you might have lost.' Yes, I was a woman who wanted to be a mother and no longer was. But I was also a sister, a friend, a daughter, a lover, a person with purpose; a woman who was hungry to experience many more facets of life than motherhood.

A few days after the surgery, I returned to work. That morning I stood on the train platform, as I had done hundreds of mornings. I stared across and saw it then: the letter 'S' on a blue sign. The first letter of the name we had given to our baby. (Had it always been there? Maybe I'd never noticed it.) In that moment I felt a surge of emotion I never had before – the exact midpoint between happy and sad. I accepted the pain and pushed forwards through it, like running through a stitch. I looked at the sign and smiled, and let myself acknowledge what for a long time I hadn't: although my baby's life was short, I did not want to forget it.

After I got off the Tube, I went to Pret. There were four people ahead of me so I waited a while, until I heard the familiar words, 'Decaf Americano?' 'No, black Americano please,' I replied. I nearly cried but didn't. 'Not decaf?' I shook my head, and he nodded awkwardly, but gently, and looked at me as if he wished he could say more. A minute or so later he handed me a coffee, and I said, 'Thank you' and nodded gently too. I walked to work and thought about the power of a tiny gesture – a glance, a smile, a nod – and how we can comfort the people we hardly know, without any words.

*

When I was a child, my mother often cried in the kitchen on New Year's Eve. My father ushered me and my brother into the other room so 'Mum can have some peace', explaining that it was the anniversary of our grandmother's death. Mum lost her mother, Pamela, when she was twenty-six and pregnant with Oliver. Today she still cries describing the experience of becoming a mother while losing her own. Back then, Oliver and I were too young to feel the weight of this annual reminder, but that was my earliest observation of grief:

tears I didn't fully understand cried on the other side of a door. Something to be shut away in another room.

Since then, as well as my miscarriage, I've experienced different versions of loss at closer proximity. I've sat in pews at grandparents' funerals. I've cried on the rainy drive back from a lover's flat, after we decided to end our relationship. I've held my arms around our family dog's neck and whispered 'I love you' in her ear, felt my wet tears on her fur, minutes before we put her to sleep. In some of those moments, the relationship between love and loss seemed simple: you lost the love, then you were left with the grief. One was the price for the other.

It wasn't until I began to understand my thoughts about miscarrying, and to speak to others about grief, that I realized love and loss were not separate, consecutive stages, but two sides of the same coin. Grief did not follow or replace love – each thing existed inside the other. And loss was not a faraway thing, but a part of every loving, fading moment. Although, mercifully, I was yet to unexpectedly lose someone close to me, I saw that it would not be possible to explore love without confronting loss too. This meant asking difficult questions: how do we accept that some people grow old with their loved ones while others lose theirs too soon? If we are gutted by a death, or marked by an absence, how do we find meaning in the life that remains, without measuring it against others? And is there anything valuable to be learnt from how we carry on loving in spite of all this? To begin my search for answers, I spoke to journalist, author and former UK editor-in-chief of *Harper's Bazaar* Justine Picardie, whose life has been shaped by loss in both painful and beautiful ways.

*

My grief after the miscarriage was for a future I never got to live. I knew I was lucky, at this point in my life, to not have been forced to mourn a past too. To not have grieved both for the memories I shared with someone and the moments we planned to experience together and never would. This dual loss is something Justine Picardie experienced twice: first when her beloved sister Ruth died, and again when her marriage ended. I wanted to ask if the first loss altered how she approached the second, and why the end of a relationship is another version of grief. Because there are obvious ways to offer comfort when a person dies: we send flowers, write letters, drop round meals, attend funerals. But when a relationship ends, there are no formalized ways to be there for someone. Perhaps by discussing heartbreak with the attention it deserves, we can find new ways to reach people in this complex form of grief, when they are mourning a person who remains part of this world, and yet no longer part of theirs.

Justine reminded me what we risk every time we choose to love someone: not just that they might outlive us, or we them, but that they might break the heart we place in their hands. It's remarkable, I think, that many of us are willing to take that risk again and again, as Justine did when she fell in love after her divorce. Her story shows we can find hope and new beginnings even when those things might feel impossible. Of course she was lucky to meet a soulmate in her forties, but luck is never enough – Justine also found the courage to love with vulnerability again. And the thing that pushed her to take that leap? The death of her sister, a loss that made her determined not to live a life governed by fear.

Finding love in the wasteland of grief, with Justine Picardie

NL: What does it feel like to grieve for the end of a marriage?

JP: Divorce can feel like a bereavement that turns your future hopes to ashes, and casts a dark shadow over the past. In my case, it was the end of an incredibly important relationship, because my ex-husband was – and still remains – the father of our sons. When he left me and our twenty-year marriage ended, I felt as if I was trying to navigate a path through a wasteland of shock and grief. It was like an immense bomb had exploded, destroying the landscape of our family life. But I managed to find my way through that challenging territory, partly because I'd done it before, when Ruth died of breast cancer at the age of thirty-three. In the immediate aftermath of her death, all I could think about was the horror of it: the physicality of her suffering and everything she endured for the last ten months of her life. But I also knew that I couldn't be completely submerged in that visceral pain, because I had two small children to look after. In a similar way, I understood that I simply couldn't go under after the end of my first marriage; I could not get lost in that wasteland, even though I had been in the relationship for most of my adult life.

When a relationship ends, people say, 'You'll get over it.' Those are the four most unhelpful words you can say to anybody who is feeling heartbroken. Because whether it's a death or the end of a marriage, the loss is not a mountain you climb up and come down the other side of. You never entirely get over it, but you do rise to the challenge, until eventually you live with the loss and it becomes part of you. I feel that way about my ex-husband. Although the ending was extremely painful, by the time we divorced we had established a cordial relationship, because I loved our sons far more than I was angry with him. I didn't want to go to war with him or undermine our shared past. Also, having survived Ruth's death, I knew that I would survive my divorce too, and that I couldn't spend the rest of my life being unhappy.

How did Ruth's death teach you to resist unhappiness and to find a way through your heartbreak?

Even when Ruth knew she was dying, she *loved* life. The little things like lipstick and flowers and chocolate cake remained very important to her. So to honour her, I had to go on celebrating life. I did so after her death, and after the end of my marriage. To find a way through losses like those, you do have to continue to cherish what is good in life: the snowdrops that you see in winter, the cake you bake with your children, the moment when you laugh with a friend. I felt it would have been a betrayal of Ruth if I hadn't celebrated life in the way that she did. And losing her taught me that optimism and faith is not enough; terrible things do happen, but that doesn't mean that you have to live in a constant state of fear. If you do, the bad things might still happen anyway, but you wouldn't have enjoyed all the pleasures of being alive.

Did losing her change your view of love?

Ruth and I were unbelievably close. I remember when she was diagnosed with terminal cancer, I felt a profound sense of failure, because I couldn't save her, I couldn't protect her. Now, whenever I write, on some level I'm always writing for her. I think about her multiple times a day. The very hard thing about losing a loved sibling is that sense of losing the one person who understands your shared past. But what I discovered is that you go on loving somebody even if they're dead. My sister is dead, but the love we shared is still astonishingly alive, and continues to be intensely meaningful to me. Our love for one another is integral to the woman I am today and, in some mysterious way, Ruth still exists within and without me.

Did the end of your marriage feel like a loss of a future, as well as a past?

I think that many of us understand the experience of relationships that have ended and yet continue in our thoughts, because we carry on thinking, 'Remember when . . .' or 'I wonder if . . .' The past, present and future are in a constant state of flux: I'll remember a former relationship or experience and, quite naturally, my thoughts will turn to a particular person, and what I might say to them were I ever to see them again. We think of our lives as linear, but they're not. Although one day follows the other, we're just as likely to be recalling what happened last week as musing on the events of a decade ago, or indeed our hopes for next year. And I feel the same way about the loss of my sister too: our past and the present and the future are threaded together.

Did the idea of falling in love again seem unrealistic in the aftermath of the divorce?

Oh God, yes. My ex-husband had fallen in love with somebody else and inevitably I felt rejected, humiliated and jealous.

So I didn't want to run the risk of falling in love again. I thought I was going to be alone for ever, and I also felt a sense of failure – not only had I failed at marriage, but I had failed to protect my beloved sons from the heartache of a broken family. At the time I thought, I'm never going to fall in love again, and I don't need to, because I have my sons, I have my friends, I have my work. I don't need or want another man. Then, out of the blue, I met somebody.

It was one of those magical moments when the universe chimes: I was invited to dinner by a friend and nearly didn't go, because I was feeling tired and a bit depressed. Eventually I changed my mind and went, only because I thought it would be rude not to. When I sat down at the table, on my right was the person I was clearly being set up with; he was very nice but there was no spark between us. And on my left, there was this interesting man who was incredibly funny and bright and original. He rang the next day to ask me out on a date to the theatre, but I said, 'I don't want to go to the theatre.' He asked, 'Why not?' and I was surprisingly straightforward about my feelings. I said, 'My marriage has ended, I've had my heart broken and I don't want to run the risk of being hurt again.'

Why do you think you were able to be so open with him?

He was remarkably easy to talk to. He said, 'Come anyway,' so we went to the theatre. Even when he took me out to dinner afterwards I kept saying, 'I'm not going on dates and I'm not going to fall in love.' That was the story I told myself. But I did fall in love with him. The funny thing is, the year before we met, I'd been asked to write a short story for an anthology about love. I didn't feel up to going to the book launch, which was on Valentine's Day – I just felt too bruised at that point. One of the book's editors rang the next day and said, 'Why didn't you come?' I said, 'Because my husband's fallen in love with somebody else, and now we're getting divorced.' She invited me for a cup of tea. Then when we met she said, 'I hope you don't mind me saying this, but sometimes I have a psychic intuition, and I really do feel I've got to tell you something important. You've got to move on from the end of your marriage, and you've got to let go with good grace, because you have two wonderful sons who are the best part of your life, and you love them, and that's an incredible gift from your ex-husband.' Which was true, I did feel that way. And then she said, 'There's somebody else out there for you. You're not going to meet him yet and he's not ready to meet you, but I hope your paths cross because, if and when they do, he's the man for you.' I asked, 'Well how am I supposed to know who he is?' and she said, 'He's called Philip and he's got an angel on the front of his house, but now you've got to forget that.' And as it happens, I did forget it – there was so much else going on in my life. Even when I eventually went to that dinner party and the man on my left was called Philip I didn't think, aha, his name is Philip.

When did you remember what she had told you?

We were walking along the road together, some time after we first met, and he said, 'This is my house,' pointing to a house with a white angel carved over the door. I said, 'Oh my God, your name's Philip and you've got an angel on the front of your house. You're my soulmate. We're meant to be together.' I told him the story and, to his credit, he didn't think

I was a mad person. Many years later, when we moved to our home in Norfolk, he commissioned a carving of a small pair of angel wings above the back door, with my initials and his initials on either side. Every time I look at it, I'm reminded of how much I love him, and how lucky we are to have found one another.

How is falling in love after divorce different to falling in love for the first time?

It's so precious when you find love in later life, whether you're in your forties or fifties or older. I think people have a great capacity to fall in love again, even after immense loss. That, to me, is the real miracle. Falling in love for the second time can feel reckless – but it's also a great act of courage. I felt blessed to have met Philip, and I had the faith to embrace our relationship. Perhaps this has something to do with what I'd learnt from my sister's death: you can't live your life fearing what lies around the corner. Also, when I fell in love for the second time, I was in my forties. What I wanted from love was very different to what I was looking for in my twenties. My ex-husband was a musician, which sounds romantic and glamorous, but it was tough, having two small children while he was often away on tour for months on end. Whereas when I fell in love for the second time, it was with someone who is very present. As soon as we met I felt I could talk to Philip about everything. I talked to him about Ruth very early on in our relationship – some people find it hard to talk about death, but there was no embarrassment or fear on Philip's part. Ruth's death is integral to who I am, and he is able to accept that. I also had to be able to trust him as a person in order to trust him to be a kind and honourable stepfather. I did have to think about that; and I didn't want to introduce him to my sons – who were fifteen and nineteen at the time – until I was certain that it was going to be a relationship that had a future. But even though I was aware of my responsibilities as a mother, and therefore behaved accordingly, I still felt the extraordinary enchantment of falling in love again. A sense of magic and possibility . . .

What do you wish you'd known about love?

If I could have given my younger self a piece of advice it would be: don't confuse love with anxiety, or the risk of danger with the thrill of romance. The harmony and the calm that comes with a true love is extremely precious. It took me many years to learn that.

*

Before speaking to Justine, I'd assumed that love is what you try to live without after a loss. In fact, her love for her sister still guides her life. It keeps Ruth close and present in her mind every day. It encourages her to cherish tiny joys, and to not let fear overshadow them. It even gave her the courage to let a new love in when she least expected to find one. Perhaps, as Justine said, getting over a loss was an impossible goal. Instead, we learn to live with our griefs inside us, and to let them transform us, until they reveal our resilience.

Our conversation reminded me of something the author Emily Rapp Black once told me. Emily's son, Ronan, died of a rare genetic disease called Tay-Sachs when he was nearly three years old. And when he had six months to live, she fell in love with the man who would become her husband. She said, 'I learnt how to love, in my best form, through Ronan. I wouldn't have been able to love in this way if I hadn't been broken open by the experience of loving and losing him.' Through her son's death, she understood that 'a broken heart is an open heart'. How extraordinary that, although both Emily and Justine's losses had stolen people from their lives, they had also deepened their capacity to love.

*

One part of loss I found particularly difficult was the way it chipped away at hope. By the time we celebrated New Year's Eve the year after the miscarriage, the optimism I had dug deep for over the last twelve months was beginning to dim, like a torch about to lose its battery. Month after month, the harder I hoped, the more I believed, the crueller the disappointment when I was proven wrong. As I made my New Year's resolutions that January I had to ask: was it still sensible to carry on hoping so blindly every month? Or might it be prudent to exercise a little caution, and think, I probably won't get pregnant this time. It might not happen. I knew this negative thinking was firmly against the strategy of acupuncturists and fertility gurus who preached a 'believe hard enough and it'll happen' philosophy, with affirmations like 'I'm letting go of any emotional blocks keeping me from conceiving'. Still, a year and a half since that first positive pregnancy test, I wondered if cynicism might add the safety net of self-protection. This new, complex relationship to hope made me think about its role after a loss. Does hope become a burden, or a guide?

Do we find it, or do we build it? And what, if anything, does it have to do with love?

The journalist Melanie Reid has a unique understanding of the connection between love, loss and hope. Melanie broke her neck and fractured her lower back in a horse-riding accident in 2010, and is now a tetraplegic, which means she is paralysed from the chest down. After her accident she lost many things: the ability to walk unaided, her physical and emotional identity, her independence and the joy of being held in a hug. The injury and limitations of her recovery also tested her love for other people – and their love for her. I had already discovered the challenges of sustaining love in the long term, but I wanted to ask Melanie: what if the test placed on love is far greater than time and complacency? Is it naive to hope that love could survive even the toughest losses?

Melanie does not sugar-coat her experiences. She does not pretend the meaning she has found in life since her accident can ever replace what she has lost. But she does invite us to ask: what will we do with the lot life has given us, however unfair it might seem?

The undercurrent of kindness and love that connects us all,
with Melanie Reid

NL: How has your accident changed your relationships and the role of love in your life?

MR: It was a nuclear explosion that blew apart not just my spine and physical life, but my family and emotional life. Since the accident, love means a different thing to me and my husband because so much has changed. Dave has to bear the burden of doing everything physical, and our intimate life has been interrupted, because we can't have sex the way we used to. It has dented the mother–son relationship too, because I can no longer be the all-solving, all-supporting mother. My son and I have reversed roles. (He was twenty when I had the accident.)

What I've realized is that what we blindly call love, we take for granted. You can forget that, for all your faults and nasty little habits – the things you do that you wouldn't want anyone to know – someone still loves you. You're a precious part of somebody's life. I think we *do* forget that. We bumble along thinking, oh, everybody's loved, the way everybody can get the bus – but they're not. I took that for granted before.

You spent a year away from your home while in hospital. When you returned, how did you and your family find a way back to each other?

The wonderful thing about Dave is he never went away, even though he was the least emotionally suited person to this job. He was the head of entertainment in our family, a sexy, funny guy who hated hospitals, hated sickness, hated ugly bodies and responsibility. Suddenly, he was landed with all those things in a package he was married to. A nurse confided to me years later that the staff were worried he wouldn't cope. Probably – privately – a lot of people were. But from the word go, he was amazing, he evolved, and as I watched him take on the huge weight of responsibility, my respect for him grew too. He'd always said to me, 'There's more to me than just the funny guy,' and then he proved it.

Early on, I was horrified at everything that had been

taken away from us, and at the burden that had been placed on him. One day I said, 'You can leave me. This has changed all the ground rules and you didn't sign up for this.' I opened the door for him because I loved him. I thought, he doesn't deserve this. Let him go. And he said, 'Don't be so bloody stupid. You're stuck with me.' To me, that was real love.

I imagine it takes great vulnerability to depend so fully on people in a physical way. What did that feel like?

When you become paralysed it's an awful rebirth. You're like a baby again, because you have to learn how to use your new body. In the beginning I sat there like a baby bird in a nest, with no choice but to take any help that was offered to me. It was when I returned home, where I used to be the practical one, that I felt the full frustration of not being able to fix fences or put water in the car windscreen washers. I was a doer who couldn't do anything.

I remember when we bought a new Hoover, I could see exactly how it needed to be assembled. I watched Dave fumble with the guide and shiny parts, like I was on a management course where you have to tell people how to do stuff rather than do it yourself. I had to be patient and not too critical, and moments like that were a tough learning curve. But isn't what I'm describing the essence of realism in love? When there's a huge change, and you learn to form a different kind of team? That's what we've done: we've both adapted, because we still want to be together.

What do you think allowed you to pull back from self-pity and see the parts of your life that you are grateful for?

I'm no saint. I still have my ten-minute pity parties when I allow myself to go into the bathroom, look in the mirror and cry. Then I suppress that self-pity, zip it up and get out there again. I have to keep going for the people I love. In that way my strength comes from love; at the roots of resilience – the ones that go deep in the earth and stop a tree getting blown over – is love. That stopped me being too selfish and kept me fighting forwards, rather than falling back into helplessness. I had this epiphany, early after my accident, when I started to play the Glad Game. I realized that if I had been brain-damaged, or paralysed higher up, I would have been on a ventilator or in 24-hour care. My husband and son would have been bound to a brain-damaged wife and mother for decades. By understanding that things could be worse, I learnt to be glad for what I had.

Do you think that losing your physical self made you notice those little details that make a life beautiful, which perhaps you overlooked before?

When you're in a wheelchair, people you love can't hug you the way they used to. You lose that everyday physical intimacy you have with friends who pat your shoulder, or with strangers you brush thighs with on the Tube. I have a hunger for the touch I have lost, but when Dave reaches out to take my hand, or anyone runs a casual hand along my shoulder, it's beautiful.

All of us take so much for granted. Life is beautiful and we don't have time to realize it. We let silly and petty things rule us and lead us into criticism. We find fault with life because we are tired and grumpy, instead of relishing the fact that we are with other people who are healthy, who love us and want to be with us.

If there are positives to be taken from my situation, one is that petty things stopped mattering. But it is tragic that we only learn these things when we experience a traumatic loss. The complacency of modern life is that a lot of us believe we are immortal, and that we deserve happiness. We think it'll come to us, when actually we need to stop and look around in order to see that it's already there.

I'm interested to know what your relationship to hope is today. Originally you seemed to focus your hope on walking again, but have you found a way to carry on hoping without pinning it all on that one goal? I ask because I had a difficult relationship to hope while trying to conceive, since, in a way, my belief that a pregnancy would hold was often what hurt me.

I was in denial in the hospital, so driven and focused on this totem of walking – like you with conceiving – that I drove myself bonkers. The yearning to walk and the yearning for a child are both primal and deep-rooted. Longing for something like that, you either fall apart or slowly learn and soften, and realize that hope should never die, whatever the outcome. To give up hope is to give up life and, in the early days, it was false hope that kept me physically alive. It puts a different filter over the eyes of your mind. You don't have to see everything through totally rose-tinted spectacles, but finding that kernel of belief makes your hunger and obsession liveable with. You also can't choke yourself on hope or your desires; you have to have a gentle approach. You never let go of that little kernel, but you grow to accept that, in the present, things are the way they are, and you better start enjoying living, not destroy yourself by thinking about things that might or might not happen. As Sydney Smith says, 'Why destroy present happiness by a distant misery, which may never come at all, or you may never live to see it? For every substantial grief has twenty shadows, and most of them shadows of your own making.' Instead, try to focus on the fact that what you have around you is love, and a good life.

Are there forms of love that are accessible to you now that weren't before?

What I have gained is a sense of being loved. I feel loved, not just by my family, but by strangers. When I meet people at book festivals or talks, or receive beautiful emails or letters, I feel incredible warmth and an overpowering sense of being loved by people I don't know. There's a tenderness between strangers when they see you in need, and sometimes that can be a moment of acute sweetness. When I was on my book tour, a friend came with me as my carer. One day, after we'd parked outside a hotel, I waited in my wheelchair while she got the cases out of the boot. Some students walked past and one of them – a young guy – stopped and said, 'Would you like me to help you?' When you receive kindness like that from someone you don't know, I think that is a form of love. It's a random connection to another soul who thinks you might need help. I now have a greater appreciation of that power of kindness and love, that beautiful undercurrent that exists between us all.

What do you wish you'd known about love?

Without love we are nothing; an isolated person, a lump of cells. Love gives everything meaning but is too easily thrown away. If we find it, we don't work hard enough at it (and you *do* have to work at it). You can't make assumptions. You can't run away from the bad stuff. Put it this way: if love between two people is profoundly tested by something, and you do get through to the other side, your relationship will be forged at a deeper level. People say marriages often break down after the loss of a child. In the same way, there are a lot of people who can't cope after a life-changing injury. They walk away. If love is tested that hard and it can't withstand it, then it can't withstand it. But what you can be sure of is that if love survives these massive tests, and you both emerge still able to enjoy life, then you've got something pretty gold-plated. My love has adapted because it was tested – and it has endured.

*

I had asked Melanie whether love could survive the loss of personal freedom and identity. But I discovered that, like Justine, at the very bottom of her loss, Melanie had found a deeper, wider love. This wasn't just a love for her husband and son, it was a love she accessed through the quiet kindness of strangers. It reminded me of the connection I had felt in the Pret barista's gentle nod. And of another time, when I called British Airways' support from the hospital and a woman called Rachel picked up. When I told her that we wouldn't be able to make our flights to Mauritius, because of the miscarriage, and needed to organize a refund, she said, 'I am so, so sorry for your loss,' and I knew that she meant it. She gave me her direct number so I wouldn't have to repeat my story to another stranger. She listened and demanded as little of me as she could. At my most fragile, she comforted me. She said, 'I'm going to see what I can do for you.'

This special love that exists between strangers – between Melanie and the student in the car park – is a form of connection we often overlook, which shows up for us when we are most vulnerable. I know this because when I asked people to share the random acts of kindness they had received, many of them had occurred during or after a painful experience. The writer Marianne Power told me that a taxi driver had comforted her during a period of depression. While driving to her destination, he opened up about his own breakdown, and told her, 'Cry as much as you need to. And watch *Paddington.*' Then the author Ella Dove revealed that, when she was lying in intensive care after losing her leg, the ward cleaner placed a packet of Jaffa cakes on her bedside table and said, 'You're doing well, girl.' Moments like these make me think that this is a strange gift of loss: how it makes us more alive to the glimmers of connection that are all around us, when we need them the most.

*

Something that struck me in this conversation was Melanie's ability to squash her self-pity into private, ten-minute moments. I was in awe of this effort, because it's easy to ask, 'Why me?' after a loss. In the times when I have slipped into self-pity – the Christmas when a relationship ended and it felt like everyone else in the world was in love – that feeling only exaggerated my sadness. I wanted to understand why our minds reach for self-pity in the face of grief, even though it hurts us more. Could there be a way to stop 'Why me?'

thoughts from escalating, even when a loss felt random and unjust? To better understand the stages of suffering – especially when a relationship ends – I spoke to the psychotherapist and bestselling author of *The Examined Life*, Stephen Grosz.

My conversation with Stephen showed me there are two types of suffering: the pain we feel from experiencing loss and the pain we can inflict upon ourselves if we get stuck in a self-pitying state where we feel that we deserved a different outcome. Although we cannot avoid the first pain, with gratitude we can lessen the second.

He also expanded my understanding of loss. Before, when I heard the word, I thought about the people we mourn, the relationships we grieve for: a painfully tiny coffin, or unwanted divorce papers in a brown envelope. But Stephen invited me to think about the 'everydayness of loss': the tender melancholy that comes with letting go of significant places – schools, universities, jobs – as we seek out new adventures. Or the loss of a youth we leave behind to build an adult future. Rather than something we experience a handful of times, I learnt that loss is part of every day, and part of love too. In this way we practise moving through it all the time, without knowing it. Sometimes it is even wrapped up with good things – because in order to accept new pleasures and adventures into our lives, we must let go of the old, and make space for what is coming next.

Life is a series of necessary losses, with Stephen Grosz

NL: Why do you think we are afraid of accepting that loss is part of love?

SG: I'm not sure it is just fear that keeps us from accepting the necessary losses that love entails. Love is something we hear about from the moment we're born. Parents say to their children, 'I love you.' They tell their children stories about princes and princesses, fairy tales in which the beautiful couple 'live happily ever after'. And yet, all love comes to an end – if not during life, then with our death. For the most part, parents don't talk to their children about the loss love entails. Talking about loss is hard for us to do. And my experience is that when we talk about love – tell our children or ourselves about love – easy narratives drive out the hard ones.

To my way of thinking, life is a series of necessary losses. From the very start, there is loss. At birth, we lose the womb to have the world: the breast, our parents, our home. In time, we give up the intimacy of breastfeeding to have solid food – new flavours, new tastes. We let go of our home to go to nursery school, then school – we have new experiences, become attached to new people, places. We make friends. Eventually, we leave our childhood home to go to university or work. Later, with any luck, we let go of our birth family to make room for a new family of our own. Life requires of us that we let go of places, things, people that we love, to make room for new life, new love. Development demands loss – it's unbearable, we resist it, but if we are to grow, we must endure this pain.

Sometimes we want the new, and yet we can't let go of the old. A lot of my work as a psychoanalyst is helping people to accept these necessary losses. In *The Examined Life*, I quote a patient who once said to me – in complete innocence: 'I want to change, but not if it means changing.'

Do you think it would help to speak to children about loss as well as love?

During the thirty-five years I've practised as a psychoanalyst, some of my patients – most of whom are adults – have described to me conversations they've had with their children about loss. These conversations – about the death of a grandparent, a pet, or divorce, for example – are enormously important to both the parent and the child. For the most part, I am unfailingly impressed by how such conversations help the child to feel that they are not alone in their loss, that their feelings are being heard, understood – that what they feel, who they are, matters. Minimizing loss does not help; it belittles the child's experience. We help children by being with them in their grief; standing with them in their experience of loss.

Do you think, if you let the fear of loss direct your life, that could also mean cutting yourself off from love?

Yes. In my book, there is a case study entitled 'How Negativity Prevents Our Surrender to Love', in which I describe a woman who is warm, thoughtful and, to all appearances, keen to meet a man – and yet, inevitably, no one is right. Consciously, she wanted to find love, but unconsciously, love meant losing herself, her work, her family and friends; it meant being emptied out, neglected and possessed. Slowly, by recollecting some of her painful early losses, as well as the deep despair she suffered at the end of her first relationship, we began to make sense of her reluctance. She was involuntarily negative because emotional surrender and attachment represented a loss, not a gain. She could not love, because she could only see the loss that love entails. Her negativity was a reaction to her positive, affectionate feelings – it was a reaction to the prospect of love.

If you are in a relationship, as you both change, you have to let go of older versions of each other and of your relationship. Is that another form of everyday loss?

The psychotherapist Julia Samuel has said that during her forty-year marriage she's been married five times – she's making the point that during a marriage our partners change and we will too; consequently, we have to find ways of renegotiating, creating new marriages. I agree with her. I sometimes say: the best marriages – by which I mean the strongest, most resilient marriages – are remarriages to the same person. Strengthened by working through their difficulties, these couples rediscover or find new aspects to love in their partner, rather than seeking another.

In my clinical work, I've seen patients – more often men than women – who repeatedly marry and divorce; some, I suspect, would have been more content if they had simply remarried the person they were originally married to. Sometimes, for example, a man remarries a younger version of his first wife. The problem is not the first wife, but the husband's difficulties in understanding, accepting his feelings. If he could have seen himself, tolerated his ambivalence – as well as his wife's ambivalent feelings towards him – things might have been different.

Iris Murdoch once said that 'love is the extremely difficult realization that something other than oneself is real.' She's right – we achieve love by overcoming our narcissism. When, as teens, we begin having relationships, we tend to do so from within our own point of view; we experience our own feelings as authentic, while the feelings of the beloved have little reality. The capacity to love – the opposite of narcissism – is the capacity to see other people, their lives and feelings, as real; the capacity to love is the ability to separate this more objective picture of the beloved from the picture that is produced by our fears and desires.

Recently, a patient of mine described to me how, in the middle of an argument with his wife, he had the thought: good Lord, she's awful! But this thought was followed by the idea: wait a minute, I'm pretty awful too – I'm being horrid to her. She really has to put up with a lot from me. This moment of realization was an instance of him tolerating his ambivalence – and accepting her ambivalent feelings towards him – seeing her point of view. We have to hear, see, feel the beloved's reality. I think if we can endure these moments of ambivalence, hear what matters to the other person, we can begin to move towards a more loving relationship.

When you see patients who are grieving over the end of a relationship, how do you help them?

It is my view that the aim of psychoanalysis is not to help the patient – it is to understand. Understanding is the medicine in psychoanalysis. Directing a patient towards any specific aim is an intrusion on their autonomy – an attack on their power to identify their own desires, or decide their own mind. Guiding the patient, even towards some benefit, limits their therapy.

'Helping the patient' can disguise an unconscious wish in the therapist to limit the patient's freedom.

None of us gets to choose what we desire. We love in our own way; we grieve in our own way. Psychoanalysis creates the conditions for the patient to speak from the heart. The process has been described as one person speaking, two people listening – the psychoanalyst listens for the unheard, the disregarded, the ignored fact, thought or feeling. Understanding the 'thing beneath notice' helps.

Thinking of different ways that love and loss are linked, I wonder if being a parent is a journey of loss too?

Speaking to a student who was leaving her clinic to set up her own practice, Anna Freud once said, 'A mother's job is to be there to be left.' Although she wasn't a mother, she was also making a larger point – that if we've done a good job as a parent, our children will grow up – become him- or herself – and leave us to create new love and life. While this is true in principle, how painful, how bittersweet this loss is.

What do you wish you had known about love and loss?

The most powerful instrument to help us understand love is suffering. It is what allows us to have knowledge of our own hearts. In 1991, after the death of a close friend and the end of a long relationship, I read a collection of autobiographical essays by the writer Andre Dubus, *Broken Vessels*.

Driving from Boston to his home in Haverhill, Massachusetts, Dubus stopped to help a brother and sister, Luis and Luz Santiago. Their car had broken down in the middle of the highway. As Dubus helped Luz to the side of the road, an oncoming car swerved and hit them. Luis was killed instantly; Luz survived because Dubus had pushed her out of the way. Dubus was critically injured and both his legs were crushed. After a series of unsuccessful operations, his right leg was amputated above the knee, and he eventually lost the use of his left leg. For the rest of his life, he was in a wheelchair. Dubus was struggling financially, drinking and depressed; his wife left him, taking with her their two young daughters.

Dubus shares this experience in the title essay 'Broken Vessels'. A candid, honest, generous writer, he portrays himself as he is: heroic and frightened, thoughtful and bombastic, loving and cruel. *Broken Vessels* is about the journey of life – 'the transcendent and common bond of human suffering'. Dubus writes:

> [I learnt] above all, our bodies exist to perform the conditions of our spirits: our choices, our desires, our loves. My physical mobility and my little girls have been taken from me; but I remain. So my crippling is a daily living sculpture of certain truths; we receive and we lose, and we must try to achieve gratitude; and with that gratitude to embrace with whole hearts whatever of life that remains after the losses.

What I take from this stark version of what we have been discussing – this most extreme point of love and loss – is that even when everything we love is gone, there is relief in gratitude.

*

Both Melanie and Stephen had talked about the importance of gratitude after loss – Melanie found it through playing the Glad Game; Stephen found it while reading Dubus's words after the death of his friend. It's a beautiful idea on the page. But how difficult it is, to find any trace of gratitude in the early, raw weeks of grief. I thought about the reader who contacted me when her sister was killed in a senseless drunk-driving accident, and the mother who told me her son had died by suicide. How could they be expected to find gratitude in these moments?

Because before we are able to 'embrace with whole hearts whatever of life that remains after the losses', first we have to accept them. Although that might sound obvious, it is easy to wrestle with a painful truth – to deny it, to try to find a reason for it, to curse the universe for its existence. It's what I had been doing while googling 'reasons for miscarriage' in the late, lonely hours of the night, long after Dan had fallen asleep, hiding my phone light under the covers. It was a way of pretending I had a scrap of control in an uncontrollable situation. But no amount of love or effort could save a life, nor will one into existence. It could not save a child, or make a parent live another month, or fill the hole an absence left. If loss was a necessary part of life, as Stephen had told me, then acceptance was too. I needed to speak to somebody who had found it, despite a crushing fact.

*

New Yorker journalist and author Ariel Levy has experienced two losses she could not control: the death of her son and the end of her decade-long marriage, weeks later. The first loss happened in Mongolia, while she was reporting on a story there. Alone in a hotel bathroom, she gave birth to her son at nineteen weeks, before he died in her hands. In her extraordinary memoir, *The Rules Do Not Apply*, she acknowledged the sadness that seemed to be 'leaking out of every orifice'. She wrote about her son, 'I saw him under my closed eyelids like an imprint from the sun.'

In the midst of her grief, Ariel also fell in love. She met John – now her husband – in the hospital clinic in Mongolia, the last place she ever saw her baby. He was her doctor, the person who answered her questions about what had happened to her body. I wanted to ask her how it felt to meet him in such a painful moment.

Speaking to Ariel reminded me that we cannot write the stories of our lives, just as we cannot protect ourselves from suffering. At first, this seemed to contradict what I had learnt in earlier interviews; that love is an active experience we have influence over, rather than a passive one. My conversations about loss had proved the opposite was true too: we are not really in control of love – or life – at all. The task for anyone who wants to love, then, is noticing the difference. Because what we can control, as Ariel told me, is whether we choose to prioritize love, even in the face of a loss as seismic as the one she had lived through. Accepting it was not a linear, simple process. But her story shows there is peace in submitting to facts that cannot be changed, instead of wrestling against them, and then choosing to be present in the life that's left behind.

Accepting what you cannot control, with Ariel Levy

NL: What was your relationship to control before you experienced loss?

AL: I'm not a Type A personality. I didn't have control issues. I just had a fundamental, privileged, underlying sense that I could bend life to my will. If you've had a tough childhood you tend to figure out early on that things don't necessarily always go your way, but if nothing has ever gone wrong for you it's easy to believe that nothing ever will.

How did losing your son change your understanding of control?

The experience taught me on a very deep level: you will not always get what you want. You control nothing. And that, in addition to being heartbreaking, is liberating.

In Al-Anon alcohol support groups [designed to support family members of addicts] they say, 'Grant me the serenity to accept the things I cannot change; courage to change the things I can; and wisdom to know the difference.' It's enormously valuable to learn to accept the things you cannot change. The tricky part is having the wisdom to know the difference between the things you can and can't. I used to believe that, whenever possible, you should assume the rules do not apply and you should try to change them. The effect of this loss on me as a human being was to switch the emphasis more to: let's look at what I cannot change and work on acceptance. That's a life's work.

In what way was that liberating?

I'm not sure how much it had to do with the loss or how much it was linked to approaching middle age, but I suddenly realized, oh, I too am going to get old and die. The liberating part is that, when you understand you can't have whatever you want, it's easier to settle down. Not if what you can't have is food and shelter, obviously, but if your options have just become more limited, it's a little easier to get on with your life instead of always thinking about how to get the best out of it. Now I find it easier to say: 'This is my life.' I don't think, could I maximize what I've got? Could it be better? Could it be different? I'm like, no, this is it. This life is the one.

Did it affect the way you approached love too?

It made me realize that all you can control is what you do with love and whether or not you choose to prioritize it. To be honest, I did prioritize love in my first marriage, and then things went haywire because my spouse was an addict. Addiction is a game-changer because it is unfathomably uncontrollable. Living with someone who is enslaved by something as mysterious as addiction feels like a betrayal, like you are being abandoned, even though they can't help it. Eventually I learnt you can't control addiction either. And understanding that lack of control gave me a conceptual framework to accept both losses. Acceptance as a coping strategy had not occurred to me before.

Although understanding we are not in control can be painful, do you think it can be beautiful too, when life gives us something we might not have chosen ourselves? For example, falling in love with the doctor who treated you after losing your son in Mongolia. What did it feel like to fall in love in the midst of grief?

Starting on that intense emotional frequency is quite something; it's the opposite of going on a date in every way. For one thing, when we met I was sobbing and covered in blood. I remember feeling that what everybody else was seeing was a lie and what he had seen was the truth. To everybody else, I was childless; to him, I was a mother who had lost a child.

More significant than the actual meeting was that when we started to fall in love I was grieving my guts out. I ask him now: how did you know I was eventually going to be fun to be around? Because I was not in a fun place. He says I was intermittently myself and then I'd be grieving. At the time we lived on opposite sides of the world, so for years it wasn't a full-time relationship and I was still busy with my pain. But emailing John was a source of joy in the midst of that. Sometimes I think it's chance that it worked. Other times I wonder if there are ways in which it was a good way to meet someone, because when you are grieving you have no choice other than to be yourself. I'll never know another way. It's just what happened.

What I will say is that when John and I fell in love, it didn't make the end of my first marriage or losing a baby any less painful. Our relationship is a beautiful thing and I value it tremendously, but it didn't fix the other things. I had to get through those.

Some people think that love fixes everything – and it doesn't. You can use it as a distraction but it's not going to remove your suffering, ever, about anything, even in little ways. You might think, I'll be less anxious if I have a partner, but you won't be, unless you figure out how to do that by yourself. Just as having a partner is not going to solve your problems, it's not going to make you into someone else.

Do you think ultimately grief is something we have to move through on our own?

I do. Grief is isolating. You're in a tunnel of all-encompassing pain. Everybody else is walking through the world and you are living in an alternate reality within that world. Other people can't relate to you there. That said, grief is also too much to bear alone, which is why Jews sit Shiva [a week-long mourning period for family]. If you're lucky, people take care of you when you are grieving so that you can bear it. But no one can suffer through your grief for you. You do that alone.

When you emerged from that reality, did you see your day-to-day life differently?

You have more empathy for people in that state. You see them in that aching, vulnerable place and you realize it can be beautiful too, because they're defenceless, humbled. You can say to them, honestly, 'This too shall pass. You will wake up again without this reality.' Because when people first experience grief they wonder: is this the new me? For a while it is – but not for ever.

Initially grief is the context within which everything else occurs. Eventually that recedes and the loss is relegated to a different role in your head. At first you live in grief, then it lives in you. It took me a couple of years to come out of that tunnel where the baseline was intense pain. It wasn't just the loss of my baby; it was the loss of my first marriage, the loss of that youthful idea that 'everything's going to work out'. I had to confront a new, more painful reality.

After that you tried IVF, another experience where you are required to confront a lack of control. How did you know when you were ready to stop treatment?

Although I stopped because I ran out of money, I'm grateful that I did. Six times was enough. IVF is all-consuming and it takes over your life, logistically and emotionally. Every day you get your blood taken, you do the injections, and all those things are related to something you want in the deepest possible way. Every time it failed I went down that dark chute of loss, with a weird primitive yearning for this baby that never really existed. To me, emotionally and chemically, that felt like the loss of a child.

I know people who have gone on and on and on with IVF, who eventually got what they wanted. That's what's so tricky about it: you don't know what will happen. Maybe if you kept going it would work. But at a certain point I couldn't do it any more. I thought, I can't live like this. I want to enjoy my life, as it is. I want to be present in my relationship. I can't live in this deep state of craving any longer.

What do you wish you had known about loss?

That it's coming, for all of us. Some people are luckier than others, obviously, but everybody's going to have the rug pulled out from under them at some point. I don't think you can know that until it happens to you. Even though you know – in theory – that you are going to lose people, until you experience it it's hard to believe it. But loss is part of the deal. It's part of being a person. It's part of what it means to be alive.

*

My grandmother had been picking strawberries on a fruit farm. Her daughter, Louisa, was in a pram beside her. There are a lot of things I don't know about this moment. I don't know what sort of day it was, whether the sky was blue or grey, whether it was a fresh morning or a sticky afternoon. I don't know what my grandmother was wearing, if her fingers were stained with strawberry juice, if she screamed when the pram collapsed, who called for an ambulance, who rang my grandfather, how he tried to comfort her, how anyone did. Louisa – my dad's sister – had been playing with the pram when she pulled off the safety catch, causing it to collapse. She died at twenty months old.

The reason I don't know the details of this day is because it is a loss my grandmother never spoke about, one I never asked about. My auntie – who was there – does not want to talk about it, which I understand, and my dad – who was at school – does not remember much about the aftermath. I didn't even know he had had another sister until I was in my twenties, when he first told me, remembering how his mother had cried every day, for around two years. How he was nine at the time, and was sent to play at his mother's friend's house after school, because she was often sad in a way he didn't fully understand.

What I do know is that my grandmother wanted a certain cross on her daughter's grave, but the church wouldn't allow it, so they argued about it, and a local paper ran a story about the disagreement. Apparently my grandmother had little time for religion after that. I know, too, that my grandfather made sure there was an investigation of the pram company, and it resulted in them changing the design, protecting other babies from the same fate. When I learn this, I wonder if that was one way he could feel useful: by taking action, by doing something, controlling something. I wonder this, because I know it's the sort of thing my dad would do too.

I know that my grandmother received an anonymous letter, accusing her of negligence. I think of this as a low form of trolling, long before the Internet. I don't know why anyone would – how anyone could – write to a woman who had lost her child with mean words instead of kind ones. Had my grandmother blamed herself, reading that letter? I hope not. I hope she had a friend who tore it up, who pointed out that often people are cruel for reasons that have little to do with those they are cruel to.

My grandmother's generation had a different relationship to loss. Death was not discussed around the kitchen table. Perhaps grief was, to her, a private thing. Or perhaps she had conversations with certain friends, or with her husband, that I'll never know about. But I think about how different her experience might have been if she was grieving today: how she might have reached out to other women online who had lost young children, or attended bereavement support groups, or posted a photo of her daughter on Instagram once a year just because she wanted the world to know she existed. Of course grief is individual as well as universal – not everyone finds peace or solace in sharing. But so many of the people I had spoken to had, and these conversations made me sad to think that my grandmother hadn't had the same opportunity. They also made me feel lucky, to live in a time where grief *is* beginning to be discussed around the kitchen table, and in offices, in books, in supermarket aisles. I know the latter is true, because after my miscarriage my mother runs into an old friend in Waitrose. When she shares my story, her friend reveals that she had multiple miscarriages a decade ago, which she never told anyone about at the time. Back then, my mum said, 'We just didn't discuss those kind of things.' Through sharing my loss, my mum had unknowingly encouraged her friend to share hers. One act of openness inspired another.

By the time I was old enough to understand the intensity of my grandmother's loss, it seemed too late to broach it. I couldn't be sure if she had ever discussed it in detail with anyone, and it didn't feel like my place to take her back to the trauma without an invitation. Maybe she didn't let herself relive the loss. Maybe she still thought about holding her daughter in her arms every day. She died last year, so I will never know. When my dad cleared out her house I asked if he found a memory of Louisa in my grandmother's bedside drawer, a photo or a lock of hair. But instead, there were letters from me and my brother, which we had written to her when we were children.

I think about my grandmother's loss when my dad offers to buy me a buggy, because he wants it to be the safest one. I think about it again at her funeral, when the vicar said she'd had a daughter called Louisa 'who tragically passed away'. It feels strange to see her name in black ink on the order of service, this little girl so rarely mentioned but who existed once. I think about all the questions that I never asked my grandmother – not about her daughter's death, but about her life – and how I never said, 'I'm sorry.' I think about how when people die, they take their stories with them, unless we make time to ask about them.

*

I would never know how – or if – talking about her daughter might have helped my grandmother. But I wanted to discover how being open about grief had helped others – and might help us all. Because for the actor Greg Wise, discussing his sister's death has been essential. Clare died of cancer in 2016, after he moved in with her to be her full-time carer. In her last months, she didn't want anyone else around – only Greg, and from time to time the 'A-Team' girls (her four closest girlfriends). When I asked Greg why, he said it was probably a combination of reasons: 'a sense of "shame" when you're really ill; a sense that you're protecting folk by them not witnessing just how ill you are; an inability or just plain not wanting to have any "difficult" conversations; and the energy required to have a visitor'. This meant that, for three months, Greg was with her full-time, 24/7. The experience of caring for his dying sister convinced him that speaking about death 'is an act of love', and something we should all do more. Now, his relationship with Clare continues through their shared history and memories, in the places they spent time together and in constant conversations with those who knew her. He passes her memory through the generations of his family and, in this way, she lives on.

How he spoke about their relationship beyond physical life reminded me of something novelist Diana Evans once said to me: 'I do sense that there isn't an end to love and that people you love never really leave you. You never lose their love because it adds something to you.' It seems we go on loving people after they die because the love we shared with them changes us, becomes a living part of us, a piece of them we can never lose.

Speaking about death is an act of love, with Greg Wise

NL: How did losing your sister Clare change your understanding of love?

GW: Firstly, I want to say that I didn't lose her, she didn't pass – Clare died. You lose someone in a shopping centre. You pass someone on the motorway. We have to be clear about our vocabulary because, unless we use the appropriate words, we can't honestly explore this topic. My sister died but oddly the relationship didn't, it just changed. The constant resonance of that love is still around me. Initially I was unable to think of Clare as my happy, healthy sister, because I had spent so much time with her when she was sick. Now I can go back to that version of her and she's very present as a hearty, happy person in any dream I have about her. We still live on the same street she used to, and most days I walk past her flat and think of her. She is an inherent part of me: so many people I know I met through her, and all the extraordinary things we witnessed together are still inside me too. Someone said it takes two generations for a person to dissipate out of the conversation and the psyche of the group of people who had witnessed and been part of that life. I hope that my daughter, who is twenty, will live into her nineties and continue to tell stories about her Auntie Bobs, and then Clare will be alive in someone else's imagination.

What was your relationship like?

A lot of people said, 'I would never have moved in and cared for my dying sister,' or, 'God, my brother would never have done that for me.' We had a particularly odd, extraordinary relationship, perhaps because she had chosen not to go down the path of romantic relationships or kids. I suppose I was the primary male figure in her life that otherwise would have been a partner, and I am extraordinarily grateful to Em [Greg's wife, Emma Thompson] for understanding and respecting that. And for once in a while saying, 'No, come on, she needs to sort it out herself,' and then also, 'No, of course you have to go.' When we got to the point where Clare required full-time care there was no question that I would be the one who did it. Obviously it's fantastically fortunate that I don't have a 'proper' job and I was able to drop everything to be there.

How has her death changed you?

We are shaped by the death of the important people around us. Clare's death taught me that, although death is a foreign language to us, it's an essential one. Speaking about death is an act of love. After all those hours by her bedside, knowing she was dying, I'm a different person but a better one. It's similar to stretching yourself by climbing a mountain; once you are able to get past the strain of a situation like that you've tested who you are. We never know if we're the type of person who will run into a burning building to save a child until we find ourselves outside a burning building with a child in it. You can't say, 'I'd do it,' because you don't know. It turns out I was able to withstand that emotional trauma, and, as a result, I have become more empathic, more grateful, more present and more hopeful. All of those things came from that painful chunk of time, which otherwise would have been viewed as a bleak moment in my life.

How did it make you more hopeful? That's an interesting word to come from something so difficult.

Hopeful in terms of what can be asked of me. I always thought when I got a terminal diagnosis I would take myself off into the hills with a bottle of whisky and opt for the lovely hypo-thermic way out. I won't do that now, because I understand it would be cruel to those who love me. That doesn't mean I won't get to the point where I say, 'Stop, enough, I'm out of here,' but I know that spending those final months with my sister created an extraordinary relationship we never would have had otherwise. The day would be dark for twenty-three hours and fifty-eight minutes, then we would find tiny gems of joy, perhaps only ten or twenty seconds long. Clare waking up with a smile on her face. Or the little victory of us laugh-ing together in a moment of pain.

I'm more able to access those moments since her death too. Just after she died I was walking on the west coast of the High-lands and I saw a golden piece of bark with the sun behind it. I found another one a few weeks ago, a peel of silver-birch bark that was paper thin, lit up by the low winter sun. It's as if I've shed a carapace, and now something can stop me in my tracks, and I am able to really see it and to just *be*. I understand that life is finite in a way I didn't before. Also, when you're a full-time carer all you can do is be present. There's nothing else to do other than to be there.

When Clare was very sick, you were living with her and caring for her, and as a result spent a lot of time alone. What was that like?

I'm not hugely social and I'm fine with my own company. Still, I did go fucking mad. The harder part of being the only person there, without a support system, was the responsibil-ity, the focus, the calmness and the compassion which that required. The local hospice was wonderful. Whenever I went there to get the prescription for her meds they'd drag me into a room and say, 'And how are you?' I'd go, 'It's not about me,' and they'd say, 'Of course it's about you.' That is the bottom line: if the carer's fucked, the care is fucked. I don't know how much longer I would have been able to do it, actually, and I'm astounded by people who do this type of caring year after year after year. There will always be times when resilience or love is harder to find because you are drained and scared. Some days it was a victory to be able to wheel her to the loo, or to swing her legs out of the bed. There is a dark mirror between the help a baby and a person at the end of their life requires. And I think we need to give the same weight we give to birth to death. Kathryn Mannix [author of *With the End in Mind: Dying, Death and Wisdom in an Age of Denial*] once said we've got two days in our lives that are under twenty-four hours: the day we were born and the day we die; and we have to be able to concentrate as totally on the second day as we do on the first day. We have to have hard conversations, because everyone on this planet is going to die. We need to ask: how would I want to die? Then talk about it with family or write it down. It's that simple. We have to be a little more grown up about it.

And it's not just death we don't have a structure for, but perhaps grief too?

Grief is interesting because you have no control over it, which is why it's mad that the UK government website guidelines are two days' leave for the death of a parent or partner. Those early stages of grief are like vomiting. You feel it starting in your knees and then it comes through your body. I would say to anyone at that stage of grief, 'Don't judge it, don't stop it – welcome it. It's an important cleanse that's part of healing.' And I grew to understand that the grief I felt equalled the love.

We also need to find a way to ask for what we want in those moments. People require different things: some want to be held, some want to sit quietly with someone. I needed to be on my own. I took myself to our cottage in Scotland and stayed there for ten days, working on the land in the air and the rain and this incredible light. Being in that wild, open space was essential for me. I became more aware that we live in a cyclical world and that life, like nature, has seasons. To see the birth-death-decay cycle in nature made it all make sense. My sister's atoms are now flying out into the universe to be reconstituted into whatever they are going to be reconstituted into. In nature, I realized, you cannot have birth without death. If dead trees fall on the floor of the forest they become nurse trees that provide the medium for the new saplings to grow. The dead tree becomes the giver of all the nutrients those little saplings need to live.

How did witnessing Clare's illness at such close proximity change your own sense of mortality?

We are the maps of our experiences. Look at my hands; this is the story of my life. I can tell you where all the various bumps and holes and scars were formed. They make me *me*. Equally, the breaks in my heart make me *me*, and completely unlike anyone else on this planet. I wasn't too upset when our daughter ran up the garden path with a cut knee, because that is part of her story now, and in forty years' time she'll be saying, 'That's where I fell off the swing when I was three,' and that will create a family narrative. So my outward shape is a result of my physical injuries over the years, and my inward shape is a result of the emotional breaks, the early heartbreaks and the more recent deaths, like Clare. We're all textured by the gaping holes that are left by the death of people close to us. Gently, over time, the emptiness softens. It'll always be there in some description and it's essential to carry these things consciously around with you, the good and the bad. When they make Moroccan rugs they sew in equal amounts of black and red: their happiness and their misfortune. Life is the balance of that, and one would hope that we can enjoy the red a bit more because the black is there.

What do you wish you'd known about love and loss?

In love, that it doesn't have to be that much work. And in loss, if someone's died, don't send their partner flowers – send them a fucking cooked chicken.

*

Talking to Greg made me think about a writer called Joe Hammond, who I interviewed while he was dying of motor neurone disease. We spoke about how the knowledge that he was going to die had changed his understanding of life, and what matters most at the end of it. He told me that his physical vulnerability made him more open, more honest. That he had learnt to let people in, to admit difficult emotions to friends, to set aside his ego. But the answer that moved me the most was about his ability to extract pleasure from less since his diagnosis. Using eye-gaze technology, he wrote:

A few days ago, Tom, my now seven-year-old son, stopped his running and floating, just for a moment, and came to a halt next to my wheelchair. He leant his cheek into the soft outer part of my upper arm and touched my bony hand with his finger. He made a sound, half-way between a hum and a squeak. All this took place over about a one-and-a-half-second period. And then he sidled off.

In that moment, and in its afterglow, the pleasure and happiness I felt matched anything my able-bodied self ever felt. To feel joy, all that matters is the desire. I can imagine the joy someone incarcerated might feel, should a solitary ant crawl through the brickwork, into their cell. A lot can be extracted from less.

I read his answer many times, trying to hang it permanently somewhere in my mind, like a poster on a bedroom wall that I could stare at and memorize every night before sleep. I thought of it again when Greg described the luminous details he accessed more easily since his sister's cancer – the victory of laughter on a bleak day; the silver-birch bark lit up by the low winter sun. *A lot can be extracted from less.* Because that is what Greg was saying too: spending a little time in death's company had made him more attuned to small shimmers of meaning.

When I interviewed Susie Orbach for a story I was working on, she told me that, as a society, unless we've been unlucky enough to have had somebody die young, we are now unused to the notion of death. People live longer, often with people of the same age – maybe a partner or children, rather than older generations – which means we exist further away from it. But Greg showed that there is much to gain from letting death back into our lives, both on a practical level (to understand how a family member might want to die) and on an emotional one (to foster hope, gratitude and resilience). We might avoid talking about death because we can't bear to think about losing the people we love, when actually, *not* talking about it is one of the reasons we can take them for granted every day. Perhaps by facing the truth – that, if we're lucky, we get to exist alongside them in this world for decades, not centuries – we will remember to look into their faces more than our phone screens.

*

We are, as Greg said, shaped and forever altered by the death of the important people around us. In the past, when I've considered how I might be changed by the loss of someone close to me, I've always thought of the negatives. The things I would be bad at doing on my own if Dan wasn't there – deciding how long to cook a piece of meat; keeping plants alive – or how sadness might burst in when something funny happened and I couldn't share it. Or when I held a saucepan handle that he had held and could no longer remember how warm his hands always were. I'd dwelt on these holes an absence would leave. I hadn't given any thought to the positive impact we have on each other, all the enduring traces of goodness we keep and learn from. How, even after we die, we are alive inside each other.

These unwanted gifts we receive from our losses offer little compensation. If we could return our loved ones and undo the heartbreak, of course we would. But I wanted to speak to someone who had been able to see clearly how knowing and loving someone had changed the direction of their life in a beautiful way, even after they were physically gone.

The journalist Gary Younge's mother, who died when he was nineteen, did exactly that. The impact she left on him exists in every decision he makes, from what to order at a restaurant to his next career move. Her death was the worst thing to ever happen to him. And yet it has also been his guide, encouraging him to pursue experience over wealth accumulation, and to prioritize present happiness over delayed gratification.

The unexpected gifts of loss, with Gary Younge

NL: What was your relationship with your mother like when you were a teenager?

GY: It went through a few iterations. She was a dominant, strict character, so we weren't mates when I was younger. It was more, 'Do as I say.' I was also the youngest, so my brothers slowly left home until it was just me and her. The turning point in our relationship came when I went to Sudan at seventeen to work in a UNHCR refugee school. I remember her insisting I took condoms, and I thought, urgh, that is horrible! (She put them in my suitcase anyway.)

When you're a teenager you're solipsistic, you often don't care about anyone else, so spending a year in a place where I had a lot of time to myself gave me time to think about what my mum had done for us as a single mum. (My dad left when I was one, so she raised us on her own.) That trip transformed our relationship, and when I came back, we were friends. I liked spending time with her. That was lucky, because she died two years later. In a way that you often don't, I absolutely got to tell her what I thought about her, even in my garbled teenage sense. I got to engage with her in a loving and more mature way than I would have done. I feel very blessed about that.

How did the suddenness of her death change your view of life?

It's difficult to know, because it's counterfactual; she never died any other way. Aren't all deaths that way? You'll never know if it would have been harder or easier if the circumstances had been different. But she was forty-four, and it was sudden. She was supposed to come up to Edinburgh, where I was at university, but the day before she took the bus to do the weekly shop, came home and died in her sleep. My lecturer told me the news and I could not take in the words. Her death left me rudderless. For a while, it also left me without a home base. The first Christmas my eldest brother kindly invited me to his house in London. After that, I spent Christmas in Edinburgh. But it wasn't home, it was where I was living in a liminal state, as you often do at university. So I was losing my grip on what it meant to have a home, just going through the motions of my life. I remember there was one bus route I took to get to university that would go over the Mound in Edinburgh. On a clear day you could see a beautiful scene of houses by the water. Every time I took that bus I looked out the window at that point and thought, I don't know what I'm doing here. This place has got nothing to do with me. Not that it couldn't have, but it didn't at that time, when I was grieving.

When did you begin to see the unexpected gifts that came with your loss?

The next year of university was a struggle and I didn't think that losing her had taught me anything. It hadn't yet, because her death didn't come with instant knowledge; I only knew that it was the most devastating event of my life. Its lessons came slowly and gradually, through experience. The most important was an acute awareness of my mortality. The understanding that no one's going to find a good life for you, you have to find it for yourself. You have to live it to the best of your ability, to the best of your knowledge. It's finite. And it can either be full of your joy, or there can be no joy at all – that's up to you.

That awareness was different from thinking you can die at any time in an anxious way; I never felt that. It's true, you can die at any time, but I've never felt my life was in immediate danger, just that it was always in danger, so I had better get on with living it. That attitude meant I refused to take a boring job, or make a decision I really didn't want to, just because it might give me enough money to do something interesting in the future. I had no time for deferred gratification. That wasted time in the present suddenly seemed too harsh a payment. It wasn't about thinking 'live fast, die young', it was more that I knew what I wanted – to be happy, fulfilled and free – and I wasn't willing to do things that weren't in pursuit of that. I became ambitious on my own terms. Obviously we all have to do things that we don't want to, but the notion that you should take a job you hate because it will make your life better years from now? It no longer made sense to me.

How does that lesson direct your life now?

It never left me. It is in the small things – like the decision to order the lobster – and the big things – like leaving my job as a columnist at the *Guardian* after twenty-six years to become an academic. That was entirely informed by that lesson. I thought, I don't want to die doing this, I want to die somewhere else. People still ask why I left, and my answer to them would be: well, if I don't want to do it, it doesn't make sense to waste any remaining years of my life on it, does it? That attitude has worked out well for me, an unlikely class-shifting dude who went from the working class into the middle class. I would often say to myself, 'What's the worst thing that can happen?' I said it so many times until I no longer needed to. Because the worst thing that could happen to me already had – my mum had died – and so that left me with a calculated sense of fearlessness. It gave me a yardstick I would use to make decisions. A lot of the time when you are making a decision you know what the answer is, you just need the courage to follow through on what you already know to be right. My mum gave me that courage, in both her life and her death.

How do you balance that understanding with a need for financial security?

That balance is important. Because when my mum died I was nineteen, and I had to be self-sufficient. Budgeting wasn't an exercise for getting older; if I didn't start then, I wasn't going to be able to eat. That financial insecurity was always there because we grew up poor, but her death amplified it. So there is an element of me that is still cautious when it comes to important things, like paying off a mortgage. But what losing my mum taught me is that I'm interested in experience, not wealth accumulation. I'm interested in surviving, in going on holiday, in having all the things I need to give my kids a safe life. But I'm not interested in saving for material things, because I know that when you die, you cannot take those things with you. And if you're always buying things, always looking to expand what you have, you're never content. I rarely see people chase wealth and become happier. It's not that material things mean nothing to me – I want financial security for my family – it's that they're the means to an end, and that end is a life. That was cemented in that moment when my mum died. I saw that the real value of her life was the impact she made and left on people.

Did her death change your approach to love too?

In the beginning, it made me defensive and bristly. I remember thinking, I'm alone in the world, I have to protect myself, I don't have the capacity to be fragile. And that's not the ideal psychological equipment to go into a relationship with.

I wasn't worried about other people I loved dying simply because she had, but I didn't want flaky people around me. My approach to dating was: if you're going to crumble at the first sign of gunfire, keep walking. If I was going to have a partner, they needed to be robust and secure and hardened. Which I guess meant I was always holding back a bit in love. I was not an easy person to be with. But it also meant I had limited tolerance for toxic relationships. The other thing was that I was busy throwing myself into life, and love was a part of life, but it wasn't all of it.

What do you wish you'd known about love and loss?

That grief evens out. I used to mark the anniversary of my mum's death, and her birthday, but I don't always now. Those milestones go as the grief spreads out over your consciousness. In the beginning it's a big leaden thing you carry around with you wherever you go. You're always aware of the weight of it. And then, as the years pass, that weight spreads throughout your life. You don't carry it any more, it just exists inside you. My mum now has a place in me.

*

By the time I spoke to Gary I saw that there was a theme running through my conversations: the problem of always wanting more. Esther Perel spoke about the consumer mentality that makes us think 'I can do better' in relationships; Ayisha Malik talked about how we are so busy chasing external things that we lose sight of who we are; and Emily Nagoski said that one reason we prioritize spontaneous desire might be because capitalism requires us to remain in a state of wanting. This constant state of craving is another enemy of love. It makes us forget that the real value of our life is the impact we have on people, like the impact Gary's mother had on him.

*

A few years ago, the magazine I work at published a letter from a reader responding to a piece about divorce. She had written in to say that her divorce felt worse than a death. She had to mourn the husband she had lost *and* the life that they had built together, which was now distorted. If her husband had died, she reasoned, at least she would be comforted by the love she had for him and he had for her. She could remember their relationship fondly, her memories unstained by rejection.

After we published that letter, we received an email complaint from another reader. This reader was appalled by the implication that divorce could be worse than death. Her husband had died; she longed for him to be alive. She was offended that anyone could compare her loss to one which did not involve death.

I understood both women's perspectives, but grief is not a game of higher or lower. We cannot line up our losses alongside each other and expect someone to confirm whose is worst. I know I have felt utterly broken after the end of a three-month relationship, and only mildly sad after a two-and-a-half-year one finished. I know that for my dad losing his dog was as devastating as losing a family member. I know friends who found the early days of parenthood more painful than their miscarriage, and others who found watching their parents grow old more difficult than watching them die. Heartbreak is too tailored and too sprawling for comparison to be of use to anyone.

The author Lisa Taddeo believes that when we compare and judge people's pain in this way, we hurt each other unnecessarily, often because of our own shame. It's why she followed the sexual and emotional lives of three women for eight years in her extraordinary, bestselling debut *Three Women*. As much as it is about sexual desire, it is a book about the way women judge each other, and the ripples of pain that causes.

In stories of loss, it's tempting to search for easier endings, in which grief grows lighter over time. But although Gary feels that his grief evened out over the years, Lisa does not. Since her parents died two decades ago – her father in a car accident, her mother from lung cancer five years later – she lives with a fear of losing people. With her, I wanted to explore the loneliness and intensity of a grief that doesn't relent, so that we might try to understand how it feels to live inside it. One thing became clear: because Lisa knows the isolation of grief so intimately, she does not want anyone else to feel as alone in it as she has. It is this longing that drives her to connect with people in pain, to share their stories. And although she still has not accepted her parents' death, this ability to reach out into the heart of another's suffering felt, to me, like an act of hope.

The loneliness of loss, with Lisa Taddeo

NL: Your parents died nearly two decades ago. How has your grief changed shape over time, and what is your relationship to it like today?

LT: My husband says I still haven't accepted my parents' death, which is true. Some people handle it better. I'm not saying that handling it better means that they are better than me, just that some people are able to process it more easily. Often people get over a loss, to the point where they look back at someone in pain and they're not able to identify with their suffering. I think that's why I've often felt alone in my loss. Plus, my identity was linked to being my father's daughter, so having that taken away left me floundering, unsure of who I was. When he died, the person I was up until then died too.

His death reshaped me. In short, I became less happy, more cynical.

How did that early loss change the way you approached love and relationships?

I think sometimes you look for the parts of yourself you've lost in a relationship. I was twenty-three when my father died, and it was almost impossible for me to think about anything else. I would wake up in the night screaming. Then when I went back to work, I started flirting with a guy in another office cubicle over G Chat. At the time I had a boyfriend of seven years, who I had neglected in the wake of my father's death. Although nothing happened with the guy at work, the excitement and newness of that was an escape.

At first I was in so much pain that I wanted to keep some-one around, a human body I could count on. But eventually, that little crush at work made me think, I don't want to do this any more, and I broke up with my boyfriend. Being interested in someone new made me realize how fake the other rela-tionship was. It saved me, in a way. In the wake of tragedy, sometimes desire is a bomb that can't be denied. Fresh loss is like defogging your eyeglasses.

Do you think, as well as a distraction, desire can feel like the opposite of loss? Perhaps through it we try to remind ourselves what it feels like to be alive?

Yes, completely. When you're in a world of grief you exist in that world. You're not connected to the place where everyone else is living. Moving through that darkness is so painful that you're looking for something – anything – that can pull you back to a happier world.

Did losing both of your parents change what you were drawn to in a partner?

Almost instantly, losing my father changed the way I looked at love and what I needed from it. It made me look for a man who had good parents, to fill that hole, and I stopped liking a lot of the men I dated in my twenties because they did not measure up to my father. I also lived alongside a fear of someone else leaving me. So I pretended I didn't need anything from anyone, because actually I needed so much that I was afraid somebody would see right through me.

Even today, I do this terrible thing – which I hope I stop doing – of putting a lot of my need to be cared for on to my partner. I want him to care for me in the same way my father did. For example, my father always filled my car with gasoline. Now if my tank is close to empty, I think, why didn't he fill it?

What was it like to watch your mother deal with her grief after your father's death? How did you manage your own grief and hers too?

It was awful, because my mum didn't drive, she didn't write cheques. She relied on my father for everything. She moved to America from Italy when she was twenty-six, had my brother, and stayed at home learning English from TV shows. At night my dad would take her discount store shopping, and that's all she liked to do. She was content and they had a lovely relationship, but when he died, it was as if she had nothing left.

After his death I moved home and took on my father's role, dealing with my own loss alongside hers. I remember I started working at *Golf Magazine* and did a story on a tournament in Avignon, in France, in the middle of spring. We stayed at a hotel with beautiful flowers and I'd never seen anything so pretty. I said, 'Mummy, look, it's so beautiful.' And she said nothing, because nothing could break through her grief. When we got home, she said, 'In retrospect that was really beautiful.' I understood why she had been unable to say that sooner, but it was hard to watch her move through life that way. It was as if she didn't want to live any more.

I think watching a parent experience grief can be scary, because it's the moment you realize they are human and fragile.

I never got to see my father as human, but I saw my mother become crippled by grief. I wonder, all the time, what would have happened if he had died second? How would he have dealt with it? I imagine he would have put a lot of focus on making sure that I was OK, whereas my mum just couldn't function, so the care-taking was flipped. I don't remember ever feeling taken care of after my father's death. I've never thought about that before, but I wonder if that is part of the reason his loss felled me in such a horrible way.

Do you still think about how your father would react to things happening in your life today?

My husband and I were talking about that last night. I asked, 'Do you think my dad would be proud of me?' and he said, 'Yes.' I think about that every day, mainly about the fact that

I have a husband and a daughter who my parents will never meet. That's brutal.

Do you think your losses are linked to your curiosity about other people's stories?

A hundred per cent. When my father died, I thought, I don't want anybody else to feel this pain. That feeling continued for years; it's still there. It's why I didn't want the women I interviewed for my book to be alone in their pain, because I know that aloneness in grief is the worst place to be.

I think when something bad happens to you, you ask yourself: how do I take what I've learnt from suffering into the world in a positive way, instead of sitting in the dark? For me, it's partly selfish. It felt good to sit and listen to someone, to disappear into their thoughts and not to be left with my own. It is helpful and healing to try to help others.

One way you've helped me is by sharing what you did about becoming obsessed with trying to conceive after your miscarriage in the first conversation we had. Hearing how much that affected you made me think, perhaps I'm not crazy!

I wasn't even sure I wanted kids before I miscarried, but as soon as I experienced that loss it felt insane to have ever considered not wanting a baby. The cruellest thing about a miscarriage is that people can't comprehend your pain. If someone's lost a cat, but the cat was the most important thing in their world, to me that needs to be taken seriously – that's as important as someone else's loss of a person. It's weird that people police grief and decide whose loss necessitates more care. Actually,

I don't think that deep loss after a miscarriage ever goes away. My husband doesn't understand why I still think about it, even now that we have a child.

What do you wish you'd known about love and loss?

I am still a walking ball of fear and I try not to lose people at every turn. But if I have learnt anything, it's that admitting you're in pain is part of how people should heal and be kind to one another. Being judgemental of someone else's pain seems bizarre to me. And often, judgement is just shame or jealousy in disguise.

*

Lisa reminded me that, as much as loss could deepen love and create meaning, it was still an ugly, ruthless thing. Because we lose more than people: Lisa lost her father, then she lost her identity; Gary lost his mother, then he lost a sense of home. First, we experience the griefs themselves, then the echoes of loss that follow them.

One particularly painful echo of loss is loneliness. The feeling that everyone else lives in a different, happier world, and you are stuck outside its window, looking in, unable to participate. But this, at least, is one facet of loss we have power over. Although no one can fix our grief, as Lisa showed me, admitting to each other that we are in pain is how we begin to heal.

*

I remember exactly where I was when I finished *When Breath Becomes Air*: on a train in Brescia in northern Italy. Dan was asleep, his head on my shoulder. As I watched him, I wondered: how many years would we get together? I silently promised to put love first in all of them, because I thought the book's lesson was that love was the most important thing in a life. It wasn't until I spoke to the author's wife, Dr Lucy Kalanithi, that I understood I had missed its full meaning.

When Breath Becomes Air is a memoir about life and death, written by American neurosurgeon Paul Kalanithi while he was dying from inoperable lung cancer. It sold over a million copies worldwide – Lucy oversaw its publication after Paul died, aged thirty-six. The experience of watching him die required her to hold death and life and love in her mind simultaneously. But Paul's book is about more than love. It is about 'relentlessly striving for something meaningful . . . and the journey to understand human suffering'. Because, as Lucy went on to say, in the end, love is not the only thing that matters.

When she told me that, I felt something I had many times during these conversations: the confusing but satisfying realignment of a thought. I felt it again when Greg Wise told me we don't lose people when they die. And again when Heather Havrilesky and Ariel Levy told me they had started their relationships over email, despite having previously thought it was not a good way to begin a romance. Every time I formed a firm opinion, another answer reshaped it. This process was a lesson in itself: however many conversations on love I had, I would never find a fixed set of responses to its challenges. As Barbara Kingsolver wrote, 'Everything you're sure is right can be wrong in another place.' It was humbling, reassuring even, to realize that the answer would always change, depending on where I was standing in the length of my life.

One thing that wouldn't change, though, was the importance of intention in love. I saw this clearly when Lucy described how Paul's death has changed the goals she has for her daughter. Instead of focusing on Cady's achievements, Lucy hopes for her to have love and connection in her life. This answer stood out, because I hadn't heard those words talked about as goals before. Goals were things filled out in an annual review at work, or resolutions made on 1st January to achieve more that year (pass a driving test; ask for a pay rise). I had never set a goal to see an old friend four times a year instead of two, or to finally invite the upstairs neighbours down for a drink, or to call my Auntie Julia who I loved speaking to but only ever saw at Christmas. How different life might be, I thought, if we made goals like these, to connect rather than to achieve.

These goals don't have to be for obvious forms of connection, either. When Lucy told me that our conversation would carry her through the rest of the day, I felt the same. Because trying to make sense of something meaningful, or taking the time to really listen to someone's story – even a stranger's – can change the direction of your day. It's another thing to be grateful for, and it's easy to miss, this way we can reach each other, and how it feels when we do.

What matters in the end, with Lucy Kalanithi

NL: How has the love you had for Paul continued to play a role in your life since his death?

LK: One of the first things that comes to mind is this C. S. Lewis quote: 'Bereavement is not the truncation of married love, but one of its regular phases . . . What we want is to live our marriage well and faithfully through that phase too.' After Paul died, I thought, oh my God, yes, this marriage is not over. Paul is my family and he's Cady's dad. I didn't break up with him. I still love him. That's not to say we're still married in a way which means I can't fall in love again. But everybody understands that if your child dies and you have another, you don't stop loving the first one. And my situation is similar when I date again – it's like being in love with two people at once.

How do you bring Paul's memory into your and your daughter's everyday life?

We go to his grave together twice a month. I love it there. Yesterday we drove through the town we used to live in, and I suddenly felt close to Paul. I was sad, too, because new restaurants had replaced the ones we used to go to on date nights. I felt a deep hate for those new restaurants. Then when I reached one of the old ones we used to visit that was still open, I kissed the air in that direction. I did that recently when I saw Paul's photo on a new edition of his book; I reflexively lifted my chin and kissed the air upward towards him. It's not a conscious thought, I just do it in situations where it feels like Paul is suddenly there: in a picture, or a memory, or a moment when I'm driving past a restaurant. Whenever I have a visceral feeling of wanting to touch him, instead I kiss the air.

There are also pictures of him in our house, and I talk about him to Cady, who is five and a half now, especially to point out the ways he's similar to her. For instance, when she wants to take a very hot bath or shower, I'll say, 'That's just like Daddy; he wanted to be so hot in the water.' I do that partly because it might be important to her at some point to understand ways in which she's like him, and partly to teach her that it is OK to talk about him. That he did exist. That he was the first person who held her.

She was eight months old when he died, and sometimes she's sad that she doesn't have any memories of him. I say, 'Sometimes you don't remember something, but you remember how it made you feel. So when you think about Daddy, if you have a cosy feeling, that is a way of you remembering him.' That seems to make sense to her.

In the final months of Paul's life, how did your love change?

It became bigger. Paul and I had been going through a hard period in our marriage, because of a lack of time and work stress. After he got diagnosed, my love for him became more unconditional. I'm not saying marital love should be unconditional – obviously there are always conditions on it in some sense – but I saw Paul with a spaciousness and a lack of resentment in a way that I hadn't before.

Mundane things melt away in the face of a serious diagnosis. There's more room for important things to take up space in your mind. I also think time changes. Obviously we knew Paul didn't have a lot of time; he had months to a few years to live when we were in that period (he ended up living twenty-two months). Suddenly, we had that knowledge and time collapsed. It felt like we were holding hands in the past and the present and the future, all at once. We knew his life was going to end, but that the truth of our love and life would not, and that, even though our time together would stop, in another sense it would never end.

Life also turns technicolour, because you're noticing it so intensely. I didn't have to remind myself to pay attention, because it was as if the only moment that existed was the present one, which felt like all moments put together. When someone's dying, time goes away and your life and your love and your relationships are there all at once, in that hospital room, in those minutes. Moments like that become part of your memory. They open up your heart in a new way.

Has that influenced the way you parent your daughter? Because for a lot of parents it can be a struggle to be present.

Yes, although being present is something I still struggle with, because sometimes parenting can be tedious. But I do have more perspective, and now, when I think about the future I want for her, it's more about wanting a meaningful life for her, not a lack of suffering – wanting her to feel resilient rather than just protected. And losing Paul reinforced for me how important love and connection are, that they're important life goals. It's important to me that Cady has those things in her life.

What has the experience of losing Paul taught you about what matters most at the end of a life?

I don't think that love is the only thing that matters. My favourite version of the meaning of life is what Viktor Frankl wrote on the topic. He says there are three sources of meaning: love (for humans and for experiences, like a sunset), purposeful work (what you're trying to do in and for the world), and the courage you find in the face of difficulty. It's not just about sitting around loving each other; the way you respond to unavoidable suffering is also a source of meaning. That resonates with me. And when Paul was dying and writing his book, trying to wrestle with the idea of mortality, he was doing the third thing: trying to make sense of human and personal suffering. Some people read *When Breath Becomes Air* and say, 'This book made me be more present in my life and made me understand that relationships are the most important thing.' And I think, no, Paul's book is also about relentlessly striving for something that's meaningful, which, for him, was medicine, and the journey to understand human suffering.

Do you think accepting that suffering is part of not just life, but love, can help us to live more meaningfully?

I do. There are two parts to it: understanding that the people you love will suffer and also that you will be there, holding their hand, and that is an important part of loving them. It's part of the deal. It's why it's brave and beautiful to love somebody.

Is there anything that can make loss easier for us to move through? Should we change the way we talk about death?

In medicine, it helps to acknowledge that you can do a lot for somebody even if you can't fix the problem. There's an essay by a doctor, Diane E. Meier, called 'I Don't Want Jenny to Think I'm Abandoning Her', which talks about how sometimes we doctors use treatments, even relentless chemotherapy, as a way to show love to our patients. But how we learn over time that just sitting with people when they're suffering, or visiting them when they're dying, is a love that patients often want. You don't always have to do something – you can just sit there. When someone's sick, people are afraid that doing that means giving up on somebody, and it doesn't. As a doctor, it's something I think about a lot: healing is different from fixing. When your family member or friend is sick, you do want to fix it, and you hardly want to say anything if you can't. But I think when you're the sick person, you want someone to witness what is happening to you. Witnessing *is* a treatment and a form of love. And you can do it, no matter what.

Losing Paul, you've said, was also a loss of identity for you. How did you begin to rebuild that?

Some of that is tied up in loneliness and purpose. I had been so focused on Paul during his illness, so when he died that section of my life went away, and so did the connection. At the time it felt like a vacuum – not like other things weren't there, but suddenly there was so much space. I had to get used to it, and then fill it back in.

Paul's book helped. And obviously I was a doctor and had a small child. Now my daughter is the person I'm here for. But so much of my life disappeared, and that felt like whiplash. When someone dies you are the same person you were five minutes ago, but suddenly you're a different person too, because your future self is no longer there. At the same time, I do think there's an essential self, and it's worthwhile to realize that we are still ourselves, even with no future. But it takes a second to remember that.

Did you have to relearn how to be on your own?

I remember it being so lonely, especially at night. My mum said, 'You'll get used to it,' and I thought, I don't even want to get used to it. A) That's impossible and B) Why would I want to get used to this? I don't think I got used to it, I just understood that you can generate your own heat and that, even when I'm alone, I will always have my love for Paul. If you have those other forms of meaning – connection, purpose (my work as a doctor) and personal reflection about suffering – at a certain point you realize: oh, I have meaning in my life and I know myself. I'm standing on solid rock, not floating. Now I have many forms of connection: to Cady, to family and friends, to co-workers and patients. Even a conversation like this feels like it's connection and purpose and a chance to make sense of suffering, all at once.

The third source of meaning – persisting despite suffering – is very important to me. I don't think that suffering makes you stronger or that we should all suffer. I think suffering creates room for connection, because you see everybody else's pain and you connect to people in a deeper way.

What do you wish you'd known about love?

I used to think the kiss was the most romantic part of a wedding. Now I listen to the vows and think, oh my gosh, you have no idea what's coming. The best-case scenario is that you'll still be together when one of you dies. What you're

really promising is to see each other through difficult times —
in sickness and in health. It's very romantic to me that what
you're signing up for are all of those hard things: the work of
long-term love, the inevitable loss, the decision not to leave
when things get tough, the beauty of suffering together. The
romance is actually in the hard part, not in the kiss.

A Leap of Faith

*'Do not now strive to uncover answers: they
cannot be given to you because you have not been
able to live them. And what matters is to live
everything.* Live *the questions for now.'*
(*Rainer Maria Rilke,* Letters
to a Young Poet)

In February of 2020, I discover I am pregnant. I sit on the loo
and there they are: two blue lines on a test, a possibility, the
start of something. I send Dan a photo of the result and a message that says, 'Buckle up!' The lightness of those two words
is a charade. I am saying to him – and to myself – be happy,
yes, but be prepared this time.

I was still wary of hope. Trying to conceive had taught me
faith was a burden: all those tortuous 'what ifs?' and 'maybes',
all the fractures in your heart that appear each time your optimism is proven wrong. I thought it would be easier to hope
if we had a little evidence, but being pregnant after a miscarriage feels like driving down a road that I have driven down
before. Last time pregnancy ended with a dead-end, and yet
people are asking me to drive down the exact same road, in the
exact same car, and somehow believe that it will take me to a
different place. I want to believe in an alternative destination,
so desperately, and I am grateful to even have the chance to

try, but I cannot force my heart to open so easily. Wouldn't disappointment hurt less if I never truly believed in a happy outcome in the first place?

A few weeks later, I wonder if Dan might be holding back too. I notice he never puts his hand on my stomach in bed at night, like he used to during the first pregnancy. One evening I ask why. 'I think this time,' he says, 'I will after the twelve-week scan.' I understand, for the same reason I have not dared to place my own hand on my stomach. Neither of us wants to believe in someone who might never come to exist, or to build and bend our lives around a question mark. At the time this seems a sensible strategy. Still, I mourn the excited parents-to-be we were first time around: so trusting, so certain; so happy to walk through galleries together, pointing to the names of paint-ers, discussing whether they might make a good name for a boy or a girl. How naive, I think, but I long for their ignorance too. There is no satisfaction in knowing more than they did.

Even when we see a galloping heartbeat on a screen at eight weeks, we continue to emotionally tiptoe around the pregnancy, careful not to connect with the life growing inside me. We do not give it a nickname. We do not tell our families. We do not discuss what sort of person he or she might turn out to be. We have too much love stored up, on hold from last time, and if we hang it on the idea of another baby it will be painful to take it down again. Don't all of us feel this way at times? People die. Hearts break. We love and we lose. And then we have to summon the courage to reckon with our losses and get back up, knowing there is no assurance we won't get knocked down again. I am even reluctant to commit this preg-nancy to words. As I write, I wonder: by the time this book is in your hands, will I have a baby with a name and a Jellycat toy bunny? Or will I have an awkward conversation with anyone who reads this chapter, about another child's future that only ever existed in my mind? I tell you this anyway, holding my breath, because I think it shows how easily we forget the lessons we learn about love, and how the task – for us all – is to keep learning them, day after day after day, even when experience distracts us. Because I was distracted by my future fears – and I succumbed to them. I was trying to achieve the impossible: to stop something that might not happen.

The problem with this cautious approach to pregnancy was similar to one I'd encountered wrapping Christmas presents a few months before. As I ran the green silk ribbon through my fingers, I worried I didn't have enough. I was careful not to use too much. But I was so concerned about running out of ribbon that I cut it too short, and it wasn't long enough to wrap around the present and tie in a bow. My fear of wasting too much ribbon meant that I had wasted it all, just as my fear of believing in this pregnancy meant that I had wasted small opportunities for love over the past months: the excited look on my mum's face; the butterflies inside my stomach; a tiny, defiant heart that seemed to say with every beat, 'I'm here, I'm here, I'm here.' Sometimes, I realized, we lose more from fear itself than the thing we are afraid of.

It is often the little things that bring us back to ourselves. A song lyric. The right sentence read at the right time. A handful of words from a loving friend. For me, it was this advice Melanie Reid gave: you mustn't 'choke on your own desires', she said, but 'slowly learn that hope should never die, whatever the outcome'. When she revealed it was her false hope that she would learn to walk again that helped her to survive after her accident, I understood that it was not about being proven right or wrong, but hoping either way. It is that inner glimmer of belief that guides us through the blackness of uncertainty. I still didn't know if my baby would live; there could be no Magic 8-Ball to ease my anxieties. All I knew was I didn't want to let my fear of loss drain any more colour from my life. Enough had been wasted.

None of us can protect ourselves from tomorrow, the next day, the next month, the next year. All we can do is try our best not to squander love on a fear of something that might or might not happen. (When I interviewed Lady Antonia Fraser for the newsletter, she told me she calls this the Great Fear, which for her meant dreading her late husband Harold Pinter's death before it happened. Now she wishes she hadn't spent a single precious minute of his life fearing it would end before it did.) I try very hard to remember this when, three days into my tenth week of pregnancy, around the same time I miscarried before, I go to the loo at work and see a familiar sight: blood in my knickers, as sudden and urgent as a shriek. I close the loo lid and sit down on it for a few minutes. I shut my eyes, tilt my head up to the ceiling and pray for my baby to live. I also realize then what had been obvious all along: I would miscarry or I wouldn't. Those were the facts. There was peace in the randomness of that and I gave myself over to it. There and then, I resigned my attempts at self-protection and decided to love a possibility, whatever happened. I said in my mind, to my baby, 'It's OK if you don't make it.'

Everything about that day seems to be a repeat run – I take the same Tube, go to the same hospital, take a urine pot from the same receptionist, stare at the same buttercup-yellow waiting-room walls. Although the people are different, they clutch the same Costa paper cups from the hospital canteen, speak in the same sad, hushed voices. Time stalls. I wait four long hours while Dan rushes from south to north London, texting every twenty minutes or so: 'I'm 55 minutes away'; '30 mins'; 'Running. Nearly there'; 'I'm here Xxx'. This race through the streets was not a romcom moment I had seen on-screen – usually a protagonist dashes across a city to say 'I love you', not to hold your hand while a doctor sticks a dildo-like plastic instrument inside your vagina. But when Dan arrives and squeezes my hand, and I kiss the side of his arm, I feel it – a deep, tender romance. It surprises me how life continues to offer up these tiny flickers of sweetness in the strangest moments. They happen all the time, even in sad waiting rooms, if we pay attention. I ask Dan then, quietly, 'What will we do if this baby dies too?' He doesn't say anything for a few seconds. Then, 'We'll go for a cocktail, we'll feel sad, and then we'll try again.' I hadn't really needed an answer; I just wanted to say our worst fear out loud to take away its power. But his reply is soothing because, although in many ways it is not that simple, in many ways it is. 'Natasha Lunn?' The doctor – the same one as before – calls us into the room. 'I remember you,' she says, with a gentle kindness that makes me want to cry. I will never forget her face. She asks me to get on to the bed while she covers the plastic instrument with cool gel. She slips it inside me. The room is quiet. I can't look at Dan. I don't know if he is looking at me. I pray to the ceiling one more time, and to the sky beyond it too. 'There it is,' she says. 'A heartbeat.'

It's hard to see clearly what you learn from what you lose. At first, I thought the lesson of my loss was to protect myself from a similar ambush in the future, by holding back love. And now? I see that the uncertainty love requires is not a problem to be fixed; it is what makes it beautiful. It invites courage. It asks us to hope, without evidence, without knowing. At times, I am able to daydream about our baby's future and, at other times, I slip up and give in to fear. I still crave a solid reassurance that she will be safe; the difference is now I know no such certainty exists, for any of us. All of love requires a risk, a moment where we have to decide to say, 'I'm all in,' even if we've been hurt before. I watch the people I love take these leaps of faith every day: to find the vulnerability to say 'I love you' for the first time, to adopt a child, to make difficult decisions about a parent's health, to end an engagement because they still believe in love and this isn't it. There can be no way of knowing if the relationship will survive, if the adoption will go through, if a parent will live a long life, or if the next person we give our heart to will treat it with care. We cannot sift the suffering out of a life. Instead, we have to let both things in – the joy and the sorrow. I understand this is not only a necessary burden; it is what makes love more tender. And that whatever we've lost, whatever life has taken from us, there will still be small moments in which we can choose to hope anyway. Will you? I am trying to. Now, when the Great Fear looms, I put my hand on my swelling stomach and feel it all – fear, courage, risk, uncertainty, joy; all the multitudes of life and loss. I whisper to my baby anyway, 'I love you. I love you. I love you!'

Conclusion

What I Wish I'd Known About Love

'Love is not the answer
But the line that marks the start'
(*Laura Marling, 'For You'*)

By the time our daughter was born, I'd spent three years asking people about love's challenges. In that period I'd also married, miscarried, lost a grandmother, seen friends miscarry, give birth, divorce, felt old friends drift away and let some new ones in too. I'd learnt about love's enemies (self-pity, neglect, ego, laziness, always wanting more) and its companions (responsibility, discipline, listening, humour, forgiveness, gratitude and hope). With this new knowledge, I anticipated I might be able to avoid future problems in love, or at least find some shortcuts. But in the first three months of parenthood, I've made many of the same mistakes, and I will no doubt make them again. The only difference now is I'm aware that I'm making them.

I did not fall in love with my daughter straight away. Despite making a commitment to love her while she was inside me, in the outside world we were starting over. The day after I gave birth, Dan asked, 'Don't you love her more than anything in the world?' And I said, 'No.' I think I shocked him, maybe worried him. I had felt a wild surge of tenderness for her in the seconds after she was born: this tiny, slimy human, climbing up my chest. I whispered, 'It's OK, you're safe now,' and I knew then that she had reassembled certain pieces of me. That I would always try to take care of her. But this was a feeling that seemed to come from my body, not my mind; one so powerful I did not need to choose it – it simply was. I had the sense it would have happened with or without much effort on my part. And love, I have learnt, is the opposite: a choice, an intention.

At the time I put this lack of love at first sight down to drugs and hormones. All I could focus on was keeping her alive: staying up all night holding one finger under her nose to check she was still breathing, or pressing two fingers lightly beneath her sleepsuit and on to her warm chest, to feel it moving up and down, so subtly, I worried I was dreaming it. Those first seventy-two hours were so full of fear, there was little room left for love.

Gradually, at home, I started to see flickers of who she might be: the way she stretched her arms in the air like Superman after she'd breastfed, or how she kicked out her legs to splash the bathwater; half excited, half nervous. Each day, I used my body to tend to her body – washing her, changing her, feeding her. In these small acts, which sometimes felt colossal, I made a daily choice to love her, even when it was hard or when I was scared. It wasn't long after that – a week, maybe two – before I looked down at her tiny eyelashes while she was asleep, like fine bristles on a paintbrush, and knew for certain that I loved her. So my love for Joni folded out into my life in the same way as it had for her father: slowly and steadily, deepening with time and knowledge, until it was as much a part of me as my organs. This shouldn't have surprised me, really, because it was one of the first lessons I learnt about love: it is not instant, like a spark, but something that grows if tended to, like a flame stoked into a fire.

I pay attention to every detail in these first months of motherhood, knowing I will never get them back, but also that the real task of loving Joni is not now. It's loving her when she throws a tantrum in a supermarket aisle, or when she throws food on the floor when I am already late to be somewhere, or when she says something spiteful to me and it stings. Love *is* a choice – and sometimes it's choosing to love someone even when we don't feel lovingly towards them. The feeling of being 'in love' comes and goes, ebbs and flows, but the action of loving is a decision. One we make every day.

It's a choice Dan and I make as we become shift workers, fumbling our way towards becoming good parents. Since Joni has reflux, we take turns to stay up with her and spend less time in the same bed. Even when we share one, we cannot hold each other fully because she sleeps on one of our chests. So I begin to miss things. The feeling of his warm thighs pressed up against mine at night. Reading side by side in bed in easy silence. Reading things and wanting to share them, like the fact that the actor James Gandolfini used to listen to *Dookie* by Green Day on repeat (one of Dan's favourite albums as a teenager); or how I've only just discovered that the chorus of David Bowie's 'Starman' was inspired by 'Somewhere Over the Rainbow'. We used to share small discoveries like these, and our big dreams for life in five years' time. Now we say, 'Was her poo green or mustard?', 'What time did you last feed her?' and 'Can you hold her while I go to the loo?' We spend more time looking into Joni's eyes, and less into each other's. And on days when we have had two and a half hours' sleep, we engage in petty contests about who is more tired. Even though we know competition is the enemy of a good relationship, sometimes we slip into one anyway.

In my teens and twenties I'd convinced myself that people who loved each other were drawn together like magnets, no matter what. But when distances like these emerge in our relationships, romantic or otherwise, we can't wait for a mystical, gravitational force to close the gap – instead we have to create that force ourselves, with honesty and empathy and forgiveness. This is what Dan and I do to stay close as new parents. We create kindness inside ordinary moments: a cup of sugary tea at 6 a.m., or a tumbler of wine poured and put beside the other on a Friday at 6 p.m. We still miss the versions of ourselves we've had to give up for a little while, but we fall in love with the new ones that are emerging too, as we crouch side by side on our knees on the bathmat, singing 'Bare Necessities' to the daughter we worried we might never have. When we can't cuddle in bed, we hold hands instead. There are always small ways to reach each other.

Just as we begin to adjust to our new world, when Joni is six weeks old Dan finds a rash on her chest. She has been quieter all week, sleeping more. That night we call 111 and they tell us to take an ambulance to the hospital. 'This seems over the top,' I say to Dan, insisting we take a cab instead. But at some point on the ride, we worry she isn't moving, isn't breathing. I stick my fingers in her mouth, pull up her eyelids, but she will not stir. I don't know the exact order of the moments that follow, only that the driver spots an ambulance on the street ahead, then Dan gets out and tells the paramedic we're not sure our baby is breathing. While he does, the driver turns to me and says, 'She'll be OK, she'll be OK,' and I feel the glow of his kindness, but can only nod in return.

In the back of the ambulance, the paramedic isn't sure she's breathing either. I watch him put a tiny gas mask over Joni's tiny mouth and nose, do tiny compressions on her tiny chest, and understand then just how precarious it is to love another person. How much we have to lose when we do. I sit in the ambulance but I am not there, as if my mind cannot take in the details of the scene, until the paramedic says, 'She's breathing, she's breathing,' and I return. Even though he runs into children's A & E shouting, 'Resus, resus,' Joni turns out to be fine. It is only a viral infection, a false alarm; she was breathing all along. They keep me in overnight anyway, and I stay up watching her sleep, listening to the light breeze of her breath. I think it will be impossible to leave her side again, but I do, because I know that loving her does not mean protecting her from the world; it means modelling courage, to help her to be independent enough to explore it. Just like in pregnancy – or in any instance when we love someone – the fear would always be there, but it would not lessen the pain of any future loss.

The next day I scroll Instagram and see a photo a father has posted of his child who died the year before. His toddler is wearing the same blue and cream John Lewis sleepsuit as Joni, and I think: we are all a phone call or a test result or a cab ride away from grief. We see other people's losses as terrible, far-away things; we say we can't imagine them, but we must. It is the only way we will get better at saying, 'I'm sorry.'

We do have this capacity, I had learnt, to be there for people we do not know. To be part of what Melanie Reid described as the undercurrent of kindness and love that exists between us all. This was something I'd often felt during these conversations, an understanding that we are all connected, and part of a bigger human family. Sometimes, I sensed a form of love between me and the person I was speaking to, as they showed me pieces of themselves, and together we tried to find meaning. While I was seeking to understand love, I had unknowingly found more of it. This made me see that the psychotherapist Dr Megan Poe was right: 'Love is a frequency we can either choose to tune into or ignore.' We can decide to move through the world in a loving way. We can look at our phone while ordering coffee in the morning, or make a connection. We can walk past the woman crying in a Soho doorway, or stop to ask, 'Are you OK?' We're all in it together, this life, and when we go through it with our individual missions, never looking up or out, we miss so much.

Just as we change, our challenges in love change too. In my twenties, friendship was effortless and romantic relationships required work. In my early thirties, marriage felt easy but I had to put more effort into friendship. And now that motherhood takes up so much space inside me, it's romantic love that requires more attention. The challenges have shifted in friendships as well: more of my friends are miscarrying, and I have to find ways to sensitively show up for them, while allowing space for any complex feelings they might have now that I'm a mother. Love will always flow through our lives in this inconsistent, unknowable way, and we cannot press pause on the joyful bits, nor fast-forward the suffering. All we can do is keep noticing when there is an imbalance, keep adjusting our efforts to make sure the people we love know that they are important to us.

I began this project hoping to solve or avoid my problems in love, rather than endure and grow from them. This aim was not that different from my first romantic fantasy – both resisted reality. Both assumed a happier ending meant skipping the harder parts of love: How vulnerable we are when we long for it. How it hurts when we lack it, or when we lose it. How it hurts when we lose ourselves. If I'd been allowed to write my own love story, I wouldn't have included any of those things. I wouldn't have imagined two decades of 'failed' relationships, or dozens of dreadful online dates, or the time I got dumped outside McDonald's in the rain. I wouldn't have included the guilt of fighting with my dad about whether I was wearing jeans or trousers on the morning of his dad's funeral, or the awkwardness of a friendship transforming, or a miscarriage, or a baby with reflux, or a husband who sometimes gets food stuck in his beard. All these mundane bits, or painful bits, I never would have picked them. And yet they are all small pieces of a reality that's more beautiful than any fantasy, than anything that I could have imagined.

Although I don't arrive at this conclusion with a magic set of answers, these conversations have altered my life in two significant ways. First, they have expanded my understanding of love into a big, boundless thing. I saw that it was in the moment Lucy Kalanithi kissed the air to remember her husband, in Ayisha Malik's connection to her faith, and in Candice Carty-Williams's birthday itinerary that her friend puts together every year. It was in the space that Diana Evans carves out for herself to write, and in the memories Greg Wise continues to share about his sister. It was in Roxane Gay's Post-it notes, in Lemn Sissay's poems, in Heather Havrilesky's reaction to her husband's grumblings about his back. Putting these conversations alongside each other showed me that love is everywhere, in so many different forms and shapes and acts. It amazes me now more than it ever has: its power and its scale, its individuality and universality.

But secondly, I am left with a fresh determination to pay attention. There is so much – so much! – to distract us from the people we love. There are practical things (life admin, work, phones) and emotional ones (the uncertainty of longing, the intensity of fear). Each day we have to fight small battles to notice the love that's right in front of us. This makes me think that one of the most important things in love is memory. We have to remember to keep up the little acts that say 'I'm here': to post the birthday card, to look into someone's eyes, to call, to kiss, to hug, to ask questions and to say 'I love you' – and not in a throwaway way. Then to remember the big things: to tell the truth, to accept impermanence, to retain separateness, to see beyond ourselves, to understand that, although other people's flaws are annoying, so are ours; and to keep catching ourselves. By 'catching ourselves' I mean tapping into a self-awareness that allows us to pull back from a mistake while we are making it. Like explaining why we are irritated, before jumping further into a fight. Or recognizing that we are distracted when someone is trying to tell us something important, then choosing to listen instead.

Some of us are good at remembering; the rest of us need a little help. As Sarah Hepola pointed out to me, the people who are the best at staying present develop certain strategies: they pray, meditate, write and run; they find tiny, significant ways to be grateful. And I hope that's what these conversations will do too: provide small but precious reminders to pay attention to the lives we are living. Through asking people how to love, all along I have been finding out how to live.

Now my aim is not to protect myself from future problems in love. Instead, my hope is that, when I am in the final weeks of my life, I will look back and know that I knew love when I felt it: how a parent's love felt like warm sun on your skin, or how being married was like singing two different notes in the same song. I hope I will remember that love is not a narrow thing. That love is what makes us care, connects us to each other and the world. That love is a quest, a promise, a home. It's the force we create to reach each other, with cups of tea and tenderness, with humour and 'I'm sorry's; and it's a world we create with another person, one truth at a time. Most of all, I hope to have noticed and been present in the love that lived in ordinary moments: the sweetness of Joni's smile first thing in the morning, the silliness of my family laughing at each other's farts on Boxing Day, the comfort of a stranger's kindness, the mystery of a clear night sky, the spontaneity of an email from Dan including only the Frida Kahlo quote, 'Take a lover who looks at you like maybe you are a bourbon biscuit,' or the deep peace of my friend's arms wrapped around me in the park on a bright autumn morning. I hope that on my last day on earth I'll look back on it all and think, love is astonishing, life is astonishing. How grateful I am, not only to have known love, but to have known just how important it was, to pay attention to it.

Further Reading

Dolly Alderton, *Everything I Know About Love* (Penguin Books)

John Armstrong, *Conditions of Love: The Philosophy of Intimacy* (Penguin Books)

Poorna Bell, *In Search of Silence* (Simon & Schuster)

Alain de Botton, *Essays in Love* (Picador)

—*The Course of Love* (Penguin Books)

Candice Carty-Williams, *Queenie* (Trapeze)

Juno Dawson, *This Book Is Gay* (Hot Key Books)

Luise Eichenbaum and Susie Orbach, *Between Women: Love, Envy and Competition in Women's Friendships* (Viking)

Diana Evans, *Ordinary People* (Vintage)

Erich Fromm, *The Art of Loving* (HarperCollins)

Roxane Gay, *Bad Feminist* (Corsair)

John Gottman and Julie Schwartz Gottman, *Eight Dates: Essential Conversations for a Lifetime of Love* (Penguin Life)

Stephen Grosz, *The Examined Life* (Vintage)

Thich Nhat Hanh, *How to Love* (Ebury)

Heather Havrilesky, *How to Be a Person in the World: Ask Polly's Guide Through the Paradoxes of Modern Life* (Doubleday Books)

Sarah Hepola, *Blackout: Remembering the Things I Drank to Forget* (Two Roads) bell hooks, *All About Love: New Visions* (HarperCollins)

Mira Jacob, *Good Talk: A Memoir in Conversations* (Bloomsbury Publishing)

Paul Kalanithi, *When Breath Becomes Air* (Vintage)

Ariel Levy, *The Rules Do Not Apply* (Fleet)

Gordon Livingston, MD, *How to Love* (Hachette)

J. D. McClatchy, *Love Speaks Its Name* (Everyman)

Joanna Macy, various books, see joannamacy.net

Ayisha Malik, *Sofia Khan is Not Obliged* (Twenty7)

Simon May, *Love: A History* (Yale University Press)

Stephen A. Mitchell, *Can Love Last?: The Fate of Romance over Time* (W. W. Norton & Company)

Vivek H. Murthy, *Together: Loneliness, Health and What Happens When We Find Connection* (Profile Books)

Emily Nagoski, *Come As You Are: The Surprising New Science That Will Transform Your Sex Life* (Scribe)

Reinhold Niebuhr, The Serenity Prayer

Mary Oliver, *Devotions: The Selected Poems of Mary Oliver* (Penguin Press)

M. Scott Peck, *The Road Less Travelled* (Ebury)

Esther Perel, *Mating in Captivity* (Hodder & Stoughton)

Philippa Perry, *The Book You Wish Your Parents Had Read (and Your Children Will Be Glad That You Did)* (Penguin Life)

Justine Picardie, *If the Spirit Moves You: Life and Love After Death* (Picador)

Susan Quilliam, *Stop Arguing, Start Talking: The 10 Point Plan for Couples in Conflict* (Vermilion)

Melanie Reid, *The World I Fell Out Of* (HarperCollins)

Adrienne Rich, 'Claiming and Education', speech delivered at the convocation of Douglass College, 1977

Rainer Maria Rilke, *Letters to a Young Poet* (Penguin Classics)

Sharon Salzberg, *Real Love: The Art of Mindful Connection* (Macmillan)

Dani Shapiro, *Hourglass: Time, Memory, Marriage* (Knopf Publishing Group)

Lemn Sissay, *Gold from the Stone* (Canongate Books)

Lisa Taddeo, *Three Women* (Bloomsbury Publishing)

Frank Tallis, *The Incurable Romantic: and other unsettling revelations* (Little, Brown)

Krista Tippett, *Becoming Wise: An Inquiry into the Mystery and Art of Living* (Corsair)

Clare and Greg Wise, *Not That Kind of Love* (Quercus)

Gary Younge, *Another Day in the Death of America* (Guardian Faber Publishing)

Acknowledgements

Just as life is made up of many different love stories, this book was built on the kindness of many different people. I have to begin by thanking all of my interviewees. Their generosity, openness and thoughtfulness not only made this book possible, but made writing it a joy. To all of you: I am so grateful.

I am also grateful to Caroline Jones, who diligently transcribed most of these interviews. Your enthusiastic emails kept me company during the solitary periods of writing. And to the incredibly talented Anna Morrison, who designed the beautiful cover. I admire your work so much and am thrilled that you are an integral part of *Conversations on Love*.

I am indebted to everyone at Penguin – thank you for believing in this book and for giving me the space and time to write it. A special thank you to Isabel Wall, my editor and fellow lover of love! Your enthusiasm and kindness turned a terrifying process into an enjoyable one. Thank you for caring so deeply about the book, and for making it better.

Thank you to the people who helped me but might not know it: to Jennie Agg, whose words made me feel less alone when I felt sad; to Pandora Sykes and Dolly Alderton, for championing *CoL* in the early days on The High Low; to Heather Havrilesky, for agreeing to be my first newsletter guest; and to Lucy Henderson, for telling me to write this book one Boxing Day.

I owe so much to my boss and friend Sarah Tomczak, who edited my writing years ago when I tried far too hard! I've learnt so much about love from watching you bring up Coco and Sylvie with grace and optimism. Thank you for always encouraging my writing, and for showing me that motherhood and purpose can coexist.

So many friends taught me about love long before I started interviewing people about it. I'm deeply grateful to Caroline Steer, Roxanne Robinson, Jennifer Livingston, Jessica Russell-Flint, Louise Waller, Ruth Lewis, Lois Kettlewell, Katy Taylor, Kristina Henderson and Katy Takla. An extra special thank you to Marisa Bate, for telling me I could write this book every time I worried I couldn't. And to Lucy Lee, for your brilliant brain and clever suggestions. You are all precious to me. I love you so much.

Thank you to Joni, for being here. If you read this book one day: I love you!

Thank you to my family – my mum Niki and dad Chris, whose love story was the first I witnessed. I used to curse them for giving me impossibly high standards in relationships, but now I see that they taught me not to settle for anything less. Thank you for creating a home that was always full of love. Being your daughter is a blast.

My brother Oliver was my earliest reader and my earliest companion. Ols: thank you for your insightful comments and for pushing me to be clearer. You were always right! Thank you also for teaching me about love from the beginning, and for reminding me that humour is a daily essential. I can't wait to dance to Springsteen together every year we have left on this Earth.

Carrie Plitt is everything I could ask for in an agent: clever, charismatic, tough, wise and always fun to talk to. Carrie: it is not a coincidence that I only started properly working on this book after we met. It would not exist without you. Thank you for being the person I always want to impress.

Thank you to my husband Dan, who so generously gave me the freedom to tell some of our stories in this book. Loving you has taught me to live expansively and courageously. Thank you for always supporting my dreams. I love you all ways, always.

And lastly, thank you to my *Conversations on Love* newsletter subscribers, particularly the ones who told me they wanted this book to exist. Whenever I got stuck, or doubted myself, I reread your emails. Your words reminded me why I wanted to write. I found love in them.

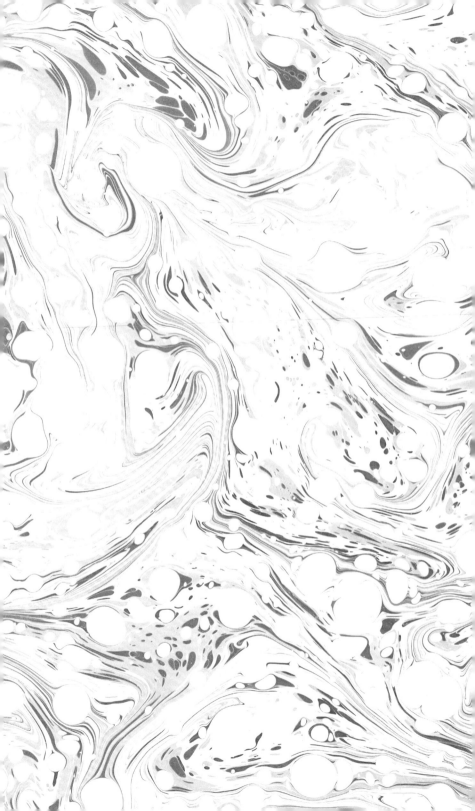